MARY LINCOLN

One of America's most compelling First Ladies, Mary Lincoln possessed a unique vantage point on the events of her time, even as her experiences of the constraints of gender roles and the upheaval of the Civil War reflected those of many other women. The story of her life presents a microcosm through which we can understand the complex and dramatic events of the nineteenth century in the United States, including vital issues of gender, war and the divisions between North and South. The daughter of a Southern, slave-holding family, Mary Lincoln had close ties to people on both sides of the war. Her life shows how the North and South were interconnected as the country was riven by sectional strife.

In this concise narrative, Stacy Pratt McDermott presents an evenhanded account of this complex, intelligent woman and her times. Supported by primary documents and a robust companion website, this biography introduces students to the world of nineteenth-century America and the first-hand experiences of Americans during the Civil War era.

Stacy Pratt McDermott is Assistant Director and Associate Editor, Papers of Abraham Lincoln.

ROUTLEDGE HISTORICAL AMERICANS

SERIES EDITOR: PAUL FINKELMAN

Routledge Historical Americans is a series of short, vibrant biographies that illuminate the lives of Americans who have had an impact on the world. Each book includes a short overview of the person's life and puts that person into historical context through essential primary documents, written both by the subjects and about them. A series website supports the books, containing extra images and documents, links to further research and, where possible, multi-media sources on the subjects. Perfect for including in any course on American History, the books in the Routledge Historical Americans series show the impact everyday people can have on the course of history.

Woody Guthrie: Writing America's Songs
Ronald D. Cohen

Frederick Douglass: Reformer and Statesman
L. Diane Barnes

Thurgood Marshall: Race, Rights, and the Struggle for a More Perfect Union
Charles L. Zelden

Harry S. Truman: The Coming of the Cold War
Nicole L. Anslover

John Winthrop: Founding the City upon a Hill
Michael Parker

John F. Kennedy: The Spirit of Cold War Liberalism
Jason K. Duncan

Bill Clinton: Building a Bridge to the New Millennium
David H. Bennett

Ronald Reagan: Champion of Conservative America
James H. Broussard

Laura Ingalls Wilder: American Writer on the Prairie
Sallie Ketcham

Benjamin Franklin: American Founder, Atlantic Citizen
Nathan R. Kozuskanich

Brigham Young: Sovereign in America
David Vaughn Mason

Mary Lincoln: Southern Girl, Northern Woman
Stacy Pratt McDermott

Mary Lincoln
Southern Girl, Northern Woman

STACY PRATT MCDERMOTT

Routledge
Taylor & Francis Group

NEW YORK AND LONDON

http://www.routledge.com/cw/historicalamericans

First published 2015
by Routledge
711 Third Avenue, New York, NY 10017

And by Routledge
2 Park Square, Milton Park, Abingdon, Oxon OX14 4RN

Routledge is an imprint of the Taylor & Francis Group, an informa business

© 2015 Taylor & Francis

Library of Congress Cataloging-in-Publication Data

McDermott, Stacy Pratt. Mary Lincoln: southern girl,
    northern woman/Stacy Pratt McDermott.
        pages cm. — (Routledge historical Americans)
    Includes bibliographical references.
    1. Lincoln, Mary Todd, 1818-1882. 2. Lincoln, Abraham, 1809-1865—Family.
3. Presidents' spouses—United States—Biography. I. Title.
    E457.25.L55M385 2015
    973.7092—dc23
    [B]
    2014030118

ISBN: 978-1-138-78680-6 (hbk)
ISBN: 978-1-138-78681-3 (pbk)
ISBN: 978-1-315-76705-5 (ebk)

Typeset in Bembo and Scala Sans
by Apex CoVantage, LLC

Printed and bound in the United States of America by Publishers Graphics, LLC on sustainably sourced paper.

In loving memory of my daughter, Mackenzie Kathleen McDermott

CONTENTS

ACKNOWLEDGMENTS

Without the encouragement of my mentor and friend Orville Vernon Burton, I never would have tackled a biography of Mary Lincoln. His unfailing faith in my abilities as a writer and historian has sustained me since my first days in graduate school at the University of Illinois.

In my life, I am fortunate to have amazing, devoted and supportive family and friends. Without them, I am a just a lonely and crazy woman. I love you all: Kevin McDermott, Savannah McDermott, Mackenzie McDermott, Marie Pratt and Mike Pollard, Dianne and Bill McDermott, Tracy Pratt and Jason Wavering, Zoe Wavering, Dave McKinney, Maureen McKinney, Alicia and Kurt Erikson, Sandra Mutman and Pat Doyle, Christi Parsons and Cody Moser. Also, thanks and puppy love to Pepper, my fluffy Pomeranian, who sat on my lap during the long writing marathons.

Every day in my capacity as the assistant director and associate editor at the Papers of Abraham Lincoln and the Abraham Lincoln Presidential Library, I am buoyed by amazing friends and colleagues. For their encouragement and good-natured teasing, I am grateful to them all: Daniel Stowell, Carmen Morgan, Marilyn Mueller, Daniel Worthington, Christian McWhirter, David Gerleman, Kelley Clausing, Boyd Murphree, Ed Bradley, Kathryn Harris and Ronda Schappaugh.

ABBREVIATIONS FOR NOTES

ALPL: Abraham Lincoln Presidential Library, Springfield, IL.

L&L: Justin G. Turner and Linda Levitt Turner, eds., *Mary Todd Lincoln: Her Life and Letters* (New York: Alfred A. Knopf, 1972).

LC: Library of Congress, Washington, DC.

INTRODUCTION

Mary Lincoln was born in 1818 in Lexington, Kentucky, into an affluent, slave-holding family, and she died in 1882 in Springfield, Illinois, the widow of a martyred president. She was a spirited, educated and cultured Southern daughter who grew up to be a strong-willed, politically opinionated, Northern political wife. The life experiences between Southern girl and Northern woman transpired during the unpredictable decades of the nineteenth century and shaped the worldview, guided the choices and defined the character of this most controversial First Lady. Mary Lincoln's life was a life of extremes and bitter ironies. The institution of slavery had been the foundation of her privileged upbringing, and the abolition of the institution of slavery became the foundation of her husband's presidency. The lively and divisive party politics of her era was a great joy of her life, yet ultimately it was a factor leading to her greatest heartbreak. After a lifelong personal pursuit of love and acceptance, she died in a darkened room without children or grandchildren around her to provide the private comfort that may have helped her come to terms with the sorrow she endured until she took her final breath.

In some ways, the personal tragedy of Mary Lincoln's life and the context of the national tragedy of the American Civil War are part of the reason she is so compelling to us today. Mary Lincoln was both a personal and a public witness to the Civil War, which was *the* defining event of her generation and one of the most intriguing historical events in our nation's history. She was raised in the South in an aristocratic family surrounded by slaves and afforded uncommon opportunities for education and cultural refinement; yet she married an uneducated, rough-hewn man of humble origins who became a middle-class lawyer and an anti-slavery politician.

The juxtaposition of those contrasting experiences makes her a fascinating historical character. Mary Lincoln did not have the historical impact that her iconic husband had on American history, but her vantage point as his wife is captivating. Mary Lincoln's life spans most of the formative years of the nineteenth century, offering a colorful historical backdrop for her experiences as a child, a wife and a mother; the life partner of an ambitious politician; First Lady of a war-torn nation; and a widow. Her experiences reveal much about Southern and Northern culture in the first half of the nineteenth century, the devastating human experiences of the Civil War and the gendered historical contexts of nineteenth-century America.[1]

However, while Mary Lincoln experienced the extraordinary position of the wife of a president, many of her life experiences were quite ordinary and illustrative of the experiences of ordinary women who were her con-temporaries as daughters, sisters, wives, mothers and widows. For example, like most people who lived in the nineteenth century, Mary, at a very young age, experienced the death of a parent. Like many—perhaps most—women of her era who suffered the loss of a child, Mary buried three of her own. The majority of women who married in the first half of the nineteenth century as Mary did lived at least for a time as widows. While Mary's educa-tional background was unique and her affluent childhood and middle-class marriage set her apart economically and socially from many less privileged women, the ordinary roles she played in her daily life were typical. We are drawn to Mary Lincoln because of the extraordinary circumstances of her life, but her life can also be an interesting focal point for understanding the lives of women more broadly.[2]

In another important way, Mary Lincoln's life is instructive. Like so many of her restless and peripatetic countrymen and women, she defies regional definitions. Her life straddled the North and the South as much as it was defined by the western frontier. Her experiences were both Southern and Northern. A slave woman helped raised her in Kentucky. A free black female dressmaker was her closest personal friend in Washington. She lost Union family members and friends during the war, but she lost Confederate fam-ily members and friends as well. All her life, she possessed some Southern sensibilities and some Northern sensibilities. She loved and prepared South-ern food. She developed friendships with abolitionists like Charles Sum-ner. She loved her native state of Kentucky as much as she wholeheartedly adopted Illinois. One might characterize Mary as a Southern belle because she was addicted to fashion and loved dancing. One might describe her as an anti-Southern Unionist because she embraced Republican politics with a personal vigor that even she admitted some might find "unbecoming."[3] Like some East Coast sophisticates who criticized the new president and his wife as western rubes, one might define her as an unrefined westerner because she arrived in Washington from the prairie state of Illinois. Mary was all of these things, but none of them alone defined her—and that is the point. Her experiences defy region, and so did the experiences of most people who lived and died in the Civil War era.[4]

Mary Lincoln was a complex individual, full of contradictions and ambiguities. This biography is going to touch on some of those contradictions and ambiguities and draw some historical meaning from the complexities of her life and the varying contexts of her experiences. One context that will be a particular focus in this biography of her life is the meaning of place. Who Mary Lincoln was, what she believed and how she behaved, was informed not only by *when* she lived but also by *where* she lived. All history takes place in some locale that is specific and unique to the people who lived there and the events that happened there. The idea that local, physical environments—like landscape, weather, population density, material culture and architecture—shape historical human experience is central to my approach to history, and my biographical portrait will pay close attention to Mary Lincoln's sense of place.[5] Mary lived for extended periods of time in Lexington, Kentucky; Springfield, Illinois; Washington, D.C.; Chicago, Illinois; Frankfurt, Germany; and Pau, France. It was within the parameters of these unique places that she experienced life, understood and navigated the joys and sorrows of human existence and searched for peace.[6]

No biography of Mary Lincoln can ignore the controversial nature of the historiography of her life. Therefore, I want to offer a brief discussion of it here. The historiography of the Mary's life story has a life of its own. Since Abraham Lincoln's death, his biographers have provided much of what we know about his wife. The sixteenth president has been the subject of thousands of books, and virtually *every* book that *anyone* has ever written about America's favorite president has provided a basic description of Mary's life, or assessed Mary as a domestic partner or as a mother, or interpreted Mary's role in Lincoln's political aspirations, or characterized the Lincoln marriage or advanced an opinion about Mary's worth as a woman or as a human being. Mostly, all seem perfectly reasonable things to do, as it is certainly natural to write about the family and personal lives of biographical subjects. In fact, a biographer would be remiss if he or she did not at least mention the fact that Lincoln was married for more than twenty-two years to a woman with whom he had four sons. What is unique in the case of Mary Lincoln, however, is that because so much has been written about her husband, the nature of what most students and general readers of history know about Mary Lincoln is filtered through the lens of biographers of Abraham Lincoln and not of Mary Lincoln herself.

Unfortunately for Mary's place in history, many of the most prominent biographers of Lincoln did not like her, and most of them have failed to understand the historical context of nineteenth-century marriage in assessing the Lincoln marriage and Mary's role within it. Because so many of these biographers have chosen to highlight infamous stories of Mary's temper, habitual spending as First Lady and episodes of mental instability, Mary's historical reputation has suffered. Look up Mary Lincoln in the index of almost any biography of Abraham Lincoln, and there will be pointers to episodes that shed unfavorable light on her. A large majority of biographers of Lincoln have vilified Mary Lincoln as a domineering, mentally disturbed shrew. Perhaps most shockingly, many biographers of Lincoln have simply dismissed Mary Lincoln as the crazy wife of our greatest president. The juxtaposition of Lincoln's good and Mary's evil has been far too irresistible for some biographers to resist.[7] Another characteristic of the historiography is that much scholarship about Abraham and Mary Lincoln has relied heavily on historically problematic reminiscences written or relayed many years after the events described within them. Reminiscent materials are seductive sources for scholars interested in the Lincoln story because Abraham and Mary Lincoln did not keep personal diaries and burned many of their personal papers before leaving Springfield for Washington in February 1861. In addition, Robert Lincoln likely purged the family papers of items he deemed unimportant or private. Reminiscent sources are attractive replacements for contemporary sources that no longer survive. The fact that Lincoln's first biographer actively collected such a large and provocative corpus of reminiscent materials for nearly two years further enhances the attraction.[8] After Lincoln's death, William Herndon interviewed more than 250 people who had known Abraham Lincoln throughout his life, and that corpus of interviews survives.[9] Reminiscences or what today we would call oral history can be valid historical sources and provide legitimate historical evidence. However, they do not carry the same level of validity as contemporary accounts like diaries, personal correspondence or other personal records like letters, business ledgers or government proceedings. Historians must weigh them very carefully and use them wisely and judiciously. For example, oral histories and written reminiscences can be particularly problematic if they were collected too many years after the fact, if the age and/or mental keenness of the narrator of the reminiscence are suspect or if the interviewer or the narrator has a particular political or personal agenda.

In 1928, Katherine Helm, Mary Lincoln's niece, published a sympathetic biography that contained recollections of Mary's sister Emilie Helm.[10] However, a full-length, scholarly biography of Mary Lincoln did not appear until 1953, when Ruth Painter Randall published *Mary Lincoln: Biography of a Marriage*. Randall's intent with her biography was to rescue Mary from the purview of the Lincoln biographers, particularly from the overwhelmingly hateful characterizations of Mary by Lincoln's law partner William Herndon in his 1889 biography of Lincoln. Randall's biography was a well-researched and engagingly written biography of Mary's entire life. It started from Mary's girlhood in Kentucky, fleshed out her life in Springfield, examined her role as First Lady and discussed at some length her seventeen years as a widow. In her effort to drown out the negative interpretations of Mary Lincoln, Randall wrote a biography that most scholars today classify as apologetic, as she downplayed the less flattering aspects of Mary's personality and life, like her excessive spending, protracted grief, interest in spiritualism and mental instabilities.[11]

In 1987, Jean Baker published what stands today as the best full-length modern biography, *Mary Todd Lincoln*. Baker's balanced approach portrayed her subject from a vantage point of women's history, drawing on new scholarship on the history of the family and approaching the Lincoln marriage in the context of that new scholarship. While Randall had been countering Herndon's negative interpretation of Mary, Baker was countering more modern Lincoln biographers. As Baker has more recently argued, "We have too many historians deciding that they don't like Mary Lincoln and with extraordinary vehemence extrapolating their personal judgments into the [Lincoln] marriage."[12] By contrast, both Randall and Baker approached Mary's life with more empathy than the mostly male biographers that published books on her husband. However, unlike Randall, Baker did not gloss over Mary Lincoln's faults. Instead she drew on the context of women's history in order to better understand Mary's human failings within the context of the era in which she lived.[13]

Before I lay out the structure of my biography of Mary Lincoln, I want to make an additional point, which will not only be illustrative of my particular viewpoint on her but also explain something of Mary's own understanding of her personal identity. For the first twenty-four years of Mary Todd's life and for her last forty years as Mary Lincoln, she was smart and intellectually curious. She held strong opinions about people and politics throughout her entire life. She was a voracious reader of literature and newspapers and periodicals of the day. She attended political rallies and public events and sat in on court proceedings. She understood politics better than many of her male contemporaries, and even when she was grief stricken or distracted by poor health or personal problems, she never abandoned her obsessive interest in political and public affairs for long. She enjoyed that engagement; it fueled her spirit and her mind, and it enriched her relationship with her famous husband. However, for all her educational opportunities, her intellect, her interests in politics and her personal ambition for her politically ambitious husband, she was, in her mind, happily just a sister and a friend, a wife and a mother and, finally, just a widow.[14] Mary Lincoln wrote many political letters, recommending individuals for appointments or writing to Lincoln's political allies about various political issues, and much of her private correspondence discussed politics. However, most of her letters were of a personal nature, gossiping about friends and family, discussing social activities and reporting on the activities of her husband and her boys. As lengthy passages throughout the biography and the full documents presented at the end of the book will reveal, Mary Lincoln's daily life and activities were mostly domestic and social, and her primary activities were within the realm of the Lincoln family and the Lincoln household. After Lincoln's death, Mary periodically experienced some public scrutiny in the press, particularly during her efforts to secure a pension from Congress, but she mostly retreated to a private, domestic life.

Only four years of Mary Lincoln's sixty-three years were spent as a public figure, yet most historians have gauged her entire life through the lens of her years in the White House. Despite the fact that Mary viewed herself primarily as a wife and a mother, a fact that her surviving correspondence does not belie, historians have tended to evaluate and to judge her entire life as a public figure in her own right. In addition, perhaps as a way to separate Mary Lincoln's identity from that of her famous husband, historians have come to identify her as Mary Todd Lincoln. This moniker is, however, historically inaccurate, and, perhaps as well, it is a primary reason why we forget to think about Mary as a married woman living within the confines of nineteenth-century domesticity. We misname her and, thus, misjudge her. At no time in her life did Mary Lincoln ever call herself Mary Todd Lincoln or sign her name Mary Todd Lincoln. When she married Abraham Lincoln in 1842, she shed her maiden name (as most women of the nineteenth century did), and she never again used it to identify herself. She was Mary Ann as a girl, Mary Todd as young woman and Molly to her Springfield friends. She always signed her personal and public correspondence Mary Lincoln, Mrs. Lincoln, Mrs. Abraham Lincoln or simply M.L. Upon her marriage, she became a partner and helpmate to her husband, and she did not view herself as separate from him, as separate in purpose or as separate in ambition. She delighted in his success and her opportunity to be a part of it, but her ambition was always channeled through her intensely confident belief in Abraham Lincoln's potential for greatness and not her own.[15]

Chapter 1, "Mary Ann Todd," will examine Mary's childhood in Lexington, Kentucky, within the context of slavery and the antebellum South. Discussion of her formative years will focus on the loss of her mother, her familial relationships, her uncommon education and her social and political upbringing. Lexington, Kentucky, was an established and sophisticated yet violent, hard-drinking town. It was in this environment of Southern honor, rabid party politics and the cruelty of slavery that Mary was a girl, a daughter, a stepdaughter, a sister and an exceptional student. Because of the absence of letters and other contemporary sources from this period of her life, this chapter will tell the story of the Todd family and will more heavily rely on historical and environmental context than will the following chapters.

Chapter 2, "From Mary Todd to Mary Lincoln," will cover the years of Mary's young, single adulthood and her courtship and marriage to Abraham Lincoln in Springfield, Illinois. The politically charged setting of Illinois's burgeoning young state capital and the rapidly changing landscape of the town and the emerging Midwest energized the Lincolns. It was in Springfield that Mary Todd separated herself from her Southern family and fell in love. A discussion of nineteenth-century courtship and marriage rituals will help the reader better understand Mary and her hopes for her domestic future. Her marriage to the rough-hewn Abraham Lincoln of Illinois may have been somewhat of a shock to her well-bred family, but it was the deliberate and wholehearted choice of the opinionated and ambitious Kentucky belle. Mary Todd chose Abraham Lincoln and, thus, chose her path.

Chapter 3, "Mrs. Abraham Lincoln," will examine Mary Lincoln's life as a mother, homemaker and the wife of a successful circuit-riding attorney and a rising politician. This chapter will also examine Mary Lincoln's social connections in Springfield, her short time in Washington while Lincoln was in Congress and the Lincoln family's personal lives in the 1850s. It will also touch on the family's political experiences during Lincoln's campaign for the U.S. Senate in 1858 and during the 1860 presidential campaign. An important component of this chapter will be the context of companionate marriage in the nineteenth century.

Chapter 4, "Mrs. President Lincoln," will analyze Mary Lincoln as First Lady, as the wife of a president and as a mother. Wartime Washington will be the dramatic backdrop of this chapter, which will cover such topics as Mary's public activities as First Lady, her interest in and limited involvement with political appointments and her controversial spending to adorn the White House and herself. Also important here will be an examination of Mary's life as both a private and public witness to the political, social and human consequences of the Civil War. Mary was a grieving mother and sister and, ultimately, widow; however, she was also the First Lady attending to wounded soldiers, managing official functions at the executive mansion and suffering as a lightning rod for public commentary about sectional politics and the war.

Chapter 5, "The Widow Lincoln," will examine Mary's life from the assassination of her husband in 1865 until her death in 1882. The noisy, sprawling and exciting vibrancy of Chicago; the refinement and sophisticated bustle of Frankfurt, Germany; and the remote haven of Pau, France, were three contrasting environments for Mary's retirement that, in some ways, exemplify her final years: mania over money, admiration for travel and culture and, ultimately, some peace and distance from the public scrutiny she endured until the end of her life. The chapter will discuss her physical and mental health issues, the latter heightened by the loss of a third son in 1871; her efforts to obtain a worthy pension; and, albeit it in more limited detail, her brief stint in a mental institution.

Finally, the documents section will give readers a chance to evaluate eleven selections written by, to or about Mary Lincoln. Presented in their entirety, these lightly edited documents will enhance the shorter selections of Mary's words presented throughout the book. The documents will give readers a sense of Mary's love for her husband and for her children, will offer evidence pertaining to the quality of her friendships and the depths of her grief, will show her love of politics and will provide a taste of public perceptions about her. The documents chosen are representative of the major themes stressed in this biography—her role as a wife and mother, her interest in politics and her grief and health problems—and also pinpoint her in time and place. There are documents from Springfield, Lexington, Washington, Philadelphia, New York, Chicago and France; the selection ranges from 1840 to 1876.

This biography seeks to find the human Mary Lincoln somewhere between the extremes and to evaluate her life both within and beyond the shadow of Abraham Lincoln. This biography is more thematic in structure and more episodic in nature—a loosely chronological narrative of Mary's life, a synthesis of secondary sources and, most importantly, a portrait predominately based on Mary's own words from the more than 600 surviving letters that she wrote from 1840 to 1882. In the absence of a personal diary or memoir, this is, I believe, the best way to understand her on her own terms. Detailed descriptions of the geographic, environmental, physical and historical settings of her life will also fill in some gaps to provide a richer tapestry of her historical experiences. The biography will highlight some of the less widely known stories and settings about Mary Lincoln's life, like her voracious appetite for politics, her travels in Europe and her medical issues and treatments. It will also rely heavily on Mary's own words, quoting her at length and letting her tell most of her own story.

Full biographies of Mary Lincoln, such as those by Randall and Baker, as well as a new volume of essays that cover a wide range of topics about her life, provided an important foundation for this biography.[16] I have also gleaned various details from the good biographies of Abraham Lincoln, and they inform and enrich this study as well. Whenever possible, Mary's voice sets the stage, the parameters and the tenor for each chapter. The goal of the five chapters and the concluding section of edited documents is to allow readers to hear Mary's own voice, to experience her triumphs and feel her disappointments and grief, to know the environments in which she lived and, most importantly, to draw their own conclusions about her life, her historical environment and her legacy. This is not simply a biography of Abraham Lincoln's wife. It is not simply a biography of an interesting First Lady. It is a biography of a nineteenth-century woman whose daily life and experiences were in many ways representative of the lives of so many others. It is a biography of a life that is illustrative of the multi-faceted and rich layers of human, female experience. It will touch on some of Mary Lincoln's extraordinary experiences as First Lady, but most of the book will contend mainly with the myriad of Mary's daily life experiences as illustrative of the thoughts and hopes of other daughters, sisters, mothers, wives and widows who were Mary's contemporaries in the nineteenth century. It is a biography of a woman who was both of her time and beyond it. However, perhaps most importantly and most simply, it is a biography of a complicated and fascinating woman in a complicated and fascinating period of American history.

Notes

1   General histories that provide sweeping narratives of the first half of the nineteenth century and that provide general historical context for Mary Lincoln's lifetime include the following: Orville Vernon Burton, *The Age of Lincoln* (New York: Hill and Wang, 2007); Daniel Walker Howe, *What Hath God Wrought: Transformation of America, 1815–1848* (New York: Oxford University Press, 2007); Charles Sellers, *The Market Revolution: Jacksonian America, 1815–1846* (New York: Oxford University Press, 1991); Drew Gilpin Faust, *This Republic of Suffering: Death and the American Civil War* (New York: Alfred A. Knopf, 2008).

2   Good studies of women's experiences in the first half of the nineteenth century that provide context for the life of Mary Lincoln include the following: Ann Braud, *Radical Spirits: Spiritualism and Women's Rights in the Nineteenth Century* (Bloomington: Indiana University Press, 2001); Catherine Clinton, *The Other Civil War: American Women in the Nineteenth Century* (New York: Hill and Wang, 1984); Catherine Clinton and Nina Silber, eds., *Divided Houses: Gender and the Civil War* (New York: Oxford University Press, 1992); Sara Evans, *Born for Liberty: A History of Women in America* (New York: Simon & Schuster, 1989), 45–144; Steven Mintz and Susan Kellogg, *Domestic Revolutions: A Social History of American Family Life* (New York: Free Press, 1988).

3   Mary Lincoln to Charles Sumner, 20 November 1864, *L&L*, 192.

4   Some of the most engaging works focusing on region include the following: Nicole Etchison, *The Emerging Midwest: Upland Southerners and Political Culture of the Old Northwest, 1789–1861* (Bloomington: Indiana University Press, 1996); Bruce Levine, *Fall of the House of Dixie: The Civil War and the Social Revolution that Transformed the South* (New York: Random House, 2013); Alice Fahs, *The Imagined Civil War: Popular Literature of the North and South, 1861–1865* (Chapel Hill: University of North Carolina Press, 2001); Colin Woodard, *American Nations: The History of the Eleven Rival Regional Cultures in North America* (New York: Penguin, 2011); Mary P. Ryan, *Cradle of the Middle Class: The Family in Oneida County, New York, 1790–1865* (New York: Cambridge University Press, 1981).

5   Thomas J. Schlereth, "Local History Is Universal History," in Joann P. Krieg, ed., *Long Island Studies: Evoking a Sense of Place* (Interlaken, NY: Heart of the Lakes Publishing, 1988), 19–20.

6 Two particularly useful books in the Abraham Lincoln historiography are focused on the significance of place. One examined New Salem, Illinois, where Lincoln found his way as a young
   adult, and the other examined Springfield, Illinois, where Lincoln made a name for himself
   professionally. Both books make the argument that Lincoln's environments played important
   roles in his development as a man, lawyer and politician. The Springfield book is instructive
   for Mary Lincoln's life as well, and this biography draws lessons from it. Benjamin P. Thomas,
   Lincoln's New Salem (Springfield, IL: Abraham Lincoln Association, 1934); Paul M. Angle, *"Here
   I Have Lived": A History of Lincoln's Springfield, 1821–1865* (Springfield, IL: Abraham Lincoln
   Association, 1935; reprint, Chicago: Abraham Lincoln Bookshop, 1971); Kenneth J. Winkle, *The
   Young Eagle: The Rise of Abraham Lincoln* (Dallas, TX: Taylor Trade Publishing, 2001).

7 Jean Baker took particular aim at Michael Burlingame and Douglas Wilson, whose books were
   particularly critical of Mary Lincoln. Jean H. Baker, *Mary Todd Lincoln: A Biography* (New York:
   W. W. Norton & Co., 1987; reprint, New York: W. W. Norton & Co., 2008); Michael Burlingame,
   The Inner World of Abraham Lincoln (Urbana: University of Illinois Press, 1994); Douglas Wilson,
   Honor's Voice: The Transformation of Abraham Lincoln (New York: Alfred A. Knopf, 1998).

   For Lincoln biographies that paint a more balanced view of Mary Lincoln and the Lincoln
   marriage, see the following: David Herbert Donald, *Lincoln* (New York: Simon & Schuster,
   1995); Benjamin P. Thomas, *Abraham Lincoln: A Biography* (New York: Alfred A. Knopf, 1952);
   Kenneth J. Winkle, *Abraham and Mary Lincoln* (Carbondale: Southern Illinois University, 2012);
   Matthew Pinkster, *Lincoln's Sanctuary: Abraham Lincoln and the Soldier's Home* (New York: Oxford
   University Press, 2003).

8 William H. Herndon and Jesse William Weik, *Herndon's Lincoln: The True Story of a Great Life*, 3 vols.
   (Chicago: Belford, Clarke & Co., 1889).

9 Douglas L. Wilson and Rodney O. Davis, eds., *Herndon's Informants: Letters, Interviews, and Statements about Abraham Lincoln* (Urbana: University of Illinois Press, 1998), xvii; Jason Emerson,
   Giant in the Shadows (Carbondale: Southern Illinois University Press, 2012), 403.

   Herndon's Informants includes a registry of all of the informants with brief biographies of each.
   Interestingly, only twenty-six were women. Some of the female informants were Mary Lincoln's
   sisters, Elizabeth Edwards and Frances Wallace, and Mary Lincoln herself. Wilson and Davis,
   Herndon's Informants, 737–78.

10 Katherine Helm, *The True Story of Mary, Wife of Lincoln* (New York: Harper & Brothers, 1928).

11 Ruth Painter Randall, *Mary Lincoln: Biography of a Marriage* (Boston: Little, Brown & Co., 1953);
   Herndon and Weik, *Herndon's Lincoln*.

   Randall published another book to counter the Lincoln narrative in 1957. Ruth Painter
   Randall, *The Courtship of Mr. Lincoln* (Boston: Little, Brown & Co., 1957).

12 Jean H. Baker, *The Lincoln Marriage: Beyond the Battle of Quotations*, 38th Annual Robert Fortenbaugh Memorial Lecture (Gettysburg, PA: Gettysburg College, 1999), 8.

13 Baker, *Mary Todd Lincoln*.

   More recent biographers, such as Jason Emerson, have accused Baker of a feminist agenda
   and of being driven by a hatred of Robert Lincoln because of his role in having Mary Lincoln
   declared insane. However, Emerson is guilty of his own agenda as a biographer of Robert
   Lincoln. The debate about the positive and negative aspects of Mary Lincoln's life continues
   today and will, perhaps, never end. Jason Emerson, "Mary Lincoln: An Annotated Bibliography,"
   Journal of the Illinois State Historical Society 103 (Summer, 2010): 194–95; Jason Emerson, *The
   Madness of Mary Lincoln* (Carbondale: Southern Illinois University Press, 2007); Emerson, *Giant
   in the Shadows*.

14 Michael Burkhimer, "The Reports of the Lincolns' Political Partnership Have Been Greatly
   Exaggerated," in Frank J. Williams and Michael Burkhimer, eds., *The Mary Lincoln Enigma: Historians on America's Most Controversial First Lady* (Carbondale: Southern Illinois University Press,
   2012), 219–36.

15 My colleague Dr. James Cornelius, the curator of the Lincoln collection at the Abraham Lincoln
   Presidential Library in Springfield, Illinois, first inspired my perspective on Mary Lincoln's name

back in 2009 when he gave a presentation entitled "What's in a Name? Cultural Onomastics and Other Scary Things about the Lincolns and Their Contemporaries" at the Annual Meeting of the Association for Documentary Editing in Springfield, Illinois.

16 Published in 2012, *The Mary Lincoln Enigma* contains some provocative essays covering such topics as Todd family life in Kentucky, Mary Lincoln's interest in fashion and travel and fictional interpretations of her life. Within this volume, some historians provide new perspectives, while others rehash some old debates. Williams and Burkhimer, *Mary Lincoln Enigma*.

PART I

MARY LINCOLN

CHAPTER 1

MARY ANN TODD

On December 13, 1818, in Lexington, Kentucky, a scrappy little town in what was then the American West, a scrappy little girl was born into the affluent Todd family. Robert and Eliza Todd and their three young children greeted the blue-eyed Mary Ann into a noisy, nine-room house on Short Street. The house was not far from the two-story, brick courthouse one block over on Main Street in downtown Lexington. Chartered in 1782, Lexington was younger than the still new American government. However, when Mary Ann Todd became its newest resident, it was one of the most populous and most wealthy towns west of the Allegheny Mountains. When Mary Ann came into the world on that winter Sunday, James Monroe was president of the United States, Kentucky's Henry Clay was Speaker of the U.S. House of Representatives, General Andrew Jackson was fighting Seminoles in Spanish Florida and Mary's future home of Illinois had just become the nation's twenty-first state. The Todd family into which Mary Ann was born was a prominent one in Kentucky. The community in which she would pass her childhood exposed her to the seedier side of the hard-drinking, slave-holding Lexington but also afforded her exceptional educational and cultural opportunities uncommon for the era. The fervent political environment in which she would come of age encouraged what became a lifelong passion for Whig and then Republican politics. The privileged family circumstances of Mary's birth, combined with the unique historical setting of her childhood, molded her personality and worldview, fueled her aspirations and provided colorful beginnings for what was to be a very interesting life.[1]

The Todd family's rise to prominence had its own colorful beginnings in Kentucky. As a member of the Kentucky militia, Mary's paternal grandfather, Levi Todd, fought in one of the final engagements of the Revolutionary War, the Battle of Blue Licks. American and Canadian loyalists and allied American and Indians defeated the Kentuckians there in August 1782. Daniel Boone and Levi's brother John Todd were two of the commanders therein engaged, and John Todd was one of sixty revolutionary fighters who died in the battle. After the war, Levi and his wife, Jane, along with his surviving brother Robert Todd, helped developed the town of Lexington, advertising a call to the East to attract settlers. Mary Lincoln's maternal grandfather and Levi Todd's cousin Robert Parker answered that call immediately after his marriage to Elizabeth Porter in Pennsylvania. The couple arrived in Lexington on horseback in 1790. It took time for more settlers to face the wilderness and the remaining Indians; therefore, the Todds and the Parkers were among a group of only 843 residents that year living in the small village, surrounded by a stockade fence.[2]

Levi Todd had parlayed his survival at the Battle of Blue Licks and the name-dropping of his deceased brother into a position as clerk of Fayette County, Kentucky. From this position, he collected the fees on all documents filed in the county. For nearly thirty years, Todd collected a fee for every deed, mortgage, marriage license or other legal document that residents filed. In his capacity as clerk, he was also privy to every land deal and construction project, collecting fees and acting on early knowledge of land sales. Fees collected and speculative land purchases made him one of the wealthiest landowners and slaveholders in central Kentucky. He built a twenty-room manor just outside of Lexington and called it Ellerslie, named for the Scottish town from which the first Todds had emigrated. Levi and his wife had eleven children, and their seventh child was Mary's father, Robert Smith Todd, who was born in Lexington on February 25, 1791.[3]

The next year, Kentucky became a state, and Lexington enjoyed steady growth and development. As the state and the city prospered, so did the Todds and the Parkers. Many settlers who arrived in the area settled in the countryside to cultivate hemp and other local crops, but Levi Todd and Robert Parker remained in town, avoiding agricultural pursuits. While Levi Todd was, as one historian has noted, a "veritable one-man government," Robert Parker was the first surveyor of Fayette County, a merchant, a miller and a member of the Lexington Board of Trustees. Both men built stately homes and accumulated substantial wealth. Parker's wealth was such that he built the first brick house in Lexington, sent his four sons to professional school and left his widow in substantial comfort when he died in 1800. Todd's wealth was even more impressive. When he died in 1807, he owned 7,000 acres of land and had personal property valued at more than $6,000. By today's standards of wealth, $6,000 in 1807 was the equivalent of more than $3.5 million in economic status and prestige, and that does not even factor in the value of his land. Both Levi Todd and Robert Parker were opportunistic and successful, carving out of the Kentucky wilderness a prominent place for themselves and their families in Lexington. While luck, rather than hard work, may have been the primary reason for their financial and political achievements, the comfortable circumstances in which they positioned their children and grandchildren advanced a family ethos of genteel comfort and entitlement.[4]

Due to his family's affluence and position, Robert Todd entered Transylvania University in Lexington at the age of fourteen and studied law. In 1811, he gained admission to the bar; however, like his father before him, he had little interest in practicing law. Instead, the War of 1812 held more allure for Robert, who had grown up with the Todd family stories of the American Revolution. If he dreamed of military glory, he must have been sorely disappointed because almost as soon as he enlisted in the army, he developed pneumonia and returned home.[5] Shortly after his return to Lexington, the tall, brown-haired, brown-eyed, twenty-one-year-old with a "ruddy complexion" caught the eye of Eliza Parker, the "sprightly" and "attractive" daughter of Elizabeth and Robert Parker. Like their brothers, Eliza and her sister Mary Ann had access to schools that cost as much as $150 per year; and likely, they attended the fashionable Lexington Female Academy. The Widow Parker was a formidable woman, with her own historical connections to the Revolutionary War. Her father was General Andrew Porter, a personal friend of General George Washington. Although she had some initial reservations about her daughter's interest in Robert Todd, she eventually consented to the marriage of her eighteen-year-old daughter to Robert, perhaps finding the union of the Todds and Parkers, two of central Kentucky's most prominent families, economically and politically advantageous. Robert and Elizabeth were second cousins, but the coupling of such closely related individuals was not uncommon in Kentucky; and certainly, it was not unusual in the Todd and Parker families. Eliza's parents were themselves first cousins; and one of Robert Todd's sisters had married a first cousin. Robert and Eliza were married on November 26, 1812, and the couple moved into a house located on her family estate where the Widow Parker could keep a close eye on the young couple. Daughters Elizabeth and Frances were born in 1813 and 1815, and son Levi in 1817, just as Todd went into business with his friend and a fellow War of 1812 veteran Sergeant Smith. Smith & Todd sold "a full line of high-grade groceries and the choicest, rarest wines, spirits, brandy, gin and whisky."[6]

By 1818, Lexington was fashionable and stood apart from other western cities of its size and age on the western frontier. One observer noted that the city's "polished" residents were "given to music and dancing" but appreciated gardens and art as well. Lexington boasted of its cultural, legal, religious and educational institutions. The town became known as the "Athens of the

West," noted for "its intelligence, appreciation of literature, its good taste and elegance" and its illumination by twenty street lamps. Lexington boasted a theatre, and citizens enjoyed productions of popular Shakespearean plays like *Macbeth*. Local taverns hosted traveling wax exhibits depicting various dramatic scenes such as the infamous duel between Aaron Burr and Alexander Hamilton. The town's newspapers and newspaper editors were leaders of the Kentucky press, widely known ministers attended the town's pulpits, some of the best lawyers in the West practiced law in Lexington and, of course, the town claimed Kentucky's favorite son Henry Clay. Lexington was also home to numerous schools and Transylvania University, which was not only a rare institution in the American West, but also a quality educational institution that had attained national and some European celebrity. The Medical Department at the university had a national reputation equal to that of Harvard. The city was brimming with learned men in fields ranging from the classics, law and medicine. Public lectures were frequent and well attended, and the weekly meetings of the Lexington Lyceum, which featured the renowned Transylvania faculty and visiting scholars, greeted crowded audiences. The city library was one of the largest in the West, and there was an established botanical garden. With its 5,279 residents, it was an impressive little metropolis, the largest city in Kentucky, and it offered cultural opportunities that belied its somewhat isolated location some seventy miles southeast of Louisville, Kentucky, on the Ohio River.[7]

However, while Lexington had developed a reputation for its educational and cultural institutions and was hailed as a refined and civilized oasis in the "wild" and "savage" West, it was a community built on the backs of slaves and sustained by the violence of slavery. Underneath the sophisticated and refined surface was a heartless and brutal environment. When Mary Todd was born, there were just over half a million people living in Kentucky, and 126,732 of them were enslaved African Americans. Slaves and a very small number of free blacks made up 40 percent of the population of Fayette County, of which Lexington was the county seat, and Lexington itself was the main slave-trading center of Kentucky. Slave-trading firms were well established in the city, slave traders were recognized as members of the business community and slave auctions were public events. Some slaves in Lexington toiled in hemp and nail factories, while others worked as domestics, some living in the homes of their masters and others in slave quarters behind houses and businesses across the city. Like other slave-holding cities of the South, Lexington tightly regulated the activities and movement of blacks. By 1820, blacks were not allowed to assemble on Saturdays and Sundays or at night, and watchmen patrolled the city's streets looking for curfew violators, runaway slaves or slaves moving about without passes. Slavery and the violence required to enforce it were on constant public display and were embedded in the daily experiences of all of the city's residents.[8]

The cruelty of slavery formed the backdrop of the violence of Lexington, and the fiery sensibilities and violent tendencies of the city's white residents went beyond the confines of slavery. Lexington was a hard-drinking, gun-toting, horse racing town, and for all of its affluence and haughty education, liquor and weapons characterized the community as much as Transylvania University and the botanical garden did. Even some of the city's most respected and refined citizens engaged in unsavory activities. For example, the highly regarded Henry Clay enjoyed liquor and card playing and was an incurable duelist. Most men carried a concealed weapon, like a pocket pistol or a knife; the homicide rate in town was four times that in eastern cities; and the culture of Southern honor and dueling encouraged physical retaliation for small slights and personal affronts. Levi Todd had known this all too well, for he himself had survived the threats of an armed group of disgruntled debtors who showed up at Ellerslie, threatening to burn it down in 1803. Lexingtonians were passionate, armed, drank too much and took their honor and their politics seriously. In fact, in Lexington, politics was often a blood sport. In 1823, for example, two political factions divided over the repeal of a Kentucky statute related to debt relief. As one observer noted, both factions employed nonviolent "argument, and invective, and sarcasm, and satire, and pasquinade, and ribaldry," but in Lexington the debate resulted in a "brick-bat war" in which the opponents faced off across the street from each other, hurling chunks of brick pavements and breaking heads and noses.[9]

Juxtaposed with the cultural refinement of upper-class white society and the gleaming architecture of white institutions, like Usher's Theatre and the city library, was Lexington's slave market. On Main Street, among the commercial establishments that helped make Lexington an economic center of central Kentucky, auctioneers sold slaves. As Lexington's residents shopped for teas and raisins at Downing & Grant, purchased boots and Irish linens at George Trotter's & Son or browsed the books at the Essex book and stationery shop, they would have seen slaves on the auction block and heard the call of the auctioneers. Lexington was, truly, a community of extremes. In the *Kentucky Gazette* printed in Lexington the week of Mary Todd's birth were announcements for the opening of Mr. Pigeon's Dancing School, the availability of Madeira wines at Smith & Todd's store, a public auction of seven slaves belonging to Coleman Rogers and two upcoming lotteries—one to benefit the Fayette Hospital (50¢ tickets) and the other to benefit the Lexington Athenaeum ($5 tickets).[10]

This was the Lexington that sustained the Todd family's provincial gentility and pretension on the one hand and on the other inspired the quick-tempered, sharp-tongued and unrestrained personalities of its men and women, boys and girls. It was to be the setting of Mary Todd's first explorations in the world beyond the Todd household, but first she would have to navigate the boisterous confines of the Todd home on Short Street. Mary was the fourth child and third daughter, and the Todd house must have been a chaotic environment with two little girls, aged five and three, a male toddler and now a new infant. Mary's father was often absent from the home for business and politics, her mother was busy with a brood of youngsters and, like most children in a large and growing family in the early nineteenth century, Mary did not receive much individualized attention.[11] Her mother, Eliza Todd, had struggled to make the transition from the comfort and conveniences of her mother's home to establishing a home of her own. Writing to her grandfather in 1813, she had complained, "I have been very busy for some time past preparing for house-keeping. I had no idea it was attended with so much trouble, it really is almost enough to deter girls from getting married. We intend residing in Lexington, it would never do for me to go far from mama as I shall stand so much in need of her instruction."[12] Eliza probably benefited more from the assistance of the slaves her mother sent to help and later from her own slaves than from any hands-on help from her own mother. She came to rely most heavily on a female slave named Mammy Sally in whom she placed the care of her children. Given the close proximity of the births of her children, it is likely that she also relied on the services of a slave as a wet nurse to her children as well.[13]

In 1820, Eliza Todd was twenty-six when she gave birth to Mary's second brother Robert P. Todd. The Todd house was brimming with active young, and as some remembered it later, undisciplined children. The siblings were competitive and impish and unmerciful in their teasing. They loved each other and fought with each other and bonded through shared experiences, and some of these sibling relationships remained important throughout their adult lives. Although probably too young herself to have been deeply affected, Mary Ann and her family experienced their first family death when fourteen-month-old Robert died suddenly of some common infection that claimed the lives of many infants in the early nineteenth century. When he died, the family's slave Nelson went door-to-door across the town, delivering funeral tickets reading: "Yourself and family are invited to attend the funeral of Robert P. Todd, infant son of Mr. R.S. Todd, from his residence on Short Street, this evening, at 5 o'clock. Lexington. July 22, 1822." Mary and her siblings likely greeted a parade of visitors into the Todd parlor, as extended family, friends and business associates paid their respects to the family. However, life continued, and just a short while after little Robert's death, Eliza was pregnant again. Mary Ann's sister Ann Marie was born in 1824. While it is quite likely that four-year-old Mary Ann was excited at the appearance of this new little girl, one wonders what she might have thought about becoming just plain Mary, as her parents dropped the Ann in her name to avoid confusion with her baby sister who was to be called Ann.[14]

Just a year and a half later, yet another Todd child was born, this one a boy named George Rogers Clark. George was born in early July, but there was no time for celebration, as Eliza developed a fever immediately following his birth. Likely, she was suffering from puerperal, or childbed, fever, which was, unfortunately, an all too common experience for women of the era. While Transylvania University had a renowned medical college, medical knowledge was limited in particulars of women's health, and medical science had not yet adopted basic techniques based on the germ theory of disease. Robert Todd sent for a bevy of doctors, certainly some of the best in the West at the time, and sent the six Todd children to their Grandmother Parker's house across the yard. Over the next twenty-four hours, the slave Nelson was seen running back and forth from the house to the drug store, collecting medicines and supplies. Sadly, despite the best medicine available, Eliza died. The family held her funeral in their home at 4 p.m. the next day, likely sending announcements similar to those circulated two years earlier for the young Robert. One can imagine the profound grief of the Widow Parker, of Robert Todd and of those six Todd children upon the death of the still young Eliza Todd. The death of any thirty-year-old woman with a household full of children was a tragedy. However, the death of children, spouses and parents was a common historical experience at a time when medical science and understanding of health and disease were far less developed than they are today. Common or not, the death of a parent was a difficult loss for any child. However, loss and sorrow were a part of life, and as it was in that hot July of 1825, Mary Todd and her siblings, spanning the ages of two days to twelve years, were motherless.[15]

Elizabeth and Frances were already attending school at this time and were old enough to be, at least mostly, self-reliant. They had teachers and friends outside of the Todd family circle to support and distract them from the difficulties at home. Levi, Mary (who was just six) and the younger children required more care and may have felt the loss of their mother more keenly. The business interests of their father occupied him entirely, and the children's needs were placed in the hands of family slaves. Soon after Eliza's death, Robert left for Frankfort, the state capital, where he was the clerk for the Kentucky legislature and would later serve as a legislator. Once in Frankfort, he almost immediately began courting Elizabeth Humphreys, the daughter of one of Kentucky's most prominent families. She was twenty-five, and a few years beyond the typical age for women to marry, but she was financially and politically well heeled. Two of her uncles were U.S. senators, and two were professors at Transylvania University. Courting a woman so soon after the death of his wife was a bit of a social faux pas, and Robert Todd's mother-in-law Elizabeth Parker was less than thrilled. Ultimately, however, she had little say in the matter. The couple did wait a respectable sixteen months before their nuptials, marrying in Frankfort on November 1, 1826. Kentucky senator John J. Crittenden, a close friend of Robert Todd, was in attendance, but the Todd children likely were not.[16]

As soon as the new Mrs. Todd—Betsey as she was called—arrived in Lexington, she was faced with rambunctious stepchildren, who certainly gave her the same varying degrees of trouble that stepchildren today heap on their own stepparents. Stepfamilies were a common reality in nineteenth-century America, but they likely had their share of difficulties. No doubt, there was an adjustment period for all concerned, and it is very likely that there were bad times as well as good times in Mary's second family. One important mitigating factor was that in the Todd household, there were slaves to tend the children. Much as Eliza Todd had done, Betsey Todd relied on the slaves to manage the growing Todd family; the slave nurses, especially Mammy Sally, provided much of the emotional support the children received. Slaves also cooked and cleaned for the children and saw them to and from school.[17] The family reliance on slaves had been a fact of life with their biological mother, and it would continue to be so with their stepmother. In actuality, Mary and her siblings may not have been any closer to their own mother than they were to their stepmother, and certainly, the smaller children never really knew their own mother well at all. Some historians have argued that Mary was more deeply affected by her mother's death and that her relationship with her stepmother was particularly stormy. There is not, however, any hard historical evidence to support this theory. Mary referred to Betsy as Ma and spoke fondly of her later in life, one time noting how "obliging & accommodating" she could be. While sectional politics would estrange the two of them in the 1860s, Mary's childhood relationship with her stepmother may not have been a close one, but it was certainly not entirely negative.[18]

Perhaps more influential than the presence of a stepmother in the Todd household was the fact that it was always packed with people. When Betsey Todd joined the family, there were already six children. The birth of Betsey's first child, Margaret, in 1828 marked the beginning of the second wave of Todd children that would not stop until 1841 when Kitty, her eighth, was born. Siblings and family slaves were constant companions of little Mary Todd, but her family extended well beyond Short Street as well. The Todd, Parker and Humphreys families were prolific in central Kentucky, and aunts and uncles and cousins were in and out of Robert Todd's house throughout the 1820s and 1830s, some even staying for months or years at a time. In addition, the children spent time at Grandmother Parker's house next door, and they visited cousins and aunts and uncles who lived in Lexington and the surrounding area. Two cousins who were particular favorites of Mary were John and Eliza Stuart, the children of Grandfather Levi Todd's daughter Hannah and her minister husband. The Frankfort house of Betsey's mother also became a destination for the Todd children. There was simply too much activity in the Todd house and too many people coming and going for Mary and her siblings to be lonely; and just when the noise and chaos might prove overwhelming to the senses and sanity, there were ample opportunities for refuge elsewhere. In a letter to Cousin Eliza written later in her life, Mary wrote: "the memory of earlier years and the memory of those who were so kind to me in my desolate childhood is ever remembered by me."[19] By desolate, she might have meant that she did not receive the individualized attention that she would have liked. Regardless, desolate is not a fitting description of the Todd house during Mary Todd's childhood. On the contrary, it was an exuberant environment. An important note here is that Mary made that comment in her later life, several years after the Civil War, during which the Todd family experienced irreparable political and personal divisions. However, during her childhood, Mary was ever surrounded by numerous family members and friends. It would have been difficult to stand out in such a large and energetic family, but if she felt lonely, it was a loneliness of her own making.[20]

Not long after the arrival of Mary's stepmother in Lexington, Mary began her formalized education. Kentucky was a unique place for private education in the early 1800s, and options for girls as well as for boys, especially in Lexington, were numerous. The public school system in Kentucky did not get started until the late 1830s, so when Mary began her education, all of the schools in Lexington were private. Private schools in Lexington were quite varied; some were rooted in particular religious denominations, like the Lexington Female Bible Society directed by Elizabeth Skillman, the Protestant Boarding School for Young Ladies and the Catholic St. Catherine's Academy founded by the Sisters of Charity of Nazareth. Most schools were segregated by gender, but some were coeducational, which was a modern approach to education; some schools taught domestic skills and the cultural arts. Lexington was home to Mrs. George P. Richardson's school for Little Misses, the Lafayette Female Academy (named for the famous Marquis de Lafayette after his visit to Lexington in 1825), Mr. Maguire's Classical, Scientific and English School for boys and girls, Cabell's Dancing School, Madame Blaique's Dancing Academy, Madame Mentelle's Boarding School for Girls, the Van Doren's Institute and Dr. Ward's Shelby Academy.[21]

It was Ward's Academy, as it was more commonly known, that Mary entered at the age of eight. Mary's older sisters had attended the Lafayette Academy, but the school had suffered some bad publicity based on accusations of lax discipline. Robert Todd had developed an interest in the new school of Dr. John Ward, an Episcopal priest and a strong advocate of serious scholarly subjects for girls. This appealed to Todd, who might have envisioned a more modern education for his daughters, as female education in the Todd family was the norm. Robert Todd's mother, stepmother, sisters and both wives attended formal schools at a time when most women did not. Even Henry Clay's wife, Lucretia, was uneducated. Robert had also been exposed to the writings of Mary Wollstonecraft, an eighteenth-century English writer who advocated for female education and women's rights. Wollstonecraft's *Vindication of the Rights of Woman* had been in Levi Todd's library at Ellerslie. Todd appreciated Ward as an innovative educator, who expected a high level of intellectual stimulation for female students. At his school, for example, he required girls to give at the end of each term public recitations, an activity that traditional educators deemed appropriate only for male students. Ward ran his school in a large, two-story building at Market and Second Streets in Lexington. Ward was a strict disciplinarian and taskmaster, but he was kind. The former rector of Christ Church, he stressed piety in his school and required the study of religion; he delivered Episcopal sermons to his students on a regular basis. The Todd family was Presbyterian. Mary attended church with her family before entering Ward's school, and her slave nanny had exposed her to her own African-Christian spiritual beliefs. However, it was at the academy where Mary acquired a strong knowledge of the Bible and developed a Christian faith she would maintain throughout her life.[22]

At Ward's Academy—where Mary attended from September through December and March through July from 1827 to 1832—she learned math, history, science, religion and French. While boys of the day studied logic, Greek and Latin as well, these subjects were not part of the curriculum at Ward's or at most other schools for girls at the time. Dr. Ward's wife, Sarah, was an important part of the academy, providing a motherly presence for the girls. Mrs. Ward also organized special events at the school. For example, in 1829, she arranged a May Day procession in which Mary and some seventy students marched through the streets of Lexington. The day school cost Mary's family $44 annually plus $8 additional for French lessons. Ward's fees were lower than other schools in Lexington but still out of reach for most families in Kentucky. In September 1827, Mary Todd began what would be a ten-year career as a student, a quite remarkable circumstance for a girl in Kentucky in the early nineteenth century. Her education was a defining experience of her life, and it was enhanced by the arrival of Lizzie Humphreys, her stepmother's niece. Lizzie moved from her home in Frankfort into the Todd house in order to attend Ward's school. Mary shared her room with Lizzie, and the two little girls walked up the hill each day to the academy and were inseparable childhood companions.[23]

Lizzie may have been her favorite, but Mary certainly had plenty of child-hood companions at school and at home as well. The Todd family continued to grow; Margaret was born in 1828, Samuel in 1830 and David in 1832. At that time, all six of the original Todd children, Mary's three little steps-siblings and Lizzie Humphreys lived in the Todd house on Short Street. In 1832, Mary completed her studies at Ward's Academy, and other significant changes in her life occurred that year as well. Her eldest sister Elizabeth married and left the household, and Mary enrolled in a boarding school, which removed her from the noisy Todd home each week from Monday morning until Friday afternoon. Another change occurred when Robert Todd moved his family to a new house on Main Street, just two blocks away. It was a brick fourteen-room house with double parlors and a wide hall in the center, and the property included a coach house, stable and slave quarters. There was a beautiful flower garden in the side lawn. A clear gentle stream ran through the yard, as did a white gravel walkway, which wound through the clipped bluegrass to the conservatory. That same year, Robert Todd had entered into a partnership with two other Kentucky businessmen to manufacture cotton yarns, and Oldham, Todd & Hemingway operated a store to sell its goods in Lexington. The new house better reflected Robert Todd's desired social and political standing within Lexington, and it met Betsey Todd's exalted requirements for a proper and refined home for entertaining. It also gave Robert and his new wife some distance from the Widow Parker, and it certainly improved the living environment of the children as well, although Mary herself would spend little time there.[24]

During Mary's teen years, the number of Todd children continued to increase. From 1833 to 1841, Martha, Emilie, Alexander, Elodie and Kitty were born. Mary would later claim that she barely knew all these children because, as she remembered it, her "early home was truly at a boarding school."[25] This comment by Mary is one of only a precious few related to her childhood that survive, and it reflects the distance she felt from her family household and from her siblings. Mary was away from the family during the week from the years 1832 to 1836, so she definitely had less time with younger children than she had had with the older ones. Mary had thirteen siblings, so it is not surprising that she had varying relationships with them. She loved some of them; she disliked others. She was emotionally connected to some, including Emilie who was born when Mary was spending much of her time away from the Todd home, and she had strained relationships with others. Not surprising in such a large family, Mary had favorite siblings, and she had siblings with whom she had little in common. Most interesting, perhaps, is the fact that her biological relationship with her siblings did not determine her closeness to them. Contrary to her statement that she barely knew the youngest of the stepsiblings, that did not keep her from having pleasant relationships with a few of them.[26]

As if immediate family members and visiting family members were not enough to overwhelm the Todd household, Robert Todd was often entertaining business and political associates at home as well. Traditionally, Kentuckians opened their homes to visitors from afar, and the Todd house was often buzzing with short-term and long-term guests. Senators Henry Clay and John Crittenden were perhaps the most prominent guests, as they were close friends of Robert Todd, but there was a steady parade of local Whig politicians through the Todd parlor. The influx of European goods in America effected the success of Todd's business interests, as did shipping and transportation networks. Therefore, Todd and other Kentucky business-men overwhelmingly supported and, in many ways, inspired the American System, an economic plan of which Henry Clay was the central congres-sional proponent. The plan advocated protective tariffs to assist American manufacturers and the expenditure of federal money to build infrastruc-ture across the developing United States. Internal improvements like roads, bridges and canals were particularly important to the growth and settlement of Kentucky, and Whig policies and Whig Party politicians like Henry Clay dominated Kentucky politics. One can imagine that much of the discussion occurring over food and the finest alcohol Todd retrieved on his travels to New Orleans centered on Whig politics, and, no doubt, there was much anti-Democratic rhetoric flying about the Todd parlor as well. Mary and all her siblings would have heard these discussions and may have even been encouraged to participate. More than her siblings, however, Mary seemed to particularly delight in the political banter. By the time she was fourteen, she was a fiery little Whig, declaring her love of Henry Clay and her disdain for President Jackson.[27]

Slavery was likely another topic of discussion in the Todd parlor. Despite the fact that Kentucky was a slave state, there was considerable anti-slavery feeling across the bluegrass. In 1833, Kentucky law forbade the importation of new slaves into the state. The auctions of slaves within the state continued in Lexington, but there was considerable debate over the issue throughout the 1830s. Mary's immediate family owned slaves and so did many members of her extended family. However, her step-grandmother Elizabeth Hum-phreys emancipated her slaves in her will, which was carried out upon her death in 1836. Mary and her siblings would also have heard talk about a notorious Lexington slaveholder and her vicious abuse of her own slaves, and the children no doubt shuddered when there were whispers in the par-lor of a particularly ugly incident in 1836 when she threw a young slave boy out of a second-story window. Mary and her siblings experienced slavery on many levels. They were privy to political discussion over it, they had personal relationships with their own family's slaves, they interacted in various ways with the slaves in the other households of family and friends and they witnessed the institution in the market place and through the business of William Pullman, a well-known slave trader, whose slave pens were adjacent to the property of Grandmother Parker.[28]

One can easily speculate that given Mary's interest in politics as an adult, the political discussions that occurred within her father's public parlor thrilled her. In addition, there is fairly good reason to believe that Robert Todd encouraged his daughter's political interests and Whig enthusiasm. In fact, this interest may have played a role in his decision to enroll her in a second school when she was fourteen. At the time, Mary's two oldest sisters Elizabeth and Frances were out of school, living at home and courting, and her brother Levi was at Transylvania University. Mary's education at Ward's Academy was rare, but it was even more uncommon that a girl of her age would remain in school past the age of fourteen. Most girls who received formalized education retired after four or five years, spending their teen years in their parent's household until they were married. This is the path that both Elizabeth and Frances were taking. Perhaps Mary advocated from her own desire to continue her studies, perhaps her father saw something in her that he did not see in his other daughters or perhaps there were tensions in the household that merited such a choice. Whatever the reason or reasons, Robert Todd enrolled Mary in Mentelle's school for young ladies. Madame Victoria Charlotte Le Clere Mentelle and her husband, Augustus, both immigrants from Paris, had fled the French Revolution in 1792, settling first in Ohio. When they arrived in Lexington, they gave lessons in French and in dancing, but after receiving a donation from Mary Todd's great aunt, Mary Wickliffe, they established a boarding school for girls across the street from Henry Clay's Ashland plantation, about a mile and a half from the Todd's home. Their home at Rose Hill housed their own family of six children, the school and its boarding students, who paid $120 annually. Madame was an attractive, large woman who was an accomplished dancer, musician and scholar. She ran her boarding schools for girls in French, requiring fluency from her students.[29]

Rising out of the American Revolution and a movement of republican motherhood, schooling for young woman was on the rise in the eastern United States, but in the newer western states such opportunities were scarce. Lexington was somewhat of an anomaly, attracting educators, like the Mentelles, who established French schools that taught logic and the classics, typically subjects reserved for boys. They often provided instruction in philosophy, history and languages, as well as in domestic and social skills, embroidery and dancing. Mentelle's school for young ladies was one of the best known academies in Kentucky, although some Lexington residents believed the Mentelles were eccentric. The school offered arrangements for boarders, but it also welcomed day students living in the area. Mary could have traveled to the school daily with little trouble, but instead she boarded at the school during the week and returned to the Todd home on the weekends. Like the choice to attend the school in the first place, the choice to live on the school's campus could be a clue about family relations; however, there is no historical evidence to explain it fully. What we do know is that Mary Todd spent four years at Madame Mentelle's school, and that experience was important in her life for three reasons. First, she became fluent in French, which was a skill she enjoyed and in which she took a lifelong pride. It would also serve her well for travels in Europe and during her four-year residence in France in her later years. Second, Mentelle's school provided literary and theatrical opportunities for students, and for Mary this was, indeed, a delight. At the school, Mary became the voracious reader that she would be for her entire life; she studied theatre, acted in plays and acquired a lifelong love of the performing arts. Third, the Mentelles were quite snobbish about the limits of Lexington society and culture. Although their daughter married Henry Clay's son Thomas, the couple found Lexingtonian manners seriously lacking. At the school, Madame Mentelle shared with her students a European perspective and opened up a world beyond Lexington and Kentucky. Very likely, this exposure to European culture and ideas as well as daily interactions with such an independent-thinking schoolmistress instilled in Mary a desire to look beyond her Kentucky home, inspired her passion for travel and new interests and encouraged a personal confidence in her own intellect and the validity of her own opinions. Mary was probably born with a fiery personality, but the experience at Montelle's encouraged her bold nature.[30]

In 1834, Mary's brother-in-law Ninian W. Edwards gained an appointment as Illinois attorney general. The following year, he resigned, and he and his young bride, Elizabeth, removed to Springfield, where they were comfortably established and prepared to receive visitors from home. In May 1835, Mary and her sister Frances accompanied their father to Springfield to visit the couple.[31] This visit likely planted the seeds of her own options for migration north following the completion of her studies at Madame Mentelle's boarding school. When she completed those studies in the summer of 1836, she was a grown woman, and returning to the congested Todd household held little appeal. There is also some evidence to suggest that the relationship between Betsey and the older children was strained at this point, heightened no doubt by the needs of the ten youngest children. Mary longed for excitement that her home could not provide. Lexington had incorporated as a town in 1832, it was connected by railroad to the state capital by 1835 and, in many other ways, it remained the beaming "Athens of the West" it had been in the early 1820s. One writer commented that "the town buildings in general are handsome, and some magnificent. Few towns in the West, or elsewhere, are more delightfully situated. Its environs have a singular softness and amenity of landscape, and the town wears an air of neatness, opulence, and repose, indicating leisure and studiousness, rather than the bustle of business and commerce." The lack of business bustle was precisely the problem. For some, the coming decade would prove to be difficult. More people filed for bankruptcy, construction slowed and forced land sales increased. As the town's economic opportunities decreased, the town failed to attract new settlers and lost many of the best and brightest of its native-born sons to Louisville, Cincinnati, St. Louis and elsewhere. Although students were still flocking to Transylvania University—among them future presidential candidate John C. Breckinridge and future Confederate president Jefferson Davis—most did not stay after graduation. The town was fading. Robert Todd remained committed to Lexington and would remain in town until his death. His oldest son, Levi, had joined him in his Lexington business interests, but he was likely not surprised when economic opportunities lured his first son-in-law to Illinois and whisked away the first of his own children, Elizabeth. Mary's second sister, Frances, then joined Elizabeth in Illinois. In 1836, Mary Todd had completed her education, and like her hometown, she was now at a crossroads. The roads in Lexington held far less appeal to her than the one her sisters had taken north. So, in the spring of 1837, Mary Todd, with her unusually sophisticated education for the period, was a Southern girl with a big brain and an even bigger personality and looked to the North as well.[32]

Notes

1 William H. Townsend, *Lincoln and His Wife's Home Town* (Indianapolis, IN: The Bobbs-Merrill Co., 1929), 50–51; George W. Ranck, *The History of Lexington, Kentucky: Its Early Annals and Recent Progress* (Cincinnati, OH: Robert Clarke & Co., 1872), 24, 219, 296; Lewis Collins, *History of Kentucky*, 3 vols. (Covington, KY: Collins & Co., 1882), 3:20.

2 Jean Baker, *Mary Todd Lincoln: A Biography* (New York: W. W. Norton & Co., 1987; reprint, New York: W. W. Norton & Co., 2008), 4; John Mack Faragher, *Daniel Boone: The Life and Legend of an American Pioneer* (New York: Henry Holt & Co., 1992), 217–21; Thomas Marshall Green, *Historic Families of Kentucky* (Cincinnati, OH: Robert Clarke & Co., 1889), 274.

3 Stephen Berry, *House of Abraham: Lincoln and the Todds, a Family Divided by War* (Boston: Houghton Mifflin Co., 2007), 6–8; Green, *Historic Families of Kentucky*, 215–16, 250.

4 Collins, *History of Kentucky*, 3:23; Baker, *Mary Todd Lincoln*, 6–8; "Major Robert Parker House, Lexington," *Herald-Leader* (Lexington, KY), 2 April 1950, 36:1–3; Samuel H. Williamson, "Seven Ways to Compute the Relative Value of a U.S. Dollar Amount, 1774 to Present," *Measuring Worth*, 2014; John J. McCusker, *How Much Is That in Real Money? A Historical Price Index for Use as a Deflator of Money Values in the Economy of the United States* (Worcester, MA: American Antiquarian Society, 2000).

5 Berry, *House of Abraham*, 6–8; Green, *Historic Families of Kentucky*, 213, 215–16.

6 Townsend, *Lincoln and His Wife's Home Town*, 45–46, 48–49; "Major Robert Parker House"; Baker, *Mary Todd Lincoln*, 10, 16–17; James Wallace Hammack, *Kentucky and the Second American Revolution: The War of 1812* (Lexington: University of Kentucky Press, 1976); Donald R. Hickey, *The War of 1812: A Forgotten Conflict* (Urbana: University of Illinois Press, 1989).

7 Ranck, *History of Lexington*, 143–44, 285, 303; Townsend, *Lincoln and His Wife's Home Town*, 16, 24; James A. Ramage and Andrea S. Watkins, *Kentucky Rising: Democracy, Slavery, and Culture from the Early Republic to the Civil War* (Lexington: University of Kentucky Press, 2011), 211–13, 228; John Dean Wright, *Lexington: Heart of the Bluegrass* (Lexington, KY: Lexington-Fayette County Historic Commission, 1982), 56; Robert V. Remini, *Henry Clay: Statesman for the Union* (New York: W.W. Norton & Co., 1991).

8 Ramage and Watkins, *Kentucky Rising*, 238; Marion B. Lucas, *A History of Blacks in Kentucky: From Slavery to Segregation, 1760–1891* (Frankfort: Kentucky Historical Society, 2003), xvi–xvii, 11, 13, 30, 87, 89; Wright, *Lexington*, 75; J. Winston Coleman Jr., "Lexington's Slave Dealers and Their Southern Trade," *Filson Club History Quarterly* 12 (January 1938): 1–23; Walter Johnson, *Soul by Soul: Life Inside the Antebellum Slave Market* (Cambridge, MA: Harvard University Press, 1999); Ira Berlin, *Many Thousands Gone: The First Two Centuries of Slavery in North America* (Cambridge, MA: Harvard University Press, 1998).

9 Ranck, *History of Lexington*, 297, 299, 301; Stephen Berry, "There's Something about Mary: Mary Lincoln and Her Siblings," in Frank J. Williams and Michael Burkhimer, eds., *The Mary Lincoln Enigma: Historians on America's Most Controversial First Lady* (Carbondale: Southern Illinois University Press, 2012), 19–21; Berry, *House of Abraham*, 7; Wright, *Lexington*, 41, 54, 57; Ramage and Watkins, *Kentucky Rising*, 32; Kenneth S. Greenberg, "The Nose, the Lie, and the Duel in the Antebellum South," *American Historical Review* 95 (February 1990): 57–74.

10 *Kentucky Gazette* (Lexington), 11 December 1818, 4:3–5; 18 December 1818, 4:1–2.

11 Berry, "There's Something about Mary," 14–15, 17.

12 Eliza Todd to General Andrew Porter, 20 June 1813, Huntington Library, San Marino, CA.

13 Baker, *Mary Todd Lincoln*, 16–18.

14 Catherine Clinton, *Mrs. Lincoln: A Life* (New York: Harper Collins, 2009), 11; Townsend, *Lincoln and His Wife's Home Town*, 51; Berry, "There's Something about Mary," 14–15.

15 Berry, *House of Abraham*, 8–9; Deborah Kuhn McGregor, *From Midwives to Medicine: The Birth of American Gynecology* (New Brunswick, NJ: Rutgers University Press, 1998), 117; Townsend, *Lincoln and His Wife's Home Town*, 53; Baker, *Mary Todd Lincoln*, 20–21; Michael R. Haines, "The White Population of the United States, 1790–1920," in Michael R. Haines and Richard H. Steckel, eds., *A Population History of North America* (New York: Cambridge University Press, 2000), 338; Wright, *Lexington*, 32.

16 *Lexington Daily Transcript* (KY), 12 December 1827, 3:1; Berry, *House of Abraham*, 9–10; Baker, *Mary Todd Lincoln*, 29; Green, *Historic Families of Kentucky*, 215.
    The political uncles of Elizabeth Humphreys were her mother's brothers Senator James Brown (1766–1835), who served Louisiana from 1811 to 1824, and Senator John Brown (1757–1837), who served Kentucky from 1789 to 1804. They were also cousins to Senator John Breckinridge, the grandfather of John C. Breckinridge, who ran for president against Abraham Lincoln in 1860. *Biographical Directory of the United States Congress, 1774–2005* (Washington, DC: Government Printing Office, 2005), 701, 720–721.

17 Townsend, *Lincoln and His Wife's Home Town*, 53–54.

18 Mary Lincoln to Abraham Lincoln, May 1848, Lincoln Papers, ALPL (this document is transcribed in its entirety in the Documents section); Mary Lincoln to Emilie Helm, 23 November 1856, *L&L*, 45–48 (this document is transcribed in its entirety in the Documents section); Baker, *Mary Todd Lincoln*, 29, 41, 49.

19 Mary Lincoln to Eliza Stuart Steele, 23 May 1871, *L&L*, 588–89.

20 Berry, *House of Abraham*, vi–vii.

21 Ramage and Watkins, *Kentucky Rising*, 14, 145–46; Ranck, *History of Lexington*, 299.

22 Baker, *Mary Todd Lincoln*, 34–35; Wright, *Lexington*, 33–34; Remini, *Henry Clay*, 30; Townsend, *Lincoln and His Wife's Home Town*, 57; *Kentucky Gazette*, 8 May 1829; Mary Wollstonecraft, *Vindication of the Rights of Woman* (1792).

23 Baker, *Mary Todd Lincoln*, 37; Clinton, *Mrs. Lincoln*, 15–18; Townsend, *Lincoln and His Wife's Home Town*, 58.

24 Articles of Partnership, 1 September 1832, evidence in *Todd v. Oldham et al.*, Fayette County (KY) Circuit Court, Kentucky Department for Libraries and Archives, Kentucky State Archives, Frankfort, KY; Berry, *House of Abraham*, vi–vii; Townsend, *Lincoln and His Wife's Home Town*, 60; Mary Lincoln to Elizabeth Keckley, 29 October 1867, transcribed in Elizabeth Keckley, *Behind the Scenes in the Lincoln White House: Memoirs of an African-American Seamstress* (Mineola, NY: Dover Publications, 2006), 135–36; Baker, *Mary Todd Lincoln*, 45–46, 57.

25 Berry, *House of Abraham*, xi–xii; Mary Lincoln to Elizabeth Keckley, 29 October 1867.

26 *L&L*, 155; Berry, *House of Abraham*, vi–vii; Ruth Painter Randall, *The Courtship of Mr. Lincoln* (Boston: Little, Brown & Co., 1957), 8.

27 Ramage and Watkins, *Kentucky Rising*, 24, 26, 30–32; *L&L*, 7; Baker, *Mary Todd Lincoln*, 33.
    In *Mary Todd Lincoln: Her Life and Letters*, the editors derived their interpretation of Mary's enthusiasm for Whig politics from Katherine Helm, *The True Story of Mary, Wife of Lincoln* (New York: Harper & Brothers, 1928) and William H. Townsend, *Lincoln and the Bluegrass: Slavery and Civil War in Kentucky* (Lexington: University of Kentucky Press, 1955; reprint, Lexington: University of Kentucky Press, 1990).

28 Wright, *Lexington*, 76; Baker, *Mary Todd Lincoln*, 67; Lucas, *History of Blacks in Kentucky*, 47; Clinton, *Mrs. Lincoln*, 25; Lowell H. Harrison, *The Antislavery Movement in Kentucky* (Lexington: University Press of Kentucky, 1978).

29 Baker, *Mary Todd Lincoln*, 40–41; Wright, *Lexington*, 3; Ruth Painter Randall, *Mary Lincoln: Biography of a Marriage* (Boston: Little, Brown & Co., 1953), 25.

30 Ramage and Watkins, *Kentucky Rising*, 165; Baker, *Mary Todd Lincoln*, 42–45; Linda K. Kerber, *Women of the Republic: Intellect and Ideology in Revolutionary America* (Chapel Hill: University of North Carolina Press, 1980), 189–231; Linda K. Kerber, "The Republican Mother," in Linda K. Kerber and Jane Sherron De Hart, eds., *Women's America: Refocusing the Past* (New York: Oxford University Press, 1991), 87–95; Kenneth J. Winkle, *Abraham and Mary Lincoln* (Carbondale: Southern Illinois University, 2012), 18.

31 Thomas F. Schwartz, "Mary Todd's 1835 Visit to Springfield, Illinois," *Journal of the Abraham Lincoln Association* 26 (Winter 2005): 42–45.

32 Ranck, *History of Lexington*, 319, 321–23; Wright, *Lexington*, 81; Berry, *House of Abraham*, 19; Answer of Elizabeth P. Edwards in *Edwards et al. v. Todd et al.*, 13 April 1852, Fayette County (KY) Circuit Court, Todd Collection, King Library, University of Kentucky, Lexington.

CHAPTER 2

FROM MARY TODD TO MARY LINCOLN

In the spring of 1837, Mary Todd was an eighteen-year-old graduate of Madame Mentelle's boarding school and one of the best-educated young women in all of Kentucky. Well versed in French, literature, poetry and the politics of the day, she was also an accomplished dancer, a brilliant conversationalist and a charming Southern belle. Grace and intellect, powerful family connections and her pretty blue eyes set her apart from other girls coming of age in Lexington's rough-hewn but still genteel Southern society. However, it was 1837, and Lexington had seen brighter economic days. While the town maintained much of its reputation as a center of educational opportunities in the West, its distance from the Ohio River limited its opportunities for future economic prosperity. Gone were many of the businesses and entrepreneurs that had once flocked to the "Athens of the West," lost to the more bustling river cities of Louisville, Cincinnati and even more distant St. Louis. Mary was bored in Lexington, and even her father agreed that some time away might be in order. Mary's sister Frances had moved to Springfield to live with their older sister Elizabeth, and Mary wished to join them. Robert Todd was unhappy at the prospect of seeing a third daughter leave Lexington, but he agreed that Mary could go so long as she returned. A shrinking pool of eligible bachelors; a household brimming with noisy, young siblings; and the pull of favored family members settled in Illinois combined to make agreeable the bargain she thus made with her father.[1]

Mary left Lexington that May, probably with her father on his way to the state capitol in Frankfort, on the Lexington and Ohio Railroad. As young women rarely traveled alone at this time, another male relative, perhaps either her father's brother Dr. John Todd or her cousin John T. Stuart, both of whom had previously settled in Springfield, accompanied Mary during the remainder of the trip to Louisville. In Louisville, she and her traveling companion boarded one of the two steamboats that left for St. Louis each week. Whenever possible, water travel was preferred for reasons of speed and of comfort. From St. Louis, a stagecoach carried them the additional 100 miles northeast to Springfield. In those days, stagecoaches stopped every 12 miles or so to rest, feed and water the horses; to drop off and pick up passengers; to deliver mail and packages; and to give passengers some relief from the bumpy terrain. The entire trip from Lexington to Springfield, which following the meandering path of the Ohio and Mississippi Rivers covered nearly 700 miles, took Mary about two weeks. Antebellum travel was slow and physically uncomfortable, but accommodations aboard railway cars and steamships offered travelers some conveniences like prepared meals, washbasins and ventilated rooms. One writer described a steamboat on the Ohio River as having "one long narrow cabin, the whole length of the boat; from which the state-rooms open, on both sides. A small portion at the stern is partitioned off for the ladies; and the bar is at the opposite extreme."[2] Stagecoach traveling was far less pleasant, as up to nine passengers in each coach experienced extreme temperatures, dirt, rugged terrain, insects and the ever-present potential for accidents.[3]

However difficult the travel, Mary arrived safely in Springfield and enjoyed a reunion with her two sisters. Her brother-in-law's home was also filled with the cries of a brand-new baby, Julia. Domestic activities, political events and parties occupied Mary's time with the Edwards family. It is entirely possible that Mary made the acquaintance of Abraham Lincoln during that summer visit. Lincoln was in Springfield much of the summer, establishing himself in his new law partnership with Mary's cousin John T. Stuart and boarding with Joshua Speed, who also had Kentucky ties. That summer, the Edwards' parlor was the scene for many Whig political discussions, including talk of John T. Stuart's potential run for Congress. The laying of the cornerstone for the new state capitol building served as an occasion for a public event featuring a speech by the popular local Whig politician Edward D. Baker. Both Mary and Abraham could likely have interacted at least casually in either of these settings. However, Lincoln was involved courting Mary Owens at this time, was focused on learning the law and was serving his second term in the Illinois General Assembly. While Mary may have enjoyed some interactions with the tall lawyer, she was engaged in social interactions with a variety of young men and women. She enjoyed a lively summer filled with fascinating social and political experiences, but she had promised her father that she would return to Lexington. In addition, the expense of her stay was likely too heavy a burden on the Edwards family. Mary hated to leave her sisters and the independence she had gained during her visit in Springfield, but there was no alternative, at least for the time being.[4]

Back in Lexington, Mary was restless. Her father was busy with business and politics, and her stepmother was preoccupied with the care of the young children and with serving as hostess for her husband's political and business associates. The Todd household was likely stifling for Mary, and given the economic difficulties that followed the depression of 1837, she might have been feeling anxious about her future prospects as well. She returned to John Ward's school as a teacher's assistant, helping Sarah Ward with the smaller children. Perhaps she even considered becoming a teacher herself. Mary was home for the birth of another sibling, Alexander, who was born in February 1839. Mary was twenty years old when little Aleck was born, and the reality of the difference in their ages presented additional evidence that it was time for her to leave her father's house once and for all. Just three months later, Mary's sister Frances was planning a wedding to Dr. William S. Wallace in Springfield. It was a happy time for the couple and for the family, but it was especially fortuitous for Mary. Frances would move into the Globe Tavern in Springfield after her marriage, opening up a bed in the Edwards' household. As soon as she possibly could, Mary packed a trunk and headed back to Springfield, perhaps arriving in time for her sister's wedding. This time, the move would be permanent.[5]

There were factors pushing Mary out of Lexington, but there was also one significant pull factor as well. The primary draw for Mary in her decision to trade in her Kentucky home for Illinois was the family network that preceded her. Mary's sisters, an uncle and three cousins were already settled and established in Springfield when Mary decided to make it her new hometown. Upland Southerners settled in Illinois in large numbers in the 1820s and 1830s, and by 1850, numbered more than 35 percent of native born immigrants in Illinois. Thirteen percent of those settlers hailed from Kentucky, mostly concentrated in two clusters: the Military Tract in Southern Illinois and another in Sangamon County, where Springfield was located. Kentucky aristocrats had played a role in the early development of Illinois. For example, Ninian Edwards, the father of Mary's brother-in-law, was the territorial governor of Illinois from 1809 to 1818 and then the third governor of the state from 1826 to 1830. Mary's cousin John J. Hardin, a Kentucky native and a graduate of Transylvania University who later served in the U.S. Congress, settled in Jacksonville in Morgan County, just forty miles west of Springfield. In September 1830, he reported home, writing that "it appears as if the flood gates of Kentucky had broken loose, and her population set free had naturally turned their course to Illinois and Missouri."[6] Core family groups characterized much of the migration stream of upland Southerners into Illinois, and the Todd family played a part in that migration to central Illinois.[7]

Dr. John Todd, Robert S. Todd's oldest brother, had left Kentucky for Edwardsville, Illinois, in 1817. When John Quincy Adams appointed him to the land office in 1827, he settled in Springfield, and thus began the Todd settlement to that city. Although slavery was illegal in Illinois, Todd had four slaves with him when he settled in Springfield. The geographic boundaries of slavery were not always so exact, and some Kentuckians like Dr. Todd bridged the divide between what defined a Northerner and what defined a Southerner. Dr. Todd's arrival marked the beginning of the movement of many members of the extended Todd family to Illinois, and he and his wife, Elizabeth, played Northern patriarch and matriarch to the extended Todd family in Springfield. After graduating from Centre College in Kentucky and gaining admission to the bar, John Todd Stuart, whose mother was Robert Todd's sister, settled in Springfield to practice law in 1828. For a short while, he lived with Dr. Todd. In 1832, another cousin, Stephen T. Logan, moved his family to Springfield, where he practiced law, served in the Illinois General Assembly and won election to a circuit court bench. In 1835, Elizabeth and Ninian W. Edwards made Springfield their home, and Mary's sister Frances was now married to a Springfield doctor. So in 1839, Mary would be the third Todd sister from Lexington to join them all.[8]

Kentucky was her past, and her future awaited her in the welcoming embrace of the Northern Todd clan in Springfield. As Mary Todd enjoyed the scenery from the stagecoach window headed northeast out of St. Louis, she may have wondered and worried about what the future would hold, but she knew she had a settled network of family to make her transition to adulthood less difficult. The Kentucky bluegrass behind her, the Illinois prairie beckoned. As a traveler from Ohio wrote in 1839: "Springfield lies on the edge of a large prairie. On the left, as you enter the village from the South, is a delightful grove . . . approaching the southern part of the town, you leave a great sweep of verdant landscape behind you, and behold almost as great a natural meadow to your right. No one can conceive the grandeur and beauty of the scenery."[9]

Yellow and red prairie flowers would have painted a colorful palette, and this was the physical tableau that greeted Mary as her stagecoach approached the thriving, developing little town of Springfield on the Illinois prairie. The vast, overwhelming landscape represented a new world for Miss Mary Todd, full of promise and adventure. As she drew nearer, the little town rose up in the midst of the prairie, and the expansive landscape might well have represented the big and bright future that she was seeking as she left her childhood behind her forever.

Once Mary Todd arrived in Springfield, the stately Edwards home on "Aristocracy Hill" duplicated many of the comforts to which Mary was accustomed back in Lexington and far fewer of the annoyances of her childhood home. The house was warmed by multiple fire places and woodstoves; it was illuminated with oil lamps and glimmering crystal chandeliers; and, as one guest exclaimed, the parlor was the scene of "the most elegant and sumptuous entertainments."[10] Much as her father's house had been open to Kentucky Whigs, the Edwards house welcomed members of the Illinois legislature and other visitors from far and wide. The houses of the Edwards family and their neighbors sat perched on a slightly elevated rise just southwest of the public square overlooking the busy little town. The people who occupied the homes in this well-to-do neighborhood formed the core of Springfield's elite society and, in a way, lorded over the expanding town below them. It was here among these people that Mary formed two important first Springfield friendships. Mercy Levering, who was living with her brother next door to the Edwards family, was the daughter of a Washington judge and would become one of Mary's most intimate female friends. Just down the street lived the Jayne family. Their energetic daughter Julia shared Mary's passion for Whig politics. While Mary certainly had some routine household duties within the Edwards home and lived somewhat under the watchful eye of her motherly sister, the social opportunities for Mary were numerous. There was also in Springfield a Southern tradition of courtly living that would have made Mary Todd comfortable in her new hometown.[11]

Springfield was the state capital as well as the seat of the Sangamon County government. It was also an economic hub for the middle section of Illinois. The city and county were thriving and expanding, and its 2,600 residents were laying claim to the opportunities created in a dynamic environment of political energy and general economic prosperity. Despite the economic difficulties of the nation following the Panic of 1837, Springfield was again booming when Mary arrived in 1839. New businesses were opening, and the construction of homes and buildings was extensive. Dozens of businesses advertised in the *Sangamo Journal*, selling a wide variety of items like fresh groceries, hardware, African cayenne, rose ointment, soda powders, expensive saddles, tea sets, boots and piano fortes. Mary had been accustomed to retail variety and the availability of special imported items in Lexington, and Springfield did not disappoint her in this regard. Various and sundry retail shops, the Sangamon County Courthouse and the shingles of law firms (including that of Stuart & Lincoln), doctors, dentists, land agents and auctioneers added to the colorful business district on and around the public square. That October, the Sangamon County Agricultural Society held an exhibition and fair, the Springfield Mechanic's Union formed, the

Young Men's Lyseum met, the Sangamon Colonization Society published proceedings of their first annual meeting and, of particular interest to the city's newest Whig Mary Todd, the Illinois State Whig Convention assembled in Springfield. No doubt, Mary quickly realized that numerous characteristics of Springfield justified her decision to join the Northern branch of the Todd family.[12]

Two characteristics must have been particularly pleasing. First, when the Illinois State General Assembly was in session, men far outnumbered women in Springfield, and eligible bachelors abounded. Second, politics was king in the state capital and county seat. When the legislature was in session and when the Sangamon County Circuit Court was sitting, legislators and lawyers flocked to Springfield for business and for politics. During the legislative winter, as citizens dubbed the annual session of the Illinois General Assembly, Springfield families opened their homes to visitors for numerous social events.[13] During these events, woman and older girls of the household were pressed into service, baking cakes, cooking food, polishing the silver and providing female social companionship to the single male visitors in town. Mary Todd enjoyed the social and political events that drew in an interesting and exciting cadre of young men with talents and ambitions that thrilled her. During her first year in Springfield, Mary was surrounded by a plethora of worthy and quite suitable suitors, many of whom were fellow Kentuckians and, better yet, many of whom were Whigs. Among the Kentucky men were shopkeeper and ladies' man Joshua Speed; Speed's gangly roommate Abraham Lincoln, the law partner of Mary's cousin John Stuart, a U.S. congressman; and Edwin Webb, a graduate of Transylvania University and a Whig in the Illinois General Assembly with Lincoln. Webb was considerably older than most of the bachelors circling around Mary Todd and her close friends Mercy Levering and Julia Jayne. He was a thirty-eight-year old widower with two children. Mary called him "a widower of modest merit," but the "principal lion" in her "society of marriageable gentlemen."[14]

This large group of male politicians and lawyers and the smaller group of educated and refined young ladies used the Edwards' home as a central meeting point. It was an exclusive clique that came to be called the Springfield Coterie, a French word defined as an "intimate and often exclusive group of persons with a unifying common interest or purpose." It is entirely possible that Mary herself was inspired by her study of French and had named this exclusive group of which she was a center of attention. The main common interest in the Springfield Coterie was definitely politics, but it was a social, educated and upwardly mobile clique that enjoyed passionate discussions over political and social issues of the day, held parties and dances, attended lectures and discussed literature and went on group sleigh rides and picnics.[15]

Politics was king, but humor and good-natured teasing was an important component of the character of Mary Todd's new circle of friends. Having grown up in a large family of boisterous Todd children, Mary had developed a keen wit and was comfortable with humorous banter. While social interactions between men and women were less formal and there were fewer restrictions governing communications between the sexes than there had been for the previous generation, the Springfield Coterie was particularly unabashed in its addiction to comedy. This trait no doubt appealed to Mary Todd and drew her closer to this Springfield group of men and women.[16] A sense of humor as well as, perhaps, the obvious shortage of women in the capital city was the motivation for a letter that four Illinois legislators wrote to Eliza Browning on December 11, 1839, praying for her to "repair, forthwith to the Seat of Government, bringing in your train all ladies in general, who may be at yo[ur] command."[17] The legislators were Abraham Lincoln, Edwin Webb, John Hardin and John Dawson; Eliza Browning was the wife of Orville Hickman Browning, who was an attorney in Quincy, Illinois. Both Mrs. Browning and her husband were good friends of the four legislators making the appeal. Hardin and Dawson were married; Lincoln and Webb were not. However, all four agreed that they needed the social services of Mrs. Browning. Hardin's wife had returned to Jacksonville, and without her and Mrs. Browning, the gentlemen felt at a loss for matronly guidance with their social affairs. To the appeal, Hardin added, "The fact is madam, that in your absence business will not progress with its accustomed facility, and now when both yourself & my distinguished lady are away, they cannot even begin operations. There is no doubt if you were here, there would be extensive improvements in the important business, of visiting conversation & amusement."[18] To add to the humorous tone, Lincoln had phrased the appeal in the form of a legal petition, and Hardin offered up the parlor of the Sangamon County Circuit Court clerk William Butler for Eliza to hold court with the men and women of Springfield society. On the need for organized conversation and amusement, Mary Todd wholeheartedly agreed.[19]

Just a couple of weeks after Abraham Lincoln wrote the letter to Mrs. Browning, he was one of sixteen men—including Ninian W. Edwards, Stephen A. Douglas, Joshua Speed and James Shields—who hosted a "Cotillion Party" at the American House hotel in Springfield. A printed invitation was distributed by the "managers" of the party, and no doubt Mary and her girlfriends were in attendance and dressed in their finery.[20] Such soirees were frequent, both at the American House and other hotels as well as in private parlors on "Aristocracy Hill" and beyond. The cotillions and parties that Mary Todd and her cohorts attended included live music, dancing, political speech-making, joke telling and the consumption of foods like oysters, quail, cake, ice creams and wine displayed on tastefully appointed buffet tables.[21]

These parties were an important setting for the young women and men of Mary Todd's generation. They provided a social environment in which the sexes could appropriately engage with each other and find companionable mates. Increasingly, men and women living in the first half of the nineteenth century were seeking partners based on mutual interests and love. Unlike their parents and other generations before them who had married mostly for economic and legal benefits, these young Americans were looking for mates who were complementary to themselves and who shared common interests. Politics was the central common interest for people with whom Mary Todd was spending her time. In Springfield, and likely in other politically minded towns of the era, politics was a popular spectator sport for both men and women. The cotillions and parties in Springfield provided a venue for men and women to discuss politics as well as to socialize. The Springfield Coterie was addicted to politics and, with the possible exception of Abraham Lincoln who felt awkward in social settings where women were in attendance, was addicted to parties as well. Mary Todd likely attended dozens of cotillions and smaller more intimate gatherings on Aristocracy Hill during the first couple of years of her residency in Springfield. It was within this spirited social environment, converging on politics and good humor, that she began assessing her possibilities for marriage.[22]

Important in this social dynamic were female friends, who offered a counterbalance to courting and marriage rituals between men and women. Mary Todd was an engaging person who enjoyed her social interactions with female family members, friends and neighbors and new acquaintances made when women visited Springfield from afar. About one visitor Mary wrote, "M[r] Edwards has a cousin from Alton spending the winter with us, a most interesting young lady, her fascinations, have drawn a concourse of beaux & company round us."[23] Not unlike female friendships today, women helped each other navigate the complexities of relationships and courting, provided emotional support, shared hopes and dreams and offered companionship through shared experiences. Like the relationship that Mary had had with her childhood friend Lizzie Humphreys her friendships with the women of the Springfield Coterie, especially with Mercy Levering, illustrate the importance of female cohorts for Mary and for her contemporaries in the early 1840s. During the nineteenth century, same-sex friendships for women, as well as for men, were framed within a societal norm of outward, emotional feeling. It was acceptable for people to exhibit love and emotional connection with their most intimate same-sex friends. Mary poured out her heart to her closest female friends, sharing joys and sorrows and ruminating on life and love. For example, while on a visit with family in Missouri, Mary made the acquaintance of the grandson of the famous American patriot Patrick Henry. It appeared to the Todd family that the young man would be an agreeable match for her, and Mary shared her deepest feelings on the subject with her friend. She wrote, "Uncle and others think, he surpasses his noble ancestor in talents, yet Merce I love him not, & my hand will never be given, where my heart is not."[24]

Mary's correspondence with female friends reflected literate, middle-class notions of female companionship. The flowery language of love, emotion and human connection was typical. "I will never cease to long for your dear presence," she wrote one friend and continued, "a cloud always hangs over me, when I think of you."[25] To another intimate friend later in her life she wrote, "The memory of your gentle kindness, is ever present, with me!"[26] In her letters with her important female friends, she used language like "your affectionate friend," "my greatest regret is that so many long weary miles divide us," "with ever so much love" and "I can never cease to love you." This language was typical in her letters to women, and it was typical in the correspondence of her contemporaries as well. Throughout her life, Mary would always be happiest when she had close female friends around her. Although she would occasionally struggle during her lifetime to maintain some of her most important female relationships, her emotional connections to women gave her strength and solace.[27]

So it was in Springfield in the winter of 1839, with close female confidants to share her innermost thoughts, with a cadre of dashing bachelors swirling around her and with a community of friends to bond over the mutual interests of politics and good humor, that Mary Todd came into her own. She was alive in spirit and heart during those first months in Springfield, and she delighted in the activities of her social circle. Her friend James Conkling called her the "very creature of excitement," adding that she "never enjoys herself more than when in society and surrounded by a company of merry friends."[28] Mary Todd no doubt was relishing the new independence she found in Springfield. There is one particular story that illustrates this point. The tale also reveals Mary's penchant for pressing the boundaries of propriety, at least a little bit, and verifies Conkling's assessment of her enthusiasm for a little excitement. During the rainy spring of 1840, Mary convinced Mercy to walk the five blocks from Aristocracy Hill to the public square. The rain and the lack of paved streets and sidewalks promised a muddy adventure, but Molly, as her new friends now called her, hatched a plan to use wood shingles to place in front of them as they walked. Thus, in full skirts and silk slippers, the two young women in all their finery made their way through the mud to the square and managed to stay clean. However, the return home was proving less successful, as the thin shingles failed to cope with the deep mud. Molly spotted a drayman named Ellis Hart and hatched another plan to get them home. Hart was the driver of a dray, or flatbed cart used for transporting goods, and Molly asked him if he would be willing to transport her and her friend the remainder of the way to the Edwards' house on his delivery cart. Mercy was horrified and refused, but Molly hopped in, unfazed by the nineteenth-century indecency of it all.[29]

A drayman's cart was a vehicle for transporting merchandise. It was not an appropriate mode of transportation for proper young ladies. Sitting on a dirty cart in fine clothes with legs dangling off the sides certainly pressed the boundaries of middle-class womanly decency. Mary Todd saw the appearance of Hart and his dray as an opportunity to get home faster and cleaner than trouncing through the mud on her own two feet. She was not deliberately trying to create a stir. If a young woman today caught a ride in the back of a pickup truck, observers might question the safety of her choice, but the scene would not shock their sensibilities of morality. However, in 1840, a climb up onto a delivery cart and the subsequent spectacle of a fine lady riding like cargo through the elite neighborhood streets of "Aristocracy Hill" would have been quite enough to draw color to the cheeks of some. For others, perhaps even for Mary's sister Elizabeth, it would have been enough evidence to pass harsh judgment on the young woman committing such a social crime. The incident, however, turned into a good joke among the Springfield Coterie, and one friend who was a ubiquitous visitor in the Edwards' parlor memorialized Mary's lapse of social decorum by writing a poem about it.[30]

> As I walked out on Monday last
> A wet and muddy day
> 'Twas there I saw a pretty lass
> A riding on a dray.
> Quoth I sweet lass, what do you there
> Said she good lack a day
> I had no coach to take me home
> So I'm riding on a dray.
> Up flew windows, out popped heads,
> To see this Lady gay
> In silken cloak and feathers white
> A riding on a dray.
> At length arrived at Edwards' gate
> Hart back the usual way
> And taking out the iron pin
> He rolled her off the dray.[31]

If any respectable ladies, especially those who were outside of the Springfield Coterie, had popped out their heads that day and laid their eyes on the spectacle, they would probably have been shocked. Yet Mary likely relished her reputation as a spirited and impulsive young woman and enjoyed the attention her ride in the drayman's cart had brought her. She also likely appreciated the humor of the poem penned in her honor. One very significant member of her social circle was still commenting on the episode a year later, as Abraham Lincoln in a letter reminded a friend about "Hart, the little drayman that hauled Molly home once."[32]

Abraham Lincoln was thirty years old when twenty-one-year-old Molly arrived in Springfield, and for the customs of the era, he was on the old side of unmarried. He was tall and gangly and unsophisticated in his manners and in his attire. His pants were too short, his hair was a mess, he was a terrible dancer and he lacked the social graces that Mary Todd had been accustomed to in the men she had known back in Lexington. However, by that time, Lincoln was an accepted member of the bar and enjoyed a growing reputation as a good lawyer. He was the law partner of a U.S. congressman, Mary's cousin John Stuart. He had won three elections of his own to the Illinois House of Representatives, and he was establishing himself as a prominent Whig in Sangamon County and throughout the state. He had been a member of a political collaborative that had successfully conspired to move the Illinois state capital from Vandalia to Springfield. Lincoln was arriving in his profession, in his political aspirations and in society. He was funny. He was intense. He was obsessed with Whig politics. He was the owner of a sharp mind. The short, slightly plump, extroverted and vivacious Mary Todd was starting to notice this quiet, intelligent, awkward man who defied in appearance all that may have made him a worthy suitor in the eyes of the Kentucky Todds and the Southern courtly society that she represented.[33]

By the summer of 1840, Mary Todd and Abraham Lincoln were spending more time together, bonding over Whig politics and the upcoming 1840 presidential election. They were socializing in the Edwards' parlor. They were attending parties at the American House and the residences of Springfield's social and political elite. They were together accompanying other members of the Springfield Coterie in social activities, like one "delightful" picnic with, as James Conkling wrote, "a profusion of delicacies which our ladies know how to prepare so well." Abraham Lincoln and Mary Todd had many common interests. They were rabid political partisans, each professing loyalty to Henry Clay and the Whig Party. They also enjoyed poetry, and probably recited favorite passages together. Observers may have been seeing the two as sweethearts. Only recently, however, Abraham Lincoln had written to Eliza Browning: "I have now come to the conclusion never again to think of marrying; and for this reason; I can never be satisfied with any one who would be block-head enough to have me."[34] "Block-head" or not, the incomparable Miss Todd was starting to make an impression on him as well.

Mary Todd was enjoying her life in Springfield and perhaps narrowing down her candidates for marriage, but a travel opportunity presented itself in July 1840. Another group of Todds who were long settled in Missouri had invited her for a visit. Loving travel and adventure and never having visited her cousins there, Mary packed her bags for Columbia. Her destination was the home of her father's brother David, who had settled in Missouri sometime before 1821, where he was first a territorial judge and then a circuit judge in the new state of Missouri. He resided in Columbia with his family, including his daughter Ann with whom Mary was close in age. During Mary's visit that summer, Todd was a delegate from Missouri at the convention that nominated William Henry Harrison (under whom Todd had fought at the Battle of Tippecanoe) as the Whig candidate for the presidency. The Missouri Todds were as serious about Whig politics as the Kentucky Todds, and during that summer visit, there was much discussion about the state of the party both in Missouri and in Illinois.[35] In mid-July, Mary and Ann traveled to Boonville, about thirty miles west of Columbia on the Missouri River. Writing home, Mary shared the news of this excursion: "I have necessarily seen more society than I had anticipated, on yesterday we returned from a most agreeable excursion to Boonville, situated immediately on the river and a charming place, we remained a week, attended four parties, during the time, one was particularly distinguished for its brilliancy & *city like* doings . . . I felt exhausted after such desperate exertions to keep pace with the music. [W]ere Missouri my home, with the exception of [S]t Louis, Boonville would certainly in my estimation have the preference a life on the river to me has always had a charm, so much excitement, and this you have deemed necessary to my wellbeing."[36] In Boonville, Mary also visited with a few former classmates and friends from Kentucky, danced and attended parties, but politics was never far from her mind. In addition to the mail that Mary received from Springfield during her stay in Columbia, she was also receiving copies of three Springfield newspapers. Numerous readers within Judge Todd's family would have been particularly interested in the *Old Soldier*, a paper dedicated to the Harrison candidacy. However, Mary likely also shared her mailed copies of the Whig *Sangamo Journal* and the Democratic *Hickory Club*.[37]

When Mary returned to Springfield, she and her circle of friends were consumed with the upcoming presidential election between Harrison and the incumbent, President Martin Van Buren, and with the upcoming elections for the Illinois General Assembly. In August, Whig friends John Hardin, Edward D. Baker, Edwin Webb, Cyrus Edwards, Josiah Francis and Abraham Lincoln all won their races. Mary was likely thrilled with the political success of her close friends, but she was enthralled with the national contest, writing after the election: "I suppose, like the rest of us <u>Whigs</u> though you seem rather to doubt my <u>faith</u> you have been rejoicing in the recent election of Gen Harrison, a cause that has excited such deep interest in the nation and one of such vital importance to our prosperity. This fall I became quite a <u>politician</u>, rather an unladylike profession, yet at such a <u>crisis</u>, whose heart could remain untouched while the energies of all were called in question."[38] Mary's discussion of politics in her letters to her friend Mercy Levering exhibits a keen understanding of the political issues of the day and illustrates her passion for the Whig Party. She was not alone in her enthusiasm and knowledge. She was one of thousands of Whig women across the country who were engaged and politically astute. In 1840, more than ever before, women were engaged and energized by the presidential campaign, especially in Whig Party political culture. Women could not vote, and constrained gender roles limited their political power; however, they were enthusiastic campaigners and political participants, and the Whig Party made efforts to win female allies. During the 1840 campaign, the Whig Party encouraged local organizations to build party unity and support by holding rallies, barbeques, speeches and picnics that included women. Whig women participated in local party activities, wrote political tracts and even gave public political speeches. Whig campaign literature reached out to female readers, educated them on the issues and solicited their participation.[39]

In addition to being a national Whig, Mary was also a voracious reader of the Springfield newspapers and well versed in the unique qualities of state and local politics as well. She was comfortable expressing her opinions and attitudes, attended events with great enthusiasm and showed unwavering support for her Whig candidates. However, Mary Todd understood that constructions of gender roles dictated certain limitations for middle-class ladies. Mary loved politics, but she also viewed her vehement attraction to politics as unladylike. For her, and many women like her, engagement in politics was a delightful hobby, but it was, in the end, a male sphere in which women could only occasionally dip their toes. However, that said, it was no accident that all of the suitors that Mary Todd seriously considered were political men.

As important as her fixation on politics that fall was her growing preoccupation with that gangly lawyer Lincoln. In matters of romance, Lincoln lacked the social charms of his friend Joshua Speed, but Mary was seeing beyond his awkward facade. In turn, Lincoln was charmed by Mary's wit and political interests. At some time in 1840, Mary Todd and Abraham Lincoln professed their love for each other and started to talk about marriage. Given Mary's social engagement with suitors during her trip to Missouri, the relationship likely escalated after she returned to Springfield. Perhaps the impassioned atmosphere of the presidential election provided or at least intensified the spark between them. In 1840, Mary Todd was in love, she had a circle of friends she adored, and her social calendar was full. Domestic responsibilities impinged on her time, and she complained to Mercy that during the miserably cold winter she had "scarce a leisure moment to call my own," having spent several weeks on a "formidable supply of sewing."[40] However, that statement was a slight exaggeration. She attended a couple of the weddings of friends within her circle, planned a "jaunt" to Jacksonville for a sleigh ride and was spending time with Mr. Lincoln with whom she was whispering of marriage.[41]

However, something happened on New Year's Day 1841 that has excited the imaginations of historians for decades. Some have speculated that Mary jilted Lincoln that day, while others have contended that Lincoln called off the affair. Lincoln's first biographer, William Herndon, forwarded a completely unfounded story that Lincoln abandoned Mary at the altar. There were also some stories that Mary was flirting with other men, including Stephen A. Douglas, and that Lincoln's jealousy led to a fight. Some historians believe that Elizabeth and Ninian Edwards did not approve of the union and pressured the couple to call off the wedding. Some historians argue that Mary and Abraham quarreled and mutually decided to part ways. Still others believe that Lincoln expressed doubts and Mary released him from his wedding promise.[42] With limited evidence, we will never know for sure, but the latter explanation seems the most plausible. Regardless of what caused the couple to cancel their nuptials, three short weeks later Abraham Lincoln was miserable. Writing to his law partner and Mary's cousin John T. Stuart, Lincoln moaned: "For not giving you a general summary of news, you must pardon me; it is not in my power to do so. I am now the most miserable man living. If what I feel were equally distributed to the whole human family, there would not be one cheerful face on the earth. Whether I shall ever be better I can not tell; I awfully forebode I shall not. To remain as I am is impossible; I must die or be better, it appears to me."[43]

Two months later, Lincoln's emotional state was only slightly improved. In a letter to Joshua Speed, he wrote: "I am not going beyond the truth, when I tell you, that the short space it took me to read your last letter, gave me more pleasure, than the total sum of all I have enjoyed since that fatal first day of Jan^y '41. Since then, it seems to me, I should have been entirely happy, but for the never-absent idea, that there is one still unhappy whom I have contributed to make so. That still kills my soul. I can not but reproach myself, for even wishing to be happy while she is otherwise. She accompanied a large party on the Rail Road cars, to Jacksonville last Monday and on her return, spoke, so that I heard of it, of having enjoyed the trip exceedingly. God be praised for that."[44]

Certainly, the tone of Lincoln's letters to Stuart and Speed revealed deep sorrow, and the melodramatic tone in each illustrated his love for the woman he had lost. As summer rolled around, Lincoln took a trip to Kentucky to stay with Joshua Speed who had recently returned to his home for good. Speed and other friends were concerned about Lincoln's well-being. Ninian

Edwards apparently declared Lincoln "crazy as a loon," and Conkling in a letter to Mercy wrote, "poor L! how are the mighty fallen."[45] Mary was lonely for Lincoln, but she stayed busy in Springfield and kept up a strong façade. Like Lincoln, she too declined to mention the name of the lamented lover, declaring to Mercy that Speed's "worthy friend deems me unworthy of notice, as I have not met <u>him</u> in the gay world for months, with the usual comfort of misery, imagine that others were as seldom gladdened by his presence as my humble self, yet I would that the case were different, that he would once more resume his Station in Society, that 'Richard should be himself again,' much, much happiness would it afford me."[46]

Clearly, Mary was lonely for her tall beau, and obviously she, like his closest friends, was worried about him. By calling him "Richard," she evoked a reference to Shakespeare's characterization of the erratic and insane King Richard II. The reference also revealed that Mary saw in Lincoln something regal beyond his humble roots and rural persona. She loved Lincoln and missed him, but unlike him, she shielded her wounded heart with social engagements. She immersed herself in her circle of friends, keeping herself busy with parties and other social events. Courtships in the nineteenth century frequently made anxious the nerves of men and women, so the parting of ways of Abraham and Mary was not so unusual. In the context of companionate marriage, there were greater emotional stakes for courting couples. Quarrels sometimes related directly to the higher marital expectations of both sexes, as men and women engaged in more hand-wringing over fears of making a wrong match.[47]

From January 1, 1841, until the summer of 1842, Abraham Lincoln and Mary Todd lived their lives apart from one another. After his initial withdrawal from work and society in January and his three-week trip to Kentucky, Lincoln was focused on his law practice and transitioning into a new legal partnership with Stephen T. Logan, another Todd relative. The social scene at the Edwards' home had quieted some, and parties in the summer of 1841 were suspended perhaps due to Mary's heartbreak. However, the June circuit court was in session, and Mary enjoyed meeting "many distinguished strangers" in the "gay capitol."[48] During this time, neither Abraham nor Mary made any attempt at a reconciliation. Fortunately, however, they had good mutual friends who believed the parted lovers were a perfect companionable match for each other and took action on their behalf. Eliza Francis, along with her husband, Simeon, who was the editor of Springfield's Whig newspaper the *Sangamo Journal*, arranged a meeting at their home for the couple sometime in the summer of 1842. After the initial meeting, it was not too long before the couple was making frequent visits in the homes of Simeon and Eliza and another mutual Whig friend, Dr. Anson G. Henry. Mrs. Francis had encouraged the couple to be friends, hoping they might eventually reconnect on a deeper level. As it happened, the timing of their reunion was opportune because a political controversy in Springfield fanned the flames of their personal political passions. Quite appropriately, the romance between Abraham Lincoln and Mary Todd that had blossomed around the national political campaign of 1840 was rekindled in the context of local partisan politics in 1842.[49]

While Mary and Abraham were spending time together, all of Springfield was talking about the closure of the State Bank of Illinois, which had ceased operations the previous February. The bank's notes were rendered worthless by the closure, and by the summer, commerce across the state was suffering because of it. Lincoln and other Whigs had supported the State Bank in the legislature and, as a result, were furious when James Shields, the state auditor, announced that the state would no longer accept Bank of Illinois paper as payment for taxes. Economically, Shields's decision was sound, but politically, it was provocative. Shields was a Democrat, and his action immediately raised the hackles of the state's Whigs. Lincoln decided to lampoon Shields in the *Sangamo Journal*. Shields was perhaps an easy target. He was a handsome man with a reputation of being vain and believing himself irresistible to women. He was also a fiery Irishman and easily unhinged. However, he had in the past been a friend of the Springfield Coterie, so politics and not personal vindictiveness motivated Lincoln. What happened next led to one of the most embarrassing moments of Abraham Lincoln's life. But, it also solidified his reconciliation with his Molly.[50]

Nineteenth-century politics was verbally vicious, and in the era of partisan newspapers, the printed word was a favored political weapon. Sarcasm, hyperbole and metaphor were popular methods of politically inspired newspaper editorials, and very frequently, the authors used pseudonyms to protect their identity and give them more freedom to vent spleens and pour on the insults. Lincoln had penned political tracts like this before, some signed and some unsigned, and his close connection to the editor of the *Sangamo Journal* ensured publication of his particularly sharp political writing. Lincoln showed a draft of his letter to Mary Todd and her good friend Julia Jayne, another Whig woman of Springfield. Thus, the trio became partners in a wicked little plot to poke fun at the haughty Democrat James Shields. Previously, the paper had printed humorous letters signed "Rebecca," and for his letter to lambast Shields, Lincoln adopted the wit and persona of that uneducated country woman from the "Lost Townships" and signed his own letter "Rebecca" as well.[51] The piece ran in the *Sangamo Journal* on August 27, 1842. In the letter, Rebecca shared a conversation with her neighbor who had worked hard to raise enough State Bank of Illinois paper to pay his taxes and was furious about Shields's decision to disallow it for payment. The neighbor asked how the state would lose anything if people paid taxes in paper and charged, "Damn officers of State . . . to have tax to pay in silver, for nothing only that Ford (the Illinois governor) may get his two thousand a year, and Shields his twenty four hundred a year."[52] Lincoln's farcical letter went on to call Shields and the Democratic Party in Illinois liars and fools, and it also spun a story about Shields spending money on ladies and declaring to them, "girls, it is distressing, but I cannot marry you all. Too well I know how much you suffer; but do, *do* remember, it is not my fault that I am *so* handsome and *so* interesting." This language was scathing and insulting, but it was not out of line for the politics of the day. However, the plot escalated two weeks later when Mary Todd and Julia Jayne decided to pen their own excoriating text using the "Rebecca" pseudonym. The letter they wrote was less elegant than Lincoln's letter, but it was no less sarcastic.[53] It utilized spelling that indicated the country woman's dialect, like "I know he's a fightin man, and would rather fight than eat; but isn't marrying better than fightin, though it does sometimes run into it? And I don't think upon the whole that I'd be sich a bad match neither—I'm not over sixty, and am just four feet three."[54] A week later, Mary and Jayne published a poem in the *Sangamo Journal* about the wedding of "Rebecca" and Shields:

Ye Jew's harps awake! The A_____'s[55] won—
Rebecca, the widow, has gained Erin's son,
The pride of the north from the emerald isle
Has been woo'd and won by a woman's sweet smile:
The combat's relinquished, old love's all forgot,
To the widow he's bound, oh! bright be his lot;
In the smiles of the conquest so lately achieved,
Joyful be his bride, "widow'd modesty" relieved.
The footsteps of time tread lightly on flowers—
May the cares of this world ne'r darken their hours.
But the pleasures of life are fickle and coy
As the smiles of a maiden, sent oft to destroy.
Happy groom! in sadness far distant from thee
The Fair girls dream only of past times of glee
Enjoyed in thy presence, whilst the soft blarnied store
Will be fondly remembered as relics of yore,
And hands that in rapture you oft would have prest,
In prayer will be clasp'd that your lot may be blest.

Cathleen.[56]

Everyone in Springfield knew about the letters and the poem lampooning Shields, and the Irishman was furious. He demanded that Simeon Francis, the newspaper's editor, reveal the name of the author who had penned such a dastardly assault on his good name and his office. Lincoln took responsibility, and Shields demanded a retraction, implying that he would fight to restore his honor. Lincoln sought the advice of his friend Dr. Elias Merryman, the man who had written the poem about Molly, who fanned the flames of the dispute that escalated into a challenge to a duel. Reluctantly, Lincoln relented, and the challenge was accepted. As was his right as the subject of the challenge, Lincoln chose cavalry broad swords, a ridiculous weapon, but perhaps a fitting one given the ridiculous nature of the feud. Dueling was illegal in Illinois, but not in Missouri. Therefore, on September 22, Shields and Lincoln, along with their seconds Dr. Merryman and General John D. Whiteside, the state fund commissioner, met at Alton and crossed the river to Bloody Island in Missouri. However, before the Whig and the Democrat could draw their ridiculous weapons and commence the fight, two mutual friends, John J. Hardin and Dr. R.W. English, intervened, and cooler heads prevailed. The duel was an embarrassing episode in Lincoln's life, but it had one positive result. Of all the women in Springfield, Miss Mary Todd best recognized Southern chivalry when she saw it. Lincoln had taken the blame for the anonymous letters and accepted responsibility for the venomous attacks on his political rival.[57] Hailing from Kentucky where Southern honor was well rehearsed and dueling was common place, Molly later noted that "Mr Lincoln, thought, he had some right, to assume to be my champion."[58]

Mary Todd was happy that her gallant beau returned from Bloody Island physically unharmed. The incident, however, was embarrassing to Lincoln, and the couple made a pact to never speak of it again. Yet, their romantic reunion in the context of partisan politics was, in the end, worth all of the trouble that their shared political passions has caused. Just a month and a half later, Miss Todd married Mr. Lincoln in a small ceremony in the Edwards' parlor, the place where they had fallen in love. Lincoln gave his new bride a wide, Etruscan gold wedding band purchased from C.W. Chatterton & Co. on the west side of the public square in Springfield. Engraved on the inside of the wedding band were the words: "A.L. to Mary, Nov. 4, 1842. Love is Eternal." Mary Todd had waited to give her hand to the man she loved, and Lincoln called the marriage a "matter of profound wonder."[59]

NOTES

1 George W. Ranck, *History of Lexington, Kentucky: Its Early Annals and Recent Progress* (Cincinnati, OH: Robert Clarke & Co., 1872), 319, 321–23; John Dean Wright, *Lexington: Heart of the Bluegrass* (Lexington, KY: Lexington-Fayette County Historic Commission, 1982), 81; Stephen Berry, *House of Abraham: Lincoln and the Todds, a Family Divided by War* (Boston: Houghton Mifflin Co., 2007), 19; Jean H. Baker, *Mary Todd Lincoln: A Biography* (New York: W. W. Norton & Co., 1987; reprint, New York: W. W. Norton & Co., 2008), 72–73; Alasdair Roberts, *America's First Great Depression: Economic Crisis and Political Disorder after the Panic of 1837* (Ithaca, NY: Cornell University Press, 2012).

2 William Bell Wait, ed., *River, Road and Rail: William Richardson's Journey from Louisville to New York in 1844* (New York: William Bell Wait, 1942), 8.

3 Baker, *Mary Todd Lincoln*, 75; Wolfgang Schivelbusch, *The Railway Journey: The Industrialization of Time and Space in the 19th Century* (Berkeley: University of California Press, 1986), 94–95; Wait, *River, Road and Rail*, 8, 13–14.

4 Kenneth J. Winkle, *The Young Eagle: The Rise of Abraham Lincoln* (Dallas, TX: Taylor Trade Publishing, 2001), 166–67; Abraham Lincoln to Mary S. Owens, 7 May 1837, Gilder Lehrman Collection, New York, NY; Baker, *Mary Todd Lincoln*, 78.

5 Baker, *Mary Todd Lincoln*, 78–79; Roberts, *America's First Great Depression*, 14–21; Gravestone of Alexander P. Todd, Lexington Cemetery, Lexington, KY; *Sangamo Journal* (Springfield, IL), 24 May 1839, 2:6; John Carroll Power, *History of the Early Settlers of Sangamon County, Illinois*, (Springfield, IL: Edwin A. Wilson & Co., 1876), 748.

6 John J. Hardin to Robert W. Scott, 24 September 1839, transcribed in Katherine Helm, *The True Story of Mary, Wife of Lincoln* (New York: Harper & Brothers, 1928), 67–68.

7 Douglas K. Meyer, *Making the Heartland Quilt: A Geographical History of Settlement and Migration in Early-Nineteenth-Century Illinois* (Carbondale: University of Southern Illinois Press, 2000), 141–46; Nicole Etcheson, *The Emerging Midwest: Upland Southerners and the Political Culture of the Old Northwest, 1787–1861* (Bloomington: Indiana University Press, 1996), 2; Robert P. Howard, *Illinois: A History of the Prairie State* (Grand Rapids, MI: William B. Eerdmans Publishing Co., 1972), 76, 145.

8 *History of Sangamon County, Illinois* (Chicago: Inter-State Publishing Co., 1881), 522; Power, *Early Settlers of Sangamon County*, 466, 696–97; Christopher C. Brown, "Major John T. Stuart," *Transactions of the Illinois State Historical Society* 7 (1902): 109–14; Mary E. Humphrey, "Springfield of the Lincolns," *Abraham Lincoln Association Papers* (Springfield, IL: Abraham Lincoln Association, 1930), 17.

    For some time after their settlement in Springfield, Ninian and Elizabeth Edwards had a male slave in their household. Office of the U.S. Census, Sixth Census of the United States (1840), Sangamon County, IL, 2.

9 Paul M. Angle, *"Here I Have Lived": A History of Lincoln's Springfield, 1821–1865* (Springfield, IL: Abraham Lincoln Association, 1935; reprint, Chicago: Abraham Lincoln Bookshop, 1971), 85.

10 Humphrey, "Springfield of the Lincolns," 28–29.

11 Angle, *Here I Have Lived*; Humphrey, "Springfield of the Lincolns," 26.

12 Joseph Wallace, *Past and Present of the City of Springfield and Sangamon County, Illinois*, 2 vols. (Chicago: S. J. Clarke Publishing, 1904), 1:10–13; Angle, *Here I Have Lived*, 88; *Sangamo Journal*, 4 October 1839, 11 October 1839, 18 October 1839; Stacy Pratt McDermott, *The Jury in Lincoln's America* (Athens: Ohio University Press, 2012), 56–58; James E. Davis, *Frontier Illinois* (Bloomington: Indiana University Press, 1998).

13 Humphrey, "Springfield of the Lincolns," 31; Winkle, *Young Eagle*, 62–63.

14 Mary Todd to Mercy Levering, 15 December 1840, Lincoln Collection, ALPL (this document is transcribed in its entirely in the Document section); *History of White County, Illinois* (Chicago: Inter-State Publishing, 1883), 305–6, 507; Ruth Painter Randall, *Mary Lincoln: Biography of a Marriage* (Boston: Brown, Little & Co., 1953), 62.

15 Ruth Painter Randall, *The Courtship of Mr. Lincoln* (Boston: Little, Brown & Co., 1957), 11.

16 Stephen Berry, "There's Something about Mary: Mary Lincoln and Her Siblings," in Frank J. Williams and Michael Burkhimer, eds., *The Mary Lincoln Enigma: Historians on America's Most Controversial First Lady* (Carbondale: Southern Illinois University Press, 2012), 14–15.

17 Abraham Lincoln and others to Eliza Browning, 11 December 1839, Rosenbach Museum and Library, Philadelphia, PA.

18 Abraham Lincoln and others to Eliza Browning, 11 December 1839. The first quotation was written by Lincoln, and the second by Hardin.

19 John Clayton, comp., *The Illinois Fact Book and Historical Almanac, 1673–1968* (Carbondale: Southern Illinois University Press, 1970), 207.

20 Invitation to Cotillion Party at the American House, 16 December 1839, Lincoln Collection, Lincoln Miscellaneous Manuscripts, box 4, folder 75, University of Chicago, Chicago, IL; Randall, *Courtship of Mr. Lincoln*, 42.

21 Humphrey, "Springfield of the Lincolns," 35–36.

22 Jean H. Baker, *The Lincoln Marriage: Beyond the Battle of Quotations*, 38th Annual Robert Fortenbaugh Memorial Lecture (Gettysburg, PA: Gettysburg College, 1999), 10; Randall, *Biography of a Marriage*, 16–19.

23 Mary Todd to Mercy Levering, 15 December 1840.

24 Mary Todd to Mercy Levering, 23 July 1840, Lincoln Collection, ALPL.

25 Mary Lincoln to Hannah Shearer, 26 June 1859, *L&L*, 56.

26 Mary Lincoln to Elizabeth Blair Lee, 11 July 1865, *L&L*, 258.

27 Carroll Smith-Rosenberg, "The Female World of Love and Ritual: Relations between Women in Nineteenth-Century America," *Signs: Journal of Women in Culture and Society* 1 (Autumn, 1975): 1–29; Mary Todd to Mercy Levering, 15 December 1840; Mary Lincoln to Hannah Shearer, 20 October 1860, *L&L*, 65–66; Mary Lincoln to Rhoda White, 8 June 1871, *L&L*, 590.

28 James C. Conkling to Mercy Ann Levering, 21 September 1840, folder 1, box 1, Conkling Family Papers, ALPL; Mary Lincoln to Hannah Shearer, 28 August 1859, *L&L*, 57–59.

29 Randall, *Courtship of Mr. Lincoln*, 4–7; Baker, *Mary Todd Lincoln*, 81–82; Office of the U.S. Census, Seventh Census of the United States (1850), Sangamon County, IL, 70.

30 "A Story of the Early Days in Springfield and a Poem," *Journal of the Illinois State Historical Society* 16 (April 1923): 146; Angle, *Here I Have Lived*, 93.

31 "Story of the Early Days," 146.

32 Abraham Lincoln to Joshua F. Speed, 19 June 1841, Lincoln Collection, ALPL.

33 Baker, *Mary Todd Lincoln*, 83; Winkle, *Young Eagle*, 62–63.

34 Abraham Lincoln to Eliza Browning, 1 April 1838, Huntington Library, San Marino, CA; Winkle, *Young Eagle*, 150–51, 207; Humphrey, "Springfield of the Lincolns," 33–36; Angle, *Here I Have Lived*, 93–95; Daniel Walker Howe, *What Hath God Wrought: The Transformation of America, 1815–1848* (New York: Oxford University Press, 2007), 597.

35 Walter B. Stevens, *Centennial History of Missouri* (St. Louis, MO: S. J. Clarke Publishing Co., 1921), 1:261, 263.

36 Mary Todd to Mercy Levering, 23 July 1840.

37 Ibid.

38 Mary Todd to Mercy Levering, 15 December 1840; Theodore Calvin Pease, ed., *Illinois Election Returns, 1818–1848* (Springfield: Illinois State Historical Library, 1923), 33, 337, 339, 344.

39 Elizabeth R. Varon, "Tippecanoe and the Ladies, Too: White Women and Party Politics in Antebellum Virginia," *Journal of American History* 82 (September 1995): 494–521; Ronald J. Zboray and Mary Saracino Zboray, "Whig Women, Politics, and Culture in the Campaign of 1840: Three Perspectives from Massachusetts," *Journal of the Early Republic* 17 (June 1997): 277–316; Kenneth J. Winkle, "'An Unladylike Profession': Mary Lincoln's Preparation for Greatness," in Williams and Burkhimer, *Mary Lincoln Enigma*, 97; Elizabeth R. Varon, *We Mean to Be Counted: White Women and Politics in Antebellum Virginia* (Chapel Hill: University of North Carolina Press, 1998); Paula Baker, "The Domestication of Politics: Women and American Political Society, 1780–1920," *American Historical Review* 89 (June 1984): 620–47; Adam Jortner, *The Gods of Prophetstown: The Battle of Tippecanoe and the Holy War for the American Frontier* (New York, Oxford University Press, 2012).

40 Baker, *Mary Todd Lincoln*, 84–89; Kenneth J. Winkle, *Abraham and Mary Lincoln* (Carbondale: Southern Illinois University Press, 2011), 40; Mary Todd to Mercy Levering, 15 December 1840.

41 Angle, *Here I Have Lived*, 95.

42 David Herbert Donald, *Lincoln* (New York: Simon & Schuster, 1995), 89; Baker, *Mary Todd Lincoln*, 89–90; Benjamin P. Thomas, *Abraham Lincoln, A Biography* (New York: Alfred A. Knopf, 1952), 87; Randall, *Biography of a Marriage*, 50–51; Randall, *Courtship of Mr. Lincoln; L&L*, 25; Angle, *Here I Have Lived*, 97.

43 Abraham Lincoln to John T. Stuart, 23 January 1841, Lincoln Collection, ALPL; Thomas, *Abraham Lincoln*, 86–91; Joshua Wolf Shenk, *Lincoln's Melancholy: How Depression Challenged a President and Fueled His Greatness* (Boston: Houghton Mifflin Co., 2005), 43–65; Donald, *Lincoln*, 85–90.

44 Abraham Lincoln to Joshua F. Speed, 27 March 1842, Lincoln Collection, ALPL.

45 Winkle, *Young Eagle*, 208; Baker, *Mary Todd Lincoln*, 90; James C. Conkling to Mercy Levering, 24 January 1841, folder 1, box 1, Conkling Family Papers, ALPL.

46 Mary Todd to Mercy Levering, June 1841, Lincoln Collection, ALPL.

47 Angle, *Here I Have Lived*, 97; Baker, *Mary Todd Lincoln*, 91–92; *L&L*, 29.

48 Mary Todd to Mercy Levering, June 1841.

49 Baker, *Mary Todd Lincoln*, 93–94, Angle, *Here I Have Lived*, 97; Winkle, *Young Eagle*, 110–11; Mark E. Neely Jr., *The Abraham Lincoln Encyclopedia* (New York, NY: DaCapo Press, 1982): 116–17; Randall, *Biography of a Marriage*, 64; Harry E. Pratt, "Dr. Anson G. Henry: Lincoln's Physician and Friend," *Lincoln Herald* 45 (October 1943): 3–17.

50 Donald, *Lincoln*, 91–93; John A. Garraty and Mark C. Carnes, eds., *American National Biography*, 24 vols. (New York: Oxford University Press, 1999), 19:838–40.

51 Lorman A. Ratner and Dwight L. Teeter Jr., *Fanatics & Fire-Eaters: Newspapers and the Coming of the Civil War* (Urbana: University of Illinois Press, 2004), 32; Winkle, "An Unladylike Profession," 100–101; Randall, *Biography of a Marriage*, 65–74.

    The previous "Rebecca" letters ran in the *Sangamo Journal* on February 10, 1838; May 5, 1838; May 26, 1838; August 10, 1842; and August 19, 1842.

52 Rebecca to the Editor of the *Sangamo Journal*, 27 August 1842, 4:1–2.

53 William C. Harris, *Lincoln's Rise to the Presidency* (Lawrence: University of Kansas Press, 2007), 25.

54 Rebecca to the Editor of the *Sangamo Journal*, 9 September 1842.

55 Perhaps in an effort to make the reference less direct, "Auditor" was not spelled out here.

56 *Sangamo Journal*, 16 September 1842, 2:7.

57 Abraham Lincoln to James Shields, 17 September 1842, *Sangamo Journal*, 14 October 1842, 2:3; James Shields to Abraham Lincoln, 17 September 1842, *Sangamo Journal*, 14 October 1842, 2:3; Abraham Lincoln to the Editor of the *Sangamo Journal*, [4] October 1842, *Sangamo Journal*, 7 October 1842, 2:6; Donald, *Lincoln*, 91–93; Baker, *Mary Todd Lincoln*, 96–97.

58 Mary Lincoln to Josiah G. Holland, 4 December 1865, *L&L*, 293.

59 Mary Lincoln to Mary Jane Welles, 6 December 1865, *L&L*, 295–96; *Sangamo Journal*, 28 October 1842, 2:7; Mary Todd to Mercy Levering, 23 July 1840; Abraham Lincoln to Samuel D. Marshall, 11 November 1842, Lincoln Collection, Chicago History Museum, Chicago, IL.

CHAPTER 3

MRS. ABRAHAM LINCOLN

Wearing a strand of pearls and a white satin dress borrowed from her sister Frances, Miss Todd married her tall Whig lawyer on Friday evening, November 4, 1842. The wedding took place in the Edwards' parlor, and the Reverend Charles Dresser, the minister of St. Paul's Episcopal Church in Springfield, officiated. Elizabeth and Ninian Edwards attended Dresser's church, and he was a family friend. As was typical for weddings of the day, it was a small affair with a simple ceremony, followed by refreshments. Elizabeth handled the arrangements. There is some reminiscent evidence to suggest that Lincoln and Mary Todd gave family and friends little advance notice of their intentions to marry and that perhaps Elizabeth and Ninian had only a day or two to prepare as hosts. A shared Todd family story records that Mary's wedding cakes were still warm when the bride and groom said their wedding vows. Yet there is no surviving correspondence that reveals such details. Etiquette of the time instructed brides to give guests one week's notice. Rarely did couples in the 1840s spend more than a week or two planning a wedding, and only rarely were weddings elaborate events. Rather, arrangements were simple, included only family and close friends and most often occurred in the bride's home. Therefore, Mary Todd's wedding was fairly typical of the weddings of her day, including the number of attendants. Mary's close friends Julia Jayne and Anna Rodney were Mary's bridesmaids, and Whig friends James Matheny and Beverly Powell stood up with Lincoln.[1]

In front of those witnesses, Abraham Lincoln slipped on his bride's finger the gold ring with "love is eternal" engraved inside the band, and Mary Todd committed what she had once called the "crime of matrimony."[2] There is no evidence in any of her own surviving correspondence that she regretted her choice of groom. The day she became Mary Lincoln and commenced her career as a married woman was a happy day for her. However, it was a modest beginning of this new chapter in her life. There was no wedding trip, and Mr. and Mrs. Lincoln moved into the Globe Tavern, a boarding house located on Adams Street just two blocks west of the public square and the new state house in Springfield. In 1842, the Globe was owned by Springfield businessmen Cyrus G. Saunders and Robert Allen and was operated by a widow named Sarah Beck. The boarding house was a large L-shaped structure, and the rooms were furnished with bedsteads, bureaus, tables, chairs and linens. The Globe Tavern, which advertised accommodations for "travelers and families," had facilities for boarding horses and a well-appointed kitchen and dining area where the residents and travelers took their meals. The Lincolns paid about $8 a week for room and board, and while there may have been some adjustment for Mary in moving from the stately home of her sister into a small space at the tavern, the Globe was not the social disappointment that many historians have interpreted it to be. The Lincolns settled into a cramped eight-by-fourteen-foot room, the same room that Dr. Wallace and Mary's sister Frances had only recently vacated after three years in residence there. John T. Stuart had also lived in the tavern before moving into his own home. There was precedence in the Todd family for making first homes in a boarding house, and it was very typical for married couples and even couples with children to live in boarding houses, especially early on in their marriages.[3]

The plain, wood-frame tavern featured a two-story porch, served breakfast and supper, offered a social community of boarders and was located for convenient access to the public square. When the newly married Lincolns moved in, there were eight rooms for boarders, and the Globe was a central office for stagecoach lines serving Springfield. That year, the tavern had undergone renovations and advertised that it could "furnish the weary with a comfortable resting place," promised that "the hungry shall always find the best table the market will afford" and assured guests that "the house shall be prudently and promptly managed." Some prominent individuals had made their home in the boarding house, including minister and Whig lawyer Albert T. Bledsoe, also a Kentuckian, who resided there when the Lincolns arrived.[4] The tavern was a lively place, as community, social and political events occurred in the public areas of the building. For example, in February 1843, General William F. Thornton threw a party at the Globe for members of the Illinois General Assembly. Certainly, the tavern did not compare to the accommodations to which Mary was accustomed in her father's home in Lexington, Kentucky, or in her sister's home on Aristocracy Hill. Its furnishings were less refined, and it offered the new couple little privacy and peace and quiet. However, the Globe Tavern was a perfectly respectable first residence.[5]

The boarding house was an economic transition into married life for the couple, while Lincoln worked to build his law practice and strive for a better financial future for his new family. Boarding house life also allowed Mary to stave off the usual responsibilities of other new wives, like housekeeping and cooking. Most importantly, though, regardless of her new modest living arrangements, the Globe Tavern was her first home with her new beloved husband. It represented her future. It represented a path chosen. It represented a new beginning. She had tied her fate to a gangly, thirty-three-year-old lawyer who might have been, in Mary's eyes at least, full of promise. However, in 1842, Lincoln was just a hardworking, circuit-riding attorney, whose political star seemed to be fading and whose economic prospects were still very much in question.[6]

When he married Miss Todd, Abraham Lincoln was no longer a representative in the Illinois General Assembly, having completed his fourth term the previous year. The legislature had provided some supplemental income—Lincoln earned $392 in his final year—but now he was solely dependent on legal fees.[7] In April 1841, Lincoln had formed a new law partnership with another of Mary's cousins, Stephen T. Logan; the office was located on Hoffman's Row, just around the corner and up the block from the Globe Tavern. The partnership with Judge Logan gave Lincoln the opportunity to enhance his growing knowledge of the law under the tutelage of a learned lawyer and judge. Although Lincoln was probably earning only one-third of the partnership's fees, he was beginning to earn more overall from his law practice. In the early 1840s, he and Logan were prolific bankruptcy attorneys, and Lincoln's experience and reputation as a lawyer traveling on the Eighth Judicial Circuit was starting to grow. However, he was still struggling financially. To her sister, Mary joked, "I often laugh and tell Mr L. that I am determined my next Husband shall be rich."[8] Several months after his marriage, Lincoln confided in his friend Speed, "I reckon it will scarcely be in our power to visit Kentucky this year. Besides poverty, and the necessity of attending to business, those 'coming events' I suspect would be some what in the way."[9]

The "coming events," as Lincoln so quietly defined them, referred to the impending birth of his first child. Immediately after their marriage, or perhaps even before, Mary became pregnant. Most couples in the first half of the nineteenth century waited a couple of years before conceiving a child, but Mary and her new husband were a bit older than typical newlyweds, so it is understandable if they were eager to start a family. In April 1843, Lincoln went back to traveling the legal circuit and was away from Springfield for days and sometimes two weeks or so at a time. He continued to keep that schedule throughout his twenty-five-year legal career. Traveling a judicial circuit was one good way for a practicing lawyer to gain experience handling a variety of cases, to earn a reputation, to generate business and to earn a living. Lincoln had been traveling the circuit since 1837, five full years before his marriage. It was a professional choice that he had made, and it was a habit that was successful for his law practice and enjoyable to him. Attorneys were not the only nineteenth-century men who traveled extensively for their livelihood. Itinerant professionals were common during this time period, as judges, politicians, doctors, ministers and businessmen traveled far and sometimes wide. Mary's father had spent much time away from his own family. While he worked in the Kentucky legislature in Frankfort and traveled to New Orleans to purchase items for his store, his family remained in Lexington. Therefore, it was not that strange that Lincoln was gone from his new wife and later from his family. He was a circuit-riding attorney, and extensive travel was a job requirement.[10]

Mary understood the reality of Lincoln's absences, and she encouraged him in his efforts to build his legal and political base.[11] Just as her mother and stepmother had done, Mary accepted the absences of her husband, yet she was no doubt very lonely. While Lincoln was earning a living for the new family, the pregnant Mary stayed alone in the Globe Tavern. During the first year of her marriage, in fact, she was mostly cooped up in her room, as it was uncommon, and some thought improper, for pregnant women to appear in public. Entertaining guests at the Globe Tavern would have been awkward, but she probably spent time with her sisters Elizabeth and Frances at their homes. Sewing occupied some of her days, but her household responsibilities were limited. No cooking or laundry was required, as she and Lincoln took their prepared meals with the other boarders at the Globe Tavern, and laundry services were included in the weekly rent. She was a voracious reader, so she likely kept herself occupied by reading books, magazines and newspapers, which maintained her knowledge of party politics during the absences of her favorite Whig. However, the transition from an active social life with frequent interactions and outings with her friends to the quiet isolation of one room in a boarding house must have been a challenging one. The transition from single adult womanhood to married life was a challenging transition for most new brides during the nineteenth century.[12]

In mid-July 1843, Lincoln returned home from the circuit and a political speaking engagement in Hillsboro, Illinois. He and Mary were looking forward to a visit from their close friend Joshua Speed and his wife, Fanny, and Mary's pregnancy was in its final month. "We shall look with impatience for your visit this fall," Lincoln wrote Speed. "Your Fanny can not be more anxious to see my Molly than the latter is to see her; nor as much so as I am. Don't fail to come. We are but two, as yet."[13] As it turned out, the couple's wait to be a family of three was short-lived, as their son arrived on August 1, 1843. Regardless of the difficulties and isolation of Mary Lincoln's confinement, the birth of Robert Todd Lincoln, named for Mary's father, changed everything. "We must derive all the satisfaction we can from our children," she believed, and the arrival of little Robert, or Bobby or Bob as the new parents would lovingly call him, was a joyous occasion for the couple. Later, in writing about Robert's birth, Mary remembered the happiness of that day, as she wrote, "it appears to me, at times, so short a time, since my darling husband, was bending over me, with such love and tenderness."[14]

It is possible that one of Springfield's twelve doctors attended to Mary's childbirth needs, perhaps even her uncle John Todd or Lincoln's friend Anson G. Henry. However, there is no surviving doctor's bill or contemporary evidence, so we can only speculate. Although medical science had improved somewhat since the death of Mary's mother from childbed fever, childbirth was still potentially dangerous for women in the 1840s. Apparently, however, Robert's birth was relatively routine, occurring in that humble room in the Globe Tavern. Robert was a healthy baby boy except for a condition called right esotropia, which caused his right eye to turn up slightly. Robert would eventually go blind in that eye much later in his life, but the condition did not hinder his early childhood. After Robert's birth, Lincoln was home for a month with Mary before returning to his work on the circuit. Mary was then alone to fend for herself and the baby. She might have had occasional help from other women living in the boarding house, but there was no money in the couple's limited budget for hiring a nurse. Since Mary's two eldest sisters were busy with their own babies, they were likely of only limited assistance to her. Younger sister Ann Todd had since joined the Edwards' household, so she, being as yet unmarried, may have helped. In Kentucky, Mary's mother and stepmother had enjoyed the help of slave nurses, but Mary and her Springfield sisters handled childrearing alone and with hired help as they could afford it. Southern slave-holding women turned childrearing over to household slaves; wealthy Northern women hired nurses to attend to their children. However, most Southern and Northern women carried this responsibility on their own shoulders. There is no indication that Mary regretted her dramatically different lifestyle from that of her Kentucky, slave-holding family. In fact, given the personal attachment that she would exhibit for all of her children, and given her and her husband's idolizing approach to their children's upbringing, she may have preferred her situation. She may well have recognized that the hands-on childrearing that she wished to provide to her own children, even in the face of much more limited financial means, was preferable to what had been the childhood experiences of her and her siblings.[15]

After Robert's birth, Mary's domestic circumstances were rapidly improving. In the fall of 1843, Lincoln moved his wife and son out of the Globe Tavern and into a small rented cottage on Fourth Street. The cottage's four rooms and private yard were a marked improvement in the family's living conditions and represented economic progress as well. That winter, Mary's father Robert Todd made a visit to Springfield to see his daughters and grandchildren and to attend to some business. In 1841, Todd had purchased 243 acres of land in Springfield as an investment. In 1843, when he tried to pay the notes on the land with Bank of Illinois money, the seller of the land refused to accept the devalued notes. That summer, Todd had retained his son-in-law to sue the seller in Sangamon County Circuit Court in Springfield. This began the first in a long line of legal work that Mary Lincoln's Northern husband would undertake for his Southern in-laws. The lawsuit probably reminded the Lincolns about the trouble that devalued bank notes had caused in their own lives back in 1842, and maybe they even temporarily broke their promise of silence regarding the duel. Regardless, the devalued bank notes caused more trouble in the family when the court ordered Robert Todd to pay the actual price of the land and not the face value of the devalued notes. Todd answered the court by settling the debt, and then he deeded eighty acres of the land at issue in the case to Mary Lincoln. The Lincoln family finances continued to improve. In May 1844, Lincoln sold a lot that he and Logan had acquired, probably in payment for legal fees, and finalized the purchase of a home from the Rev. Charles Dresser. That month, the Lincoln family of three moved into the house, which was located on Eighth and Jackson Streets southeast of Springfield's public square.[16]

Lincoln paid $1,500 for the home, which was a modest, one-and-a-half-story frame cottage. His new home ownership was symbolic of his movement into middle-class respectability. However, for Mary Lincoln, the home was symbolic of a domestic achievement that most middle- and upper-class nineteenth-century American women prized, particularly because the "covered" legal status of women denied them property rights. In the context of middle-class values and proscribed gender roles, the lives of women in the middle and upper classes were defined by their domestic sphere. It was within that domestic sphere that they enjoyed some power over their own lives. Mary was now a wife and a mother keeping house, which were the essential roles of nineteenth-century womanhood. It was the job of middle-class married women to provide an appropriate family environment for their husbands and their children. The establishment of a home was an important step in anchoring a woman's life, providing economic stability and emotional security.[17] This fact is particularly important with respect to the overall picture of Mary Lincoln's life. Being settled in her own home was at least as important to Mary Lincoln's mental and emotional stability as were her human connections to her husband, her children and her female friends. The house on the corner of Eighth and Jackson Streets would shelter the Lincolns for the next seventeen years. In no other place would Mary ever spend more time or be more fulfilled and at peace. Reflecting later on that happy spring of 1844, Mary wrote, "A nice home—loving husband and precious child are the happiest stages of life,"[18] a time when "you are a happy, laughing, loving Mama."[19] From May 1844 until February 1860, with the exception of one year away from Springfield when Abraham Lincoln served a term in the U.S. Congress, Mrs. Lincoln focused primarily on those three happy stages of her life.[20]

In this perspective of home and security, Mary Lincoln was not alone. Most nineteenth-century women played the three vital roles of homemaker, wife and mother, and many of them in this era of companionable marriage found happiness within the family domain. Victorian gentility regarded the peaceful home created by a loving wife and mother as an oasis from the bustle of public life, and Mary desired to provide such a space for her family.[21] Her house, her husband and her children provided the most significant context of Mary Lincoln's life experiences. It was during these Springfield years that she made her most critical impact on the world, nurturing and providing intimacy and companionship to her husband and raising four little boys. The story of Mary Lincoln's marriage and the childhood experiences of her sons will reveal much about her personal needs and her values. In addition, this story illustrates how women of her generation and of her economic and social class experienced domesticity. After her marriage, Mary remained a strong-willed and opinionated woman and an avid reader, maintained an enthusiastic interest in politics and ultimately returned to keeping an active social calendar. In marrying, Mary Lincoln did not surrender all of herself to Abraham Lincoln and the family she raised. However, in her years as the lady of the house on Eighth and Jackson Streets, raising a family was her primary goal, and in addition, it represented her primary joy.[22]

The little cottage that became the setting for Mary Lincoln's joy was many blocks removed from Aristocracy Hill. It reflected her husband's more modest means but also his more modest sensibilities. Sitting on lot number eight and a small sliver of lot number seven in Elijah Iles's Addition to Springfield, the sturdy frame house with a loft sat on one-eighth of an acre and had at least one out-building when the family moved in that spring. In the 1840s, city homes were heated with fireplaces and wood-burning stoves, water was drawn from backyard wells outfitted with hand pumps, horses and other animals lived in stables in close proximity to the home and outdoor privies were standard. In regard to these characteristics, the Lincolns' home was typical. The Lincoln family had a small woodshed in a deep yard with a barn, where they kept a horse and milk cow. It was in the size and fine details of Lincoln house and in the neighborhood that Mary's new home differed more strikingly from the home of her eldest sister. In the beginning, the Lincolns could afford only simple furnishings, and the neighborhood in which their house was located was far more retiring and more economically and ethnically diverse than the pretentious estates on the Hill. Among the family's neighbors were European immigrants, lawyers and politicians, African Americans and widows; many of these neighbors were close friends of the Lincolns over the years. Their modest home and surroundings reflected the financial means of the Lincoln family at the time they purchased their house, but the location may have been a more deliberate choice on the part of Abraham Lincoln and better reflected his own simple and humble tastes. In addition, Mary may have preferred some distance from her eldest sister, who had taken on a motherly role with her younger Springfield sisters.[23]

The family had moved into their new home between Lincoln's circuit travels to Urbana at the end of April and Tremont in the first week of May. Having not yet accumulated many household items, moving meant unpacking a couple of trunks, mostly consisting of clothing and sundry personal items. During the first year in the house, Mary tended the baby, cooked and cleaned and purchased items for the home. The records of Mary's separate purchases at Irwin's Dry Goods store included a fireplace shovel and tongs, baby shoes, loaf sugar, gunpowder tea, cups and saucers, needles and $10 worth of yard goods and buttons for her sewing projects. By October of that year, the Lincolns had hired a girl to assist Mary with the baby and the household chores. It was very common for middle-class families to hire domestic help; nearly one in four households in Springfield by 1850 enjoyed the services of a live-in female servant. Over the years, Mary would employ a number of servants, including some that lived with the family, but she preferred to do much of the work herself. Even as her economic fortunes increased, Mary Lincoln continued to perform more of her own domestic tasks than other women with the same economic status did. In late 1844 and early 1845, the hired girl who purchased items for the family at Irwin's was likely employed to do light housekeeping and run errands, and she did not live in the Lincolns' home. The Lincoln family of three was already crowded enough.[24]

The clapboard house became even more congested on March 10, 1846, when twenty-seven-year-old Mary gave birth to a second son. Edward Baker Lincoln was named for Edward D. Baker, a lawyer and Illinois Whig legislator. Baker had previously defeated Lincoln to earn the Whig nomination for Congress, but theirs was a friendly rivalry. The Lincolns admired his gifted oratory, Mary appreciated his English nativity and Baker and his wife were favorites among their friends.[25] The Lincoln household was chaotic with two children, and although they remodeled to add another bedroom downstairs, the family was outgrowing the cottage. There is no indication that Mary minded her cramped little house, but she did no entertaining during this time period. There was no formal dining space in the house, and the family was still on a limited budget. Lincoln reported Eddy's arrival in the world to his friend Joshua Speed and included a story, which offers some insight about the rowdiness of the Lincoln toddlers and something of the difficulties Mary faced in trying to corral them: "We have another boy, born the 10th of March last. He is very much a child as Bob was at his age—rather of a longer order—Bob is 'short and low,' and, I expect, always will be. He talks very plainly, almost as plainly as any body. He is quite smart enough. I some times fear he is one of the little rare-ripe sort, that are smarter at about five than ever after. He has a great deal of that sort of mischief, that is the offspring of much animal spirits. Since I began this letter a messenger came to tell me, Bob was lost; but by the time I reached the house, his mother had found him, and had him whip[p]ed, and, by now, very likely he is run away again."[26]

The year that little Eddy was born, the Springfield Todds celebrated two weddings. Mary's younger sister Ann married Clark M. Smith, a Springfield merchant, and Mary's cousin Eliza Todd wed Harrison Grimsley. Eliza, with whom Mary would remain close throughout her life, was the daughter of Mary's uncle Dr. John Todd of Springfield, and Harrison Grimsley was a local Whig. It was a busy time for Abraham Lincoln, too, as he was campaigning for a seat in the U.S. Congress. In those days, it was typical in party politics to set in place a chain of succession for various offices, sharing opportunities for service among the party faithful. For example, John J. Hardin had served in the Twenty-eighth Congress from 1843 to 1844, and then stepped aside for Edward Baker to serve in the Twenty-ninth Congress from 1845 to 1846. It was Lincoln's turn as the next Whig to represent Illinois' Seventh Congressional District in the Thirtieth Congress, but Hardin decided he wanted to return to Washington himself, and he put up some good resistance. We can only imagine how Mary might have felt about her cousin's rivalry with her husband, but it was her husband who won the fight. Lincoln used his circuit travels to garner support, secured the nomination and won the election on August 3, 1846, with 56 percent of the vote. Mary Lincoln was now married to a future U.S. congressman.[27]

Politics was one of the central factors tying the Lincolns together, and Mary was no doubt thrilled that her husband had achieved this important political milestone. In their political sensibilities, they were of like minds, but personality wise, they were quite different. Mary was an exuberant social person, emotional and high strung. Lincoln was brooding, laid-back and absentminded. She was well-bred and culturally high-minded, while he was informal and sometimes coarse in his appearance and interactions with people. Because there is no surviving correspondence between the Lincolns during the early years of their marriage, we know very little about how they were settling in with each other. However, no doubt there was an adjustment period for both. Mary admitted later on that she likely "trespassed, many times & oft, upon his great tenderness & amiability of character," but she also noted that her husband was not a "demonstrative man, when he felt most deeply, he expressed, the least."[28] She clearly understood that they handled their emotions in vastly different ways. Mary's intensity and directness would often clash with Lincoln's periods of silence and brooding, but those difficulties did not overshadow the love and companionship that the Lincolns shared. When Lincoln wrote to friends and colleagues, he mentioned Mary, or Molly as he called her, and those letters suggested that they shared each other's correspondence, talked about the boys and other family members with each other and planned activities and social engagements together. Given Lincoln's extensive travels, it probably took the couple longer to get acquainted with each other, but they managed well; the home that Mary was making for her husband and the couple's two little boys was a happy one. Lincoln enjoyed his time on the circuit, but his wife and darling boys represented home, and home was a welcome retreat from the far less hospitable accommodations Lincoln experienced on the circuit.[29]

Because of the scheduling of Congress in the 1840s, it would be more than a year before Lincoln would begin his service in the U.S. Congress. Therefore, the patterns of their family life continued as they had before, with Lincoln away for much of the time and Mary at home with the boys. In December, Mary Lincoln purchased two books, *Miss Leslie's Cookery* and *Miss Leslie's Housekeeper*. Eliza Leslie was a popular author whose cookbooks and advice on housekeeping and childrearing appealed to middle-class women like Mary Lincoln. The purchase of these volumes illustrates Mary's desire to attend to her household duties properly. The Lincoln family's domestic life was fairly quiet, at least as quiet as was possible with two noisy little boys, but the Mexican War caused worries for Mr. and Mrs. Lincoln. Several of their Illinois friends, including Edward Baker and John Hardin, and Mary's fourteen-year-old brother, David, from Kentucky were serving in the U.S. Army. The couple's fears were realized when on February 23, 1847, Hardin was killed in the Battle of Buena Vista in Mexico.[30]

Late that summer, Lincoln was busy with Whig politics, and in August he hosted twenty delegates from the Illinois Constitutional Convention at his home. Mary was not present for the event, but she no doubt played some role in the details. Judge David Davis, a close friend of Mr. Lincoln's, was in attendance, and writing of the visit to his wife, he noted that "Mrs. L. I am told accompanies her husband to Washington next winter. She wishes to loom largely. You can't make a gentleman in his outward appearance, out of Lincoln to save your life." Davis's tone reveals some frustration with Lincoln but even more with the new congressman's wife, and this may be the first evidence of Lincoln's political allies chafing at Mary Lincoln's interest in her husband's political life. In the coming months, Lincoln kept an active schedule in his law practice, traveling to Tremont, Bloomington and Clinton, while Mary prepared herself and the boys for their upcoming departure from Springfield. In October, the Lincolns started making plans for a visit to Kentucky that would precede their long journey to Washington, and on October 23, Lincoln rented the family's home to Cornelius Ludlum, a local railroad agent, for $90. The Lincolns moved their furniture and other belongings into one of the rooms in the loft of their home. Two days later, Mary Lincoln, her congressman-elect husband, four-year-old Bobby and eighteen-month-old Eddy left Springfield on a stagecoach bound for St. Louis. The *Illinois Journal* reported the Lincoln family's departure and added, "Success to our talented member of Congress! He will find many men in Congress who possess twice the good looks, and not half the good sense, of their own representative."[31]

It was of no matter to Mary Lincoln that her husband would not be the best-looking member of Congress. He was her member of Congress, and that is all that mattered. Mr. and Mrs. Lincoln were excited as they began their first big adventure together away from Springfield, and with their little boys in tow, they looked forward to Lincoln's first visit to the Todd family home in Lexington. "A Lincoln and Family" registered at Scott's Hotel in St. Louis to await the departure of the steamboat that would take them to Frankfort, Kentucky. Located on the southwest corner of Third and Market Streets, the hotel was in the heart of the city. Mary was fond of St. Louis and loved the bustle of a city. "You know I enjoy, city life," she once told a friend.[32] Likely, the Lincolns strolled the busy streets and did some shopping. On October 28, they boarded a steamship and arrived in Frankfort on November 2 or 3. From there, they took a train the rest of the way to Lexington, and a favorite Todd family story about that train ride offers another glimpse of the Lincoln children. Apparently, a Todd cousin who was staying with Robert and Betsey Todd had been on the train from Frankfort with the Lincolns but had no knowledge of who they were at the time. When he arrived at the Todd house on Main Street, he complained to his Aunt Betsey that on the train he had suffered the rambunctious behavior of two wild boys whose long-legged father delighted in their antics and offered no amount of discipline to quiet or control them whatever. The cousin was sharing this story when a carriage pulled up in front of the house. When the Lincoln family emerged from within, the cousin was horrified to see that the brats had followed him home.[33]

Mary had not been home in seven years, and her husband had never met her stepmother or younger siblings. The family's three-week visit gave the Todds some time to become acquainted with Mary's husband and the boys. Mary showed off her Whig husband to all of her Lexington relatives, and her father introduced him to his Whig friends. Partisan politics dominated many parlor discussions, and since Mary's stepbrother David had run off to fight in the Mexican War, the conflict and the politics surrounding it were ripe for debate as well. During their visit, Henry Clay delivered an anti-war speech in Lexington, which Lincoln attended, likely with his father-in-law. While Lincoln was practicing Whig politics with Robert Todd, Mary got reacquainted with her younger siblings. Since she had moved to Springfield, sisters Elodie and Kitty had been born, and Emilie and Alexander whom Mary had barely known before were now eleven and eight, respectively. Mary's stepbrother Sam visited from nearby Centre College to roughhouse with Mary's boys, stepmother Betsey seemed charmed by Lincoln's knowledge of poetry and Mary enjoyed the company of all of the younger girls. Lincoln also enjoyed the younger Todd children, and he and Mary developed a particular attachment to Emilie. The Lincolns shared a love of children, which along with politics, was another important shared interest that solidified their marital relationship.[34]

After the visit in Lexington, the Lincolns packed up their little boys and boarded a stagecoach for Virginia. When they arrived in Washington, they spent one night in a hotel and then settled in at Mrs. Sprigg's boarding house, where other Whigs were in residence. In the Thirtieth Congress, only 73 of the 230 congressmen had their wives with them, and even fewer had children with them. Most of those who were in the city with wives and children were rich enough to afford stately residences, so the Lincolns' domestic situation was a bit unusual. The boarding house was just fifty feet from the national capitol grounds, and Mary Lincoln found the location convenient to shopping and the accommodations amenable albeit not spacious. Most of the house's boarders were men, and the rowdy Lincoln children greatly annoyed some of them. Mary did not quietly let slide criticisms of her darling boys, so some of her relationships with fellow boarders were strained. There were slave servants at the house who helped watch the boys when Mary was away, but the nasty winter weather kept the family inside much of the time. While Mary enjoyed keeping some company with her husband, who was busy learning the ropes as a freshman member of the U.S. House of Representatives, the living arrangements became a burden for both of them and for the cooped-up boys.[35]

Five months of those conditions proved enough, and in April 1848, Mary Lincoln returned to Lexington with her toddlers. The three of them stayed in her father's house on Main Street, but they also spent time at the family summer home, Buena Vista. The estate, which had been in Betsey Todd's family, was a tall frame house situated on a knoll and surrounded by large locust trees. There was a double portico in front and a long side porch that connected the dwelling with two stone slave cabins. There was room for the children to run and breathe fresh air, a marked improvement over the cramped boarding house and the chilly wet weather in Washington City. However, despite the improved amenities and restful lifestyle, Mary was lonely, and so was her husband. It was during this separation that we can learn something of their love and passion for each other, as a few of their letters from this period survive.[36] Not long after Mary left Washington, Lincoln lamented, "In this troublesome world, we are never quite satisfied. When you were here, I thought you hindered me some in attending to business; but now, having nothing but business—no variety—it has grown exceedingly tasteless to me."[37] His letters to Mary reveal his love for his children, his worries over her health and his desire for her. Language like "Eddy's dear little feet" and the "blessed fellows" characterize his feelings for the boys, and his free talk of Mary's weight reveals the physical intimacy he enjoyed with his wife. His letters to her were addressed to "My Dear Wife" and signed "Affectionately, A. Lincoln." In turn, Mary's letters to her husband illustrate her loneliness without him. "My Dear husband," she pined, "How much, I wish instead of writing, we were together this evening."[38] In June, Mary wanted to return to Washington, and Lincoln asked her, "Will you be a good girl in all things, if I consent?" He continued, "Come on just as soon as you can. I want to see you, and our dear-dear boys very much. Every body here wants to see our dear Bobby."[39] By July, Lincoln was the one more anxious for a family reunion. "Father expected to see you all sooner," he wrote Mary, "but let it pass; stay as long as you please, and come when you please. Kiss and love the dear rascals."[40] This final letter enclosed $100 intended for Mary's expenses for traveling back to Washington.

Taken together, the letters show a contented couple. There was talk of politics, news about family and friends and discourse regarding family matters. The tone of each of the letters illustrates desire and longing, care and concern, respect and friendship. Clearly, Mary Lincoln and her husband shared intimacy, talked about problems, teased one another and enjoyed each other's stories. No doubt there were difficulties that the letters fail to reveal, but the marriage was working for both of them, and the family was a functional one. In mid-July, Mary and the boys rejoined Lincoln in the capital for the next six weeks, while Lincoln wrapped up his first session of Congress. In early September, the family left Washington together, bound for a tour of New England, where Lincoln delivered a series of political speeches, and the family enjoyed some sightseeing. On this summer vacation with the boys they visited Niagara Falls, which became a favorite place for Mary and her husband. After viewing the spectacular natural wonder, Lincoln jotted some notes about the experience and declared that the falls possessed the "power to excite reflection, and emotion." Mary agreed that it was an interesting location. Much of the family's travel was by rail, as the railroads were better developed in New England than they were yet back in Illinois, and the boys probably annoyed East Coast passengers at least as much as they had annoyed Mary's cousin in Kentucky. After seeing Niagara Falls, the family boarded the aptly named steamer *Globe* in Buffalo, New York, and left for Chicago on Sunday, October 1, 1848. Several years earlier, a St. Louis newspaper had marveled at the convenience of steamboat travel, noting that the distance from Buffalo to Chicago was 1,047 miles and could be traveled in sixty hours, which was "record" time.[41]

The Lincolns stopped over in Chicago for three days, checking into the Sherman House on October 5. The next day, Mary and the boys were in attendance on the public square when Lincoln delivered a two-hour political speech supporting the election of Zachary Taylor, the Whig candidate for president. The next day, the *Chicago Daily Democrat* reported that "Hon. A. Lincoln and Family passed down to Springfield this morning on his way home from Congress," and they arrived at home on October 10, 1848. They had been gone an entire year. The Lincoln home was still being rented, so the family moved back into the Globe Tavern. Lincoln traveled some on political business, while Mary and the boys settled back into a rhythm of domestic life, and Mary began her winter sewing. At the end of November, Lincoln left Springfield to return for the second session of his term in Congress. On this trip to Washington, he was alone. Eddy was ill, the trip was expensive and the Lincolns decided it best for the family to remain in Springfield. Mary then endured what would be Lincoln's longest absence from his family.[42]

Lincoln returned home on Saturday evening March 31, 1849, and while he was thrilled to kiss his wife and hug his boys, who had grown like weeds, he was dejected. During his term in Congress, he had made numerous friends, but his political performance had been something of a disaster. Noted mostly for delivering his "Spot Resolutions," an anti–Mexican War speech that proved unpopular with Democrats and Whigs back in Illinois, Lincoln came home disappointed with himself and disillusioned over the future prospects of the Whig Party, which some believed Lincoln had hindered. To top it off, he had necessarily neglected his law practice for seventeen months, and he needed to get back to work. That spring, Lincoln lobbied for and lost an appointment in the General Land Office, and then he rejected a consolation appointment as secretary of Oregon Territory. At the last minute, the Taylor administration offered Lincoln the governorship of the territory instead. The $3,000 annual salary was tempting, but Mary was not interested in moving the children to the wilderness, away from family and the life she was building in Springfield. Lincoln agreed and declined the appointment, took a step back from politics and hunkered down with the law.[43]

While Lincoln turned his attention to his law career, Mary focused on her home and her children. That spring, she hired a painter to spruce up the house, and she did a great deal of shopping at Jacob Bunn's large store on the public square. The Sangamon & Morgan Railroad reached Springfield in July 1849, and Bunn and other merchants were expanding their inventories in quantity and variety. Mary Lincoln and her friends must have been pleased with the increase of goods that were available in downtown Springfield. That month, however, bad news arrived from Kentucky.[44] On the sixteenth, Mary's father died of cholera while campaigning for reelection to the Kentucky State Senate. Despite his frequent absences from home and his limited interaction with his children, Robert S. Todd had been the heart of the Todd family. He was the biological father to all fourteen of the children raised in his household, and his death exposed deep fractures within the family. In his will, Todd had left his house, furnishings and slaves to his wife Betsey. However, George, the child whose birth had claimed the life of Todd's first wife, successfully contested the validity of the will and launched an assault on the stepmother who had raised him. Robert Todd's death, George's vendetta against Betsey Todd and the series of legal cases that grew out of the settlement of Todd's estate upended Betsey and three of Todd's sons. More interestingly, perhaps, the legal cases that should have been simply routine legal avenues for distributing property, paying debts and settling business partnerships, instead devolved into a decade of family drama that divided Todd's children along biological and sectional lines. The family fighting pitted the biological children of Betsey Todd against her stepchildren, and it divided the Northern siblings in Springfield, Illinois, from the Southern siblings in Lexington, Kentucky. Mary Lincoln and her husband found themselves in the middle of the Todd family turmoil.[45]

There was simply no relief from unhappy events in the Lincoln household. In December, Eddy Lincoln became ill. At first the family thought it was diphtheria, but when the child had not improved by January 1850, there were more serious concerns. Consumption was the likely culprit. In the nineteenth century, consumption (pulmonary tuberculosis) was a common ailment that claimed the lives of many children. In the 1850s, half of all deaths in Springfield were children under the age of five, and many of those were the result of consumption. Eddy's condition continued to deteriorate. There is some evidence that he had always been a frail child. The family trip in New England back in the summer of 1848 had been sidetracked for several days with one of his illnesses. However, the infectious disease from which he was likely suffering was an extremely dangerous one even for healthy children. As the disease ravaged Eddy Lincoln, it exacted a heavy emotional toll on his parents who helplessly watched over him as he suffered. Mary nursed her son day and night for fifty-two days, bearing witness to his fevers and chills and cycles of coughing and restless sleep. On February 1, 1850, his wracked little body could take no more, and Eddy Lincoln, just shy of his fourth birthday, died at home in the arms of his weeping mother. Most parents in the mid-nineteenth century suffered the death of a child, but shared historical circumstances were no consolation for grieving mothers who had to bury their babies. The Rev. Dresser was out of town, so James Smith, the pastor of the First Presbyterian Church nearby, came to the Lincoln home to conduct the service and offer prayers for the family. Abraham Lincoln participated in the procession and burial service in Hutchinson's Cemetery just west of the public square, and Mary's sisters consoled her in the privacy of her own home, as was the custom of the time. Unfortunately, Mary would also have to provide emotional support for her sisters as well. Elizabeth lost a son in 1853, and Ann's son died in 1860 of typhoid fever, of which Mary wrote, "I trust never to witness such suffering ever again. He is to be buried this afternoon. The family are almost inconsolable, & for the last week, I have spent the greater portion of my time, with them."[46] In the Victorian era, women provided a network of emotional comfort for each other within the private confines of the domestic sphere.[47]

Eddy's death was a terrible loss for Mr. and Mrs. Lincoln, but within a few weeks, Mary was pregnant again. Anticipation of a new baby in the house helped the grieving couple to move on with their lives. Yet, the family tragedy had two lasting effects. First, it reinforced the Lincolns' doting and permissive approach to their children. Afterward, Mary also developed a type of mania regarding the well-being and safety of her sons, and both she and her husband hugged their "little codgers," as Mr. Lincoln called them, a little tighter and loved them a little harder than ever before.[48] The Lincolns both adored their children, and their shared affections for them became an even more significant bond between them. Second, the tragedy brought Mary Lincoln to the First Presbyterian Church, where she became a member and avid attendee of the services of the Rev. Smith. When her husband was in Springfield, he also attended Sunday services with her. "From the time of the death of our little Edward," Mary wrote, "I believe my husband's heart, was directed towards religion."[49] Lincoln most likely attended at Mary's behest, as he never became a member of the church. However, he did purchase a family pew and supported his wife's religious spirit and connection to the church because it brought her so much comfort. Religion played an important role in the lives of the Lincoln children, who attended Sunday school, revivals and church social events and who accompanied their mother to charitable sewing circles.[50]

After Eddy's death, Lincoln returned to his circuit travels in early April, and his wife focused on Robert and the family home, where two more little boys would soon be born. William Wallace "Willie" Lincoln arrived on December 21, 1850. Named for the husband of Mary's sister Frances, Dr. William S. Wallace had lovingly tended to Eddy during his final illness. Mary nursed Willie for more than the year that was typical in the nineteenth century, and soon after he was weaned, she was pregnant with her fourth and last child. On April 4, 1853, the Lincoln family of four welcomed Thomas Lincoln, named for his paternal grandfather who had died in 1851. The youngster was not long for that name, however, because as soon as Abraham Lincoln laid eyes on the squirming little newborn with an enormous head, he likened him to a "Tadpole." Like his three older brothers, Tad gained an affectionate nickname from his loving parents. Mary was thrilled with her little brood of boys, but Tad's birth had been a difficult one and had badly injured his mother. This childbirth experience likely left her unable to bear more children, and the resulting gynecological problems plagued her for the remainder of her life. Describing an episode of poor health to a close female friend in the late 1860s, Mary wrote, "My disease is of a womanly nature," adding that "since the birth of my youngest son, for about twelve years I have been more or less a sufferer."[51]

Mary Lincoln was certainly not alone in this type of suffering. Many women in the nineteenth century endured painful and inconvenient women's health issues that today have simple and effective surgical cures and medicinal remedies. The science of gynecology was in its very early stages, and Victorian perspectives of woman's emotional frailty minimized for male doctors the severity of women's physical complaints.[52] Despite her childbirth injuries and the resulting gynecological difficulties and despite the migraine headaches she endured, Mary Lincoln energetically maintained a household and raised her boys with interest and passion that was somewhat uncommon among her contemporaries. She also continued to do many of her own household chores and took on most of the childrearing responsibilities, although she did employ live-in servants at various times throughout the 1850s. Lincoln chided Mary for refusing to relinquish more responsibilities to hired girls, but she was stubborn and particular about how she wanted tasks completed. Her high expectations led to difficulties with hired help, and while she may have had more trouble than her sisters or her friends, many Springfield women complained about the quality of available domestic help. On the one hand, Mary Lincoln created a household that exemplified nineteenth-century expectations about motherhood and family life. She cooked and cleaned, instilled moral and religious values and nurtured her husband and her children by providing a safe and warm oasis from the chaos of the outside male world. On the other hand, Mary Lincoln created a unique environment for her boys, engaging in some parenting activities that were unheard of in the 1850s. She played games with her sons, threw them elaborate birthday parties, took them on trips, allowed pets in the house and made educational decisions for them at a time when education fell decidedly in the purview of fathers. During the 1850s, Mr. Lincoln, Bobby, Willie and Tad were the center of Mrs. Lincoln's universe, and the house on Eighth and Jackson Streets was filled with love and laughter and a menagerie of animals.[53]

Mary Lincoln was probably generally happy during these Springfield years, as she felt "enriched by the most loving and devoted of husbands," she wrote a friend. Her "dear little" children kept her life busy and contented. Robert was helpful, keeping his younger brothers occupied and running errands for his mother on Saturdays when his father was away at court. There were sleigh rides, state fairs, Independence Day celebrations, barbeques, parades and frequent trips with their father to his law office that each enriched the childhood experiences of the Lincoln boys.[54] There were illnesses and occasional scrapes and bruises, but the children lived in a loving, indulgent household. The Lincoln home was also mostly a loving environment for the Lincoln marriage as well. However, like all marriages it had its share of difficulties. Mary made sacrifices in her marriage to Lincoln, as he was sometimes a difficult man with whom to communicate. Sometimes he was gloomy and depressive, and sometimes he played the role of a careless daydreamer who was lost in his own thoughts or spinning stories for the boys when he should have been stoking the fire or helping with some other household chore. By the same token, Mary was quick-tempered, emotional and jealous of her husband's time. There were arguments between them that sometimes extended to the lawn outside, where neighbors had a view of the drama. However, those incidents were not the norm. For the most part, Mary accepted the laid-back gentle nature and somber moods of her husband, and he attributed her tantrums to her headaches and his own limitations as a husband. About Lincoln, Mary wrote, "My beloved husband, was my all, I almost worshipped him & his deep loving nature."[55] Despite his faults, she believed, "There never existed a more loving & devoted husband & such a Father, has seldom been bestowed on children."[56] Most of all, Abraham and Mary Lincoln were well matched and enjoyed a companionate union that enriched each of their lives on various levels. They enjoyed a healthy sex life, shared ideas about childrearing, teased each other, talked about politics together and laughed a whole lot more than they cried.[57]

In the fall of 1854, Mary Lincoln sold the eighty acres that her father had given her ten years earlier. The Lincolns likely applied that $1,200 to improvements to their property and, ultimately, to an extensive expansion of the Lincoln home. At first, they updated the back privy and had a brick wall and wooden fence installed across the front and south sides of the property along the public street. The wall was functional, keeping water from damaging the foundation of the house and coming into the basement, and was decorative as well. There were also small interior projects, including the purchase of some wallpaper. There may have been a small fire in the home around this time, which prompted some of the renovations, but the family of five had outgrown the small cottage. The need for more space required a move or an extensive addition to the house. As Lincoln's income from his law practice increased, so did Mary's desire for a bigger house with finer appointments. She wanted her three growing boys to have more space, but she also likely desired a home that would better reflect the rising professional status of her husband and the family's growing social status in Springfield.[58]

On Saturday, January 20, 1855, a blizzard hit central Illinois, and the heavy snow and high wind continued for two days. Travel was impossible, trains were stranded on the prairies, telegraph lines were downed, the mails ceased delivery and churches canceled services. Luckily, Lincoln was at home when the snowstorm hit, as all of Springfield was snowbound for nearly a week. On Tuesday, Lincoln trudged through the snow to the public square to buy overshoes and cotton flannel. Four days later, the first train from the south made it to Springfield from Alton, but huge snowdrifts barricaded the northern part of town until January 28, when a train from Bloomington finally arrived. Roads were still partially blocked February 1. The Lincoln family spent time together cooped up in the house, but perhaps they took advantage of the wintery opportunity to use the $30 sleigh that Lincoln had purchased from his carriage maker the previous winter. The Lincoln family had always enjoyed quiet time together in the evenings, playing games like checkers and chess and blind man's bluff. Therefore, the snowstorm just afforded them an opportunity to have a week at home together.[59]

Being snowbound also gave the couple time to discuss politics. The previous November, Lincoln had won a seat to the Illinois House of Representatives, but he resigned in order to be a candidate for the U.S. Senate. At that time, the Illinois General Assembly elected senators, so it was necessary for Lincoln to garner support among the members of that body. When Springfield was snowed under, Lincoln filled small notebooks with the names of Illinois legislators, their county and their party affiliation, and Mary helped him calculate his chances of a successful vote. They determined that Lincoln had the support of the thirty-seven Whigs and there was reason to believe that all or most of the nineteen Anti-Nebraska Democrats would support him as well. On February 8, the Illinois legislature convened in the state capitol. Mary Lincoln, Elizabeth Edwards and Emilie Todd, Mary's younger sister visiting from Lexington, ventured out in the cold winter wonderland to watch the vote that would surely send Mrs. Lincoln's husband to the U.S. Senate. The women took seats in the balcony, and after the first balloting, Lincoln was leading with forty-four votes to forty-one for James Shields, the man that Lincoln and Mary had ridiculed in the newspaper.

Lyman Trumbull had four votes.[60] Trumbull was now the husband of Mary Lincoln's best friend Julia, the same Julia who had also been involved in the kerfuffle with Shields. Soon, however, it became clear that many of the Democrats and Anti-Nebraska Democrats supported Joel Matteson and not Shields. Lincoln knew he was beaten and threw his votes to Trumbull. Julia Jayne, and not Mary Lincoln, was now married to a U.S. senator-elect. It was the end of Mary's relationship with her old friend. Unfairly, she blamed her husband's defeat on them both, dismissing him as a "sordid selfish creature" and her as "cold" and "unsympathizing." Although capable of warmth and deep friendship, Mary could also rage with extreme jealousy and pettiness; once she rejected a friend, whatever the reason, she exhibited those very characteristics that she so angrily ascribed to others.[61]

Abraham Lincoln moved past the disappointment more quickly, but eventually Mary moved on as well. A house full of boys was her primary distraction in the coming year. However, the following spring, a big change was in store at the Lincoln home. On April 3, 1856, Mary Stuart, the wife of Mary's cousin John, reported to her daughter Bettie that "Mr. Lincoln has commenced raising his back building two stories high." Springfield builders Hannon & Ragsdale had finally begun the construction work that spring on the Lincoln home. The expansion would cost $1,300 and required the raising of the roof of the original structure. Although Lincoln approved of the remodeling, he left it entirely to Mary to oversee the construction and the decorating. In May, Mary purchased wallpaper from John Williams & Co., so the remodeling was proceeding quickly. When the construction was complete, the family had more than doubled their living space. The first floor featured a large double parlor that functioned as the public area of the house. There was also a small, private sitting room where Mr. and Mrs. Lincoln would gather with the boys in the evening. At the back of the house was a formal dining space, which the cottage had not had, a kitchen with a new stove and two porches. Upstairs were two bedrooms to the south for the boys and for guests, a maid's room at the back of the house and two large adjoining bedrooms, one for Mr. Lincoln and one for Mrs. Lincoln. Separate marital bedrooms were a common status symbol of the nineteenth century, so this characteristic of the remodeled Lincoln home reflected that trend and not a rift in the Lincoln marriage. For the public areas of the house, Mary had purchased fashionable, brightly patterned wallpapers and vibrant carpets, which revealed her elaborate tastes and reflected the decorating trends of the nineteenth-century middle and upper classes. When it was completed in 1856, the Lincoln residence was "an elegant two-story dwelling, fronting west, of pleasing exterior, with a neat and roomy appearance, situated in the quiet part of the town surrounded with shrubbery." The attractive façade and green spaces around the house as well as the colorful interior of the public spaces within the home presented Mr. and Mrs. Lincoln as the prominent Springfield couple they had become.[62]

As the Lincolns passed the first winter in their expanded home, scarlet fever hit Springfield hard in January 1857. "The first part of the winter was unusually quiet, owing to so much sickness among children with scarlet fever," Mary wrote to her sister, "in several families, some two & three children were swept away."[63] Mary Welles, a friend of the Lincolns, lost her three daughters to the disease that month just two and one-half years after losing her husband and young son in an outbreak of cholera. Yet despite sickness and a financial panic in 1857, Springfield was growing. "You can scarcely image a place, improving more rapidly than ours," Mary wrote in another letter that fall, "almost palaces of homes, have been reared since you were here, hundreds of houses have been going up this season and some of them, very elegant. Gov Matteson's house is just being completed the whole place has cost him he says $100,000."[64] In 1860, Matteson owned more than $500,000 in real and personal property, and his residence was the most impressive mansion on Aristocracy Hill. The Matteson estate was not the only architectural improvement in Springfield. In 1857, the new governor's mansion had been completed, Ridgeley's Cottage Garden had become a favorite public space for Springfield's residents and Cooke's Hall and the city's brand new Metropolitan Hall were gracious structures that hosted that year the noted American Poet Park Benjamin and the famous actor Charles Walter Couldock, among many others.[65]

While the architectural character and cultural life of Springfield was on the rise, so was the professional and political status of Mr. Lincoln, who celebrated his forty-eighth birthday in February 1857. He was now a leading lawyer in the state, he was sought after in appellate cases from across Illinois and he was handling nationally important trials. He was also at the center of the development of the new Republican Party in Illinois. His law practice was providing a comfortable middle-class lifestyle for his wife and sons. In 1857, Robert turned fourteen and was a student at an academy in Springfield, Willie turned seven and Tad turned four. Mary was thirty-nine, although she had reported to the census taker back in 1850 that she was twenty-eight that year, and she would report to the census taker in 1860 that she was only thirty-five then. The Todd women were legendary for lying about their ages. Mary was not fourteen years and ten months younger than her husband, as she would later tell a friend, but regardless of how old she wanted to be or how young she may have felt, in 1857 she was no longer the mother of babies. In addition, she had a beautifully renovated home in which to entertain, and she was now playing hostess to Springfield's social, economic and political elite just like her sister Elizabeth had been doing when Mary first arrived in Springfield in 1839. Mary was, once again, in her element, attending parties and hosting her own. From 1857 to 1860, the Lincoln home was a private living space for the Lincoln family, but it was also a political and public arena for Mr. Lincoln as well.[66]

There was much excitement in the Lincoln home and within the state's Republican camp when William H. Bissell was inaugurated as the first Republican governor of Illinois. The Lincolns attended three gala events in January and February.[67] In February, the Lincolns hosted their own celebration, a party one rainy and foggy winter evening. "I may perhaps surprise you, Mary reported to her sister, "when I mention that I am recovering from the slight fatigue of a very large & I really believe a very handsome & agreeable entertainment, at least our friends flatter us by saying so—About 500 hundred [sic] were invited, yet owing to an unlucky rain, 300 only favored us by their presence."[68] From the tone of the report, Mary was beaming. All of 1857 and 1858 were a blur of political speeches, parties and social events, as Mr. Lincoln was delivering Republican speeches across the state and maintaining a hectic schedule with his law practice as well. Mary continued to run the house, chase the boys and sew, but her social responsibilities were dramatically increasing. Mary also began to accompany her husband on his trips with considerable frequency. In the fall of 1857, she traveled to Chicago with him while he was engaged in the important *Effie Afton* steamboat case in federal circuit court. This was only one of numerous business trips on which she tagged along, providing companionship but also political help entertaining the wives of Lincoln's legal associates and political allies as well. Also that year, the Lincolns had a chance for an extensive leisurely trip. Perhaps funded by a $5,000 fee that Lincoln had earned representing the Illinois Central Railroad in a critical tax case, that summer the Lincolns traveled back to New York, where they again enjoyed the beauty of Niagara Falls.[69]

In June 1858, the State Republican convention nominated Lincoln as their candidate for the U.S. Senate, and Lincoln delivered his "House Divided" speech, accepting the nomination in Springfield on the sixteenth. Dinners, speeches and short trips occupied Lincoln that summer. In July, Lincoln agreed to terms for a series of seven debates with his opponent Stephen A. Douglas to take place in each Illinois congressional district. Between August 12 and October 30, Lincoln delivered sixty-three speeches and traveled hundreds of miles, and during that time Mary rarely saw him. Mary stayed home for her husband's first six debates with Douglas, but she kept the house ready to receive Lincoln and his political allies when they were in Springfield. It is also entirely possible that she is the one who created the newspaper scrapbook of the debates that Lincoln scholars still use today. On October 15, 1858, Mary and Robert Lincoln, who was wearing his Springfield Cadets blue coat with gold trim, boarded a railcar on the Sangamon & Alton Railroad and traveled to Alton for the final debate. Mary had, of course, heard and read about the crowds that had assembled for each debate, but she must have gasped to witness it firsthand. Even though the Alton debate had the second-smallest crowd, 5,000 people were in attendance, waving their banners and cheering for her husband and his opponent while bands played. The festive political scene and her husband's participation in the debate must have provided a great deal of satisfaction to Mary Lincoln that day, for she had seen what many observers believed was the best of Lincoln's seven performances.[70]

The next month, the Democrats won more legislative seats than the Republicans, so Stephen Douglas was returned to the U.S. Senate. Lincoln had failed a second time to win a seat in that body. However, he had made a mark on Republican politics. His now famous debates with Senator Douglas had made Lincoln a national figure in the party, and there was soon talk of him as a presidential candidate. The year 1859 was another busy one for the Lincoln family. In August, Robert and his friend George Latham traveled to Massachusetts to gain admission to Harvard College. It is very likely that Mary Lincoln had been a strong influence in this decision, although she was sad to see him go. "I am feeling quite lonely," she wrote a friend, "as Bob, left for College, in Boston, a few days since, and it almost appears, as if light & mirth, had departed with him. I will not see him for ten months."[71] Both boys failed to gain admission, as their education in Springfield had not adequately prepared them, but the failure did not bring Bobby home. Instead, he enrolled in Phillips Academy in Exeter, New Hampshire, for a college preparatory curriculum that would increase his prospects for another attempt at Harvard admission. Back in Springfield, the Lincoln home was the scene of parties and teas, and there was a steady stream of political guests. There was a large evening party after the court sessions concluded in February and another in June. Orville Hickman Browning and his wife from Quincy; state auditor Jesse K. Dubois and his wife, who were also neighbors and friends; Illinois secretary of state Ozias M. Hatch; and Judge David Davis were frequent guests in the Lincoln home during this time. All four of the men were Republicans and very strong supporters of Mr. Lincoln. In Lincoln's parlor, the men had serious discussions about Lincoln's political prospects in 1860, while Mary served tea and her renowned white cake to them and visited with the ladies. With the exception of Tad's brief illness with a lung fever, it was a thrilling and happily exhausting year filled with entertaining interesting guests and traveling with Lincoln to various events.[72]

The Lincolns closed out the year with a big party for Willie's ninth birthday. Mary Lincoln prepared handwritten invitations and addressed them directly to the young guests. An invitation to one of the invited boys, the six-year-old son of a Springfield druggist, survives. Written on the front in Mary Lincoln's neat hand is "Little Isaac Diller." Some fifty or sixty boys and girls attended the party on December 21. While some believed that such an elaborate party for a child was a "nonsensical affair," Mary did not agree. "I had long promised him a celebration," she wrote a friend, "duly it came off."[73] In the midst of perhaps the most disruptive year of the Lincolns' lives to date, Mary had planned a birthday party for her son, and both she and her husband indulged their child and played happy hosts to a whole hoard of Springfield's youngsters.[74]

That frenzied year, Mary had passed one pleasant and quiet week in St. Louis with cousins, taking a much needed break. The chaos that had become her life was taking its toll, making her feel uncertain and unsettled. She was enjoying the steady stream of political company, she was supportive of her husband's political ambitions and she willingly played the role of a political wife. However, she was lonely. Her husband had been gone most of the year, her oldest son had moved away and she had little time for intimate female companionship. "What would I not give," she wrote Hannah Shearer, her close friend and former neighbor, "for a few hours conversation, with you this evening. I hope you may never feel as lonely as I sometimes do, surrounded by much that renders life desirable."[75] Clearly, Mary understood that she had no reason to be unhappy. In another letter, she complained, "I miss Bob, so much, that I do not feel settled down, as much as I used to & find myself going on trips quite frequently."[76] Mary Lincoln had described herself as the "staid matron, & moreover the mother of three noisy boys," and with Robert gone and Lincoln's political career drawing her away from the family that had rooted her, it is no wonder that she was feeling unsettled.[77]

The Lincoln family's hectic schedule continued in 1860. There were more speeches, more visitors and more trips, and there was the very real possibility that Lincoln might be a candidate for president of the United States. In February, Lincoln traveled to New York to deliver a speech on his political positions on the issue of slavery at the Cooper Institute. After the speech, Lincoln traveled to Exeter, New Hampshire, to see Bob and make a few speeches in the area. He enjoyed the time with his son and his son's friend George Latham, who was also in school at Exeter. Lincoln took them with him on "a little speech-making tour." "This is Sunday morning," Lincoln wrote home to Mary, "and according to Bob's orders, I am to go to church once to-day." As he knew his wife would be waiting to know, he added, "The speech at New-York, being within my calculation before I started, went off passably well, and gave me no trouble whatever."[78] Passably well, indeed. The speech was widely hailed, printed broadly and made Lincoln a serious contender. Going into the Republican National Convention in Chicago, however, William H. Seward, a Republican senator from New York, was still the favorite.[79]

Lincoln attended the Republican state convention in Decatur on May 9 and 10 and then returned home to await the results of the national convention in Chicago. On May 18, 1860, Mary was at home and Lincoln was in the *State Journal* office. At noon, the telegraph wire buzzed with the latest message from Chicago. The telegrapher wrote on a scrap of paper, "Mr. Lincoln, you are nominated on the third ballot," and he sent a boy to deliver the note to Lincoln. Lincoln took the paper in his hand and examined it quietly as loud cheering had broken out around him. He stood up and softly remarked, "There's a little woman down at our house would like to hear this. I'll go down and tell her."[80] From that day on, Mary Lincoln was no longer just a wife, mother and homemaker. She was now the wife of a presidential candidate, and the family and home she had built in Springfield was about to be on full public display. Soon she would be swept up by remarkable historical circumstances and events that would dramatically alter her world and complicate her happiest stages of life.

By the time Lincoln arrived at his home just past noon on Friday, May 18, the entire town of Springfield was already pulsating with the news that one of their own residents was the Republican Party's candidate for president of the United States. A 100-gun salute was resounding, people were cheering, pistol shots were firing, flags were flying and plans were underway for an evening celebration. At 8 p.m. that evening, a large crowd gathered at the state house for speeches and music, and then an hour later, the Young America Band led a procession to the Lincoln home. The crowd called for Mr. Lincoln, and he emerged from the house to deliver brief impromptu remarks. Afterward, Mr. and Mrs. Lincoln greeted throngs of friends, neighbors and well-wishers into their home.[81] The next evening, a special excursion train on the Central & Great Western Railroad arrived in Springfield, carrying a committee from the national Republican Convention in Chicago. A large crowd, along with the Springfield Lincoln Club and the German Saxe Horn Band, met the visiting party at the train depot and led the group to the public square, which was "brilliantly illuminated" and where the crowd gave "vent to their enthusiasm in almost continual cheers." The impressive group of delegates included Congressman Francis P. Blair of Missouri, New York governor Edwin D. Morgan, former Massachusetts governor George S. Boutwell, abolitionist judge William D. Kelley of Pennsylvania, and New York lawyer William M. Evarts, among others.[82]

Detailed stories of the committee's visit to the Lincoln home appeared in numerous newspapers over the coming days. The *New York Daily Tribune* offered two such stories, one of the Lincoln boys on that Saturday, and the other of Mary Lincoln. As the committee arrived, "passing in at the gate and up the steps," recounted the *Tribune*, "two handsome lads of eight or ten years met them with a courteous 'good morning, gentlemen.' 'Are you Mr. Lincoln's son?' said Mr. Evarts. 'Yes, Sir,' said the boy. 'Then let's shake hands'; and they began greeting him so warmly as to excite the younger one's attention, who had stood silently by the opposite gate-post, and he sang out, 'I'm a Lincoln, too,' whereupon several delegates, amid much laughter, saluted the young Lincoln." So went the introduction of Willie and Tad to the American public.[83] While the boys had been waiting outside to receive the committee members, Mary Lincoln was inside in the small family parlor on the south-west corner of the house. "It will no doubt be a gratification to those who have not seen this amiable and accomplished lady to know that she adorns a drawing-room, presides over a table, does the honors on an occasion like the present, or will do the honors at the White House with appropriate grace," wrote the *Tribune*. "She is one of three sisters noted for their beauty and accomplishments ... Mrs. Lincoln is now apparently 35 years of age, is a very handsome woman, with a vivacious and graceful manner; is an interesting and often sparkling talker," concluded the story. Obviously, Mary had told yet another lie about her age, for in May of 1860, she was actually forty-one. Yet the newspaper was correct in make the following observation: "Standing by her almost gigantic husband, she appears petite, but is really about the average height of ladies."[84]

Mary Lincoln made a good impression on her guests that day. George Ashmun, the Republican committee chairman, wrote Lincoln later to say, "I may possibly be pardoned for saying that I shall be proud, as an American citizen, when the day brings her to grace the White House."[85] It was only the beginning of the attention that the Lincoln family would garner from the press and from the public. Not all of the attention would be of such a positive nature; however, in the beginning at least, there was nothing but enthusiasm for Honest Abe and his gracious little wife. James A. Briggs, the Republican lawyer who had invited Lincoln to speak at the Cooper Institute in New York the previous February, was charmed by the Lincoln romance. "You will pardon me for saying, there was to me a touching tenderness & beauty, and a real wealth of affection, in your remark upon the receipt of the telegraph announcing your nomination, 'There's a little woman down at our house would like to hear this. I'll go down & tell her,'" Briggs wrote to Lincoln on May 25. "To you, at that moment, the shouts of the great world had no music. Your heart in that moment of conscious pride, was with the mother of your boys—the chosen one of your affections; she was more than all the world beside." Briggs continued, "God bless her & the boys: and I believe a kind Providence will take care of you. I hope to see that 'little woman' The Lady President."[86]

Notes

1 Marriage License of Abraham Lincoln and Mary Todd, 4 November 1842, Abraham Lincoln Papers, ALPL; Jean H. Baker, *Mary Todd Lincoln: A Biography* (New York: W. W. Norton & Co., 1987; reprint, New York: W. W. Norton & Co., 2008), 97; James T. Hickey, "A Family Album: The

Dressers of Springfield," *Journal of the Illinois State Historical Society* 75 (Winter 1982): 309–20; Paul M. Angle, *"Here I Have Lived": A History of Lincoln's Springfield, 1821–1865* (Springfield, IL: Abraham Lincoln Association, 1935; reprint, Chicago: Abraham Lincoln Bookshop, 1971), 98; Kenneth J. Winkle, "'An Unladylike Profession': Mary Lincoln's Preparation for Greatness," in Frank J. Williams and Michael Burkhimer, eds., *The Mary Lincoln Enigma: Historians on America's Most Controversial First Lady* (Carbondale: Southern Illinois University Press, 2012), 101; Kenneth J. Winkle, *Abraham and Mary Lincoln* (Carbondale: Southern Illinois University Press, 2011), 45–46.

2   Mary Todd to Mercy Levering, 15 December 1840, Lincoln Collection, ALPL (this document is transcribed in its entirely in the Documents section).

3   Angle, *"Here I Have Lived,"* 87; James T. Hickey, "The Lincoln's Globe Tavern: A Study of Tracing the History of a Nineteenth-Century Building, *Journal of the Illinois State Historical Society* 56 (Winter 1863): 629, 638–39, 650; Abraham Lincoln to Joshua F. Speed, 5 October 1842, Abraham Lincoln Papers, ALPL; *Sangamo Journal* (Springfield, IL), 19 January 1843, 1:5.

4   Bledsoe would later become the Confederacy's assistant secretary of war, be an apologist for the Confederacy after the war and found *The Southern Review*. John A. Garraty and Mark C. Carnes, eds., *American National Biography*, 24 vols. (New York: Oxford University Press, 1999), 3:11–12; William Murrell Hays, *Polemics and Philosophy: A Biography of Albert Taylor Bledsoe* (Ann Arbor, MI: University Microfilms, 1971); Albert Taylor Bledsoe, *Is Davis a Traitor or Was Secession a Constitutional Right Previous to the War of 1861?* (Baltimore, MD: Innes and Co., 1866).

5   *Sangamo Journal*, 14 October 1842, 4:6; Hickey, "Lincoln's Globe Tavern," 639; John Palmer, ed., *The Bench and Bar of Illinois: Historical and Reminiscent*, 2 vols. (Chicago: Lewis Publishing Co., 1899), 1:174; William Hyde and Howard L. Conard, *Encyclopedia of the History of St. Louis*, 4 vols. (St. Louis, MO: The Southern History Company, 1899), 1:106–7.

6   Baker, *Mary Todd Lincoln*, 99–101; Hickey, "Lincoln's Globe Tavern," 632–33.

7   Harry E. Pratt, *Personal Finances of Abraham Lincoln* (Springfield, IL: Abraham Lincoln Association, 1943), 31–32, 144.

8   Mary Lincoln to Emilie Helm, 20 September 1857, *L&L*, 49–51.

9   Abraham Lincoln to Joshua F. Speed, 18 May 1843, Abraham Lincoln Papers, ALPL; David Herbert Donald, *Lincoln* (New York: Simon & Schuster, 1995), 94–95.

10   Winkle, *Abraham and Mary Lincoln*, 47, 54–55; Baker, *Mary Todd Lincoln*, 102; Martha Benner and Cullom Davis, eds., *The Law Practice of Abraham Lincoln: Complete*, 2nd ed. (Springfield: Illinois Historic Preservation Agency, 2009), www.lawpracticeofabrahamlincoln.org (hereafter cited as *LPAL*); Guy C. Fraker, *Lincoln's Ladder to the Presidency: The Eighth Judicial Circuit* (Carbondale: Southern Illinois University Press, 2012).

   During the 1840s, Lincoln's circuit travels took him as far north as Pontiac in Livingston County (100 miles from Springfield), as far south as Shelbyville in Shelby County (100 miles), as far east as Danville in Vermilion County (120 miles) and as far west as Havana in Mason County (50 miles). Before the development of railroads in Illinois in the 1850s, Lincoln made his trips on horseback, extending his time away from home. During his marriage, Lincoln traveled about half of the time and spent the other half in Springfield handling cases in local, circuit and federal courts and in the Illinois Supreme Court. *LPAL*.

11   Don E. Fehrenbacher, *Prelude to Greatness: Lincoln in the 1850s* (Stanford, CA: Stanford University Press, 1962); Fraker, *Lincoln's Ladder to the Presidency*; Kenneth J. Winkle, *The Young Eagle: The Rise of Abraham Lincoln* (Dallas, TX: Taylor Trade Publishing, 2001).

12   Winkle, *Abraham and Mary Lincoln*, 46–47; Baker, *Mary Todd Lincoln*, 100; *Illinois State Register* (Springfield), 28 July 1843, 2:7.

13   Abraham Lincoln to Joshua F. Speed, 23 July 1843, Abraham Lincoln Papers, ALPL.

14   Mary Lincoln to Rhoda White, 20 December 1869, *L&L*, 536.

15   Baker, *Mary Todd Lincoln*, 101–3; Pratt, *Personal Finances*, 84; Jason Emerson, *Giant in the Shadows: The Life of Robert T. Lincoln* (Carbondale: Southern Illinois University, 2012), 8, 26; Stephen

Berry, *House of Abraham: Lincoln and the Todds, a Family Divided by War* (Boston: Houghton Mifflin Co., 2007), 37.

16 Baker, *Mary Todd Lincoln*, 103; Pratt, *Personal Finances*, 64–66; Mortgage of Robert S. Todd to Nathaniel A. Ware, 8 September 1841, *Todd v. Ware*, Sangamon County (IL) Circuit Court, Herndon-Weik Collection, LC; *Todd v. Ware, LPAL*; Deed of Robert S. Todd and Elizabeth Todd to Mary Lincoln, 3 March 1844; Contract between Charles Dresser and Abraham Lincoln, 16 January 1844; Deed of Charles Dresser and Louisa Dresser to Abraham Lincoln, 2 May 1844, all in Abraham Lincoln Papers, ALPL.

17 Sara M. Evans, *Born for Liberty: A History of Women in America* (New York: Free Press, 1997), 95–97; Winkle, *Abraham and Mary Lincoln*, 50–51.

18 Mary Lincoln to Mary Harlan Lincoln, 22 March 1869, *L&L*, 504.

19 Mary Lincoln to Emilie Helm, 20 February 1857, *L&L*, 49–50; Winkle, *Abraham and Mary Lincoln*, 47–48.

20 Richard Lawrence Miller, "Life at Eighth and Jackson," in Williams and Burkhimer, *Mary Lincoln Enigma*, 60–81.

21 Winkle, *Abraham and Mary Lincoln*, 51.

22 Mary Lincoln to Mary Harlan Lincoln, 22 March 1869.

23 Deed of Charles Dresser and Louisa Dresser to Abraham Lincoln, 2 May 1844; Winkle, *Abraham and Mary Lincoln*, 48.
    In 1850, two mulatto families lived in proximity to the Lincoln family, Office of the U.S. Census, Seventh Census of the United States (1850), Sangamon County, IL, 118–20.

24 William E. Baringer, ed., *Lincoln Day by Day: A Chronology, 1809–1865*, 3 vols. (Washington, DC: Lincoln Sesquicentennial Commission, 1960), 1:228–325, passim; Baker, *Mary Todd Lincoln*, 105.

25 Baker, *Mary Todd Lincoln*, 104; Harry C. Blair and Rebecca Tarshis, *Lincoln's Constant Ally: The Life of Colonel Edward D. Baker* (Portland: Oregon Historical Society, 1960); Donald, *Lincoln*, 107, 111.

26 Abraham Lincoln to Joshua F. Speed, 22 October 1846, Lincoln Collection, ALPL.

27 Donald, *Lincoln*, 107, 113; *Sangamo Journal*, 29 October 1846, 2:6; *Sangamo Journal*, 30 July 1846, 2:7; Theodore Calvin Pease, *Illinois Election Returns, 1818–1848* (Springfield: Illinois State Historical Library, 1923), 141, 148, 159; Baker, *Mary Todd Lincoln*, 136.

28 Mary Lincoln to Josiah G. Holland, 4 December 1865, *L&L*, 293.

29 *L&L*, 32–33; Jean H. Baker, *The Lincoln Marriage: Beyond the Battle of Quotations*, 38th Annual Robert Fortenbaugh Memorial Lecture (Gettysburg, PA: Gettysburg College, 1999), 22–26; Abraham Lincoln to Joshua F. Speed, 18 January 1843, 18 May 1843 and 22 October 1846, all in Abraham Lincoln Papers, ALPL.

30 Baringer, *Lincoln Day by Day*, 2:281; Patrick Dunne and Charles L. Mackie, "Philadelphia Story," *Historic Preservation* 46 (July/August 1994): 72–103; Garraty and Carnes, *American National Biography*, 2:7–8; Proceedings of the John J. Hardin Memorial Meeting regarding the Battle of Buena Vista, 5 April 1847, *Sangamo Journal*, 8 April 1847, 2:2; Mark E. Neely Jr., *The Abraham Lincoln Encyclopedia* (New York: McGraw Hill, 1982), 139–40; Berry, *House of Abraham*, 38–40; *Sangamo Journal*, 15 July 1847; Robert W. Merry, *A Country of Vast Designs: James K. Polk, the Mexican War and the Conquest of the American Continent* (New York: Simon & Schuster, 2009); Karl Jack Bauer, *The Mexican War: 1846–1848* (Lincoln: University of Nebraska Press, 1992).

31 David Davis to Sarah W. Davis, 8 August 1847, folder B-2, David Davis Family Papers, Springfield, IL; Abraham Lincoln to Buckner S. Morris and John J. Brown, 19 October 1847, Roy P. Basler, ed., *The Collected Works of Abraham Lincoln*, 8 vols. (New Brunswick, NJ: Rutgers University Press, 1953), 1:405–6; Wayne C. Temple, *By Square and Compass: Saga of the Lincoln Home* (n.p.: Ashlar Press, 1984; reprint, Mahomet, IL: Mayhaven Publishing, 2000), 61; Contract between Abraham Lincoln and Cornelius Ludlan, 23 October 1847, Lincoln Collection, ALPL; *Illinois Journal* (Springfield), 28 October 1847, 2:2.

32 Mary Lincoln to Hannah Shearer, 26 June 1859, *L&L*, 56–57.

33 *Daily Era* (St. Louis, MO), 28 October 1847; Mary Lincoln to Mercy Levering, 23 July 1840, Lincoln Collection, ALPL; John W. Starr, *Lincoln and the Railroads: A Biographical Study* (New York: Dodd, Mead, 1927), 47; Berry, *House of Abraham*, 38.

34 Berry, *House of Abraham*, 38–40; Robert V. Remini, *Henry Clay: Statesman for the Union* (New York: W. W. Norton & Co., 1991), 692; Baker, *Mary Todd Lincoln*, 137.

35 Starr, *Lincoln and the Railroads*, 48; Allen C. Clark, *Abraham Lincoln in the National Capital* (Washington, DC: W. F. Roberts Co., 1925), 3; Baker, *Mary Todd Lincoln*, 139; Abraham Lincoln to Mary Lincoln, 16 April 1848, Lincoln Collection, ALPL (this document is transcribed in its entirety in the Documents section); Paul Findley, *A. Lincoln: The Crucible of Congress* (New York: Crown Publishers, 1979).

36 William H. Townsend, *Lincoln and His Wife's Home Town* (Indianapolis, IN: The Bobbs-Merrill Co., 1929), 164.

37 Abraham Lincoln to Mary Lincoln, 16 April 1848.

38 Mary Lincoln to Abraham Lincoln, May 1848, Lincoln Papers, ALPL (this document is transcribed in its entirely in the Documents section).

39 Abraham Lincoln to Mary Lincoln, 12 June 1848, Lincoln Papers, ALPL.

40 Abraham Lincoln to Mary Lincoln, 2 July 1848, box 5, Lincoln Papers, University of Chicago, Chicago, IL.

41 Starr, *Lincoln and the Railroads*, 49–51; Summary of Speech of Abraham Lincoln at Worcester, Massachusetts, 12 September 1848, *Boston Daily Advertiser* (MA), 14 September 1848, 2:2–3; Summary of Speech of Abraham Lincoln at Boston, Massachusetts, 15 September 1848, *Illinois State Register*, 13 October 1848, 2:4; Fragment of Notes regarding Niagara Falls, September 1848, Abraham Lincoln Papers, LC; Mary Lincoln to Henry C. Deming, 16 December 1867, transcribed in Thomas F. Schwartz and Kim M. Bauer, "Unpublished Mary Todd Lincoln," *Journal of the Abraham Lincoln Association* 17 (Summer 1996): 13–14; Mary Lincoln to Edward Lewis Baker Jr., 4 October 1879, Lincoln Collection, ALPL; *St. Louis Gazette* (MO), 9 July 1839.

42 Blain Brooks Gernon, *The Lincolns in Chicago* (Chicago: Ancarthe Publishers, 1934), 13; *Illinois Gazette* (Lacon), 14 October 1848, 2:2; *Chicago Daily Democrat* (IL), 7 October 1848; Summary of Speech of Abraham Lincoln at Chicago, Illinois, 6 October, 1848, *Illinois Gazette*, 14 October 1848, 2:2; *Illinois State Register*, 13 October 1848; Temple, *By Square and Compass*, 57; Baringer, *Lincoln Day by Day*, 2:323.

43 *Illinois Daily Journal*, 2 April 1849, 2:2; "Spot Resolutions in the United States Congress," 22 December 1847, Abraham Lincoln Papers, LC; Donald, *Lincoln*, 125–40; Baker, *Mary Todd Lincoln*, 144–45; Thomas F. Schwartz, "An Egregious Political Blunder: Justin Butterfield, Lincoln, and Illinois Whiggery," *Journal of the Abraham Lincoln Association* 8 (Winter 1986): 9–19; Donald, *Lincoln*, 140–41; *L&L*, 39–40; Daniel Walker Howe, *What Hath God Wrought: The Transformation of America, 1815–1848* (New York: Oxford University Press, 2007), 762–65.

44 Baringer, *Lincoln Day by Day*, 3:11; Angle, "Here I Have Lived," 159.

45 *Observer and Reporter* (Lexington, KY), 18 July 1849, 3:2; Berry, *House of Abraham*, 40–43; *L&L*, 40; *Todd et al. v. Edwards et al.*, *Todd v. Todd et al.* and *Edwards et al. v. Todd et al.*, all in *LPAL*.

46 Mary Lincoln to Adeline Judd, 13 June 1860, *L&L*, 64–65.

47 Baker, *Mary Todd Lincoln*, 125–26; Winkle, *Abraham and Mary Lincoln*, 57; Mary Lincoln to Henry C. Deming, 16 December 1867, *L&L*, 463–64; *Sangamo Journal*, 6 September 1853, 3:2; *Sangamo Journal*, 13 June 1860, 2:5; Glenna Schroeder Lein, *Lincoln and Medicine* (Carbondale: Southern Illinois University Press, 2012), 11–13, 40–41; Samuel P. Wheeler, "Solving a Lincoln Mystery: 'Little Eddie,'" *Journal of the Abraham Lincoln Association* 33 (Summer 2012): 34–36.

48 Abraham Lincoln to Mary Lincoln, 2 July 1848.

49 Mary Lincoln to James Smith, 9 June 1870, *L&L*, 566–68.

50 Winkle, *Abraham and Mary Lincoln*, 57–59; Baker, *Mary Todd Lincoln*, 128; Abraham Lincoln to Mary Lincoln, 2 July 1848; Emerson, *Giant in the Shadows*, 23.

51 Mary Lincoln to Rhoda White, 2 May 1868, *L&L*, 475–77; Family Record in the Lincoln Family Bible, Lincoln Collection, ALPL; Lincoln Family Record, Lincoln Collection, Chicago History Museum, Chicago, IL; *L&L*, 41; Baker, *Mary Todd Lincoln*, 129; Catherine Clinton, *Mrs. Lincoln: A Life* (New York: Harper Collins, 2009), 88–89, 197.

52 Carroll Smith-Rosenberg, "The Hysterical Woman: Sex Roles and Role Conflict in 19th-Century America," *Social Research* 39 (Winter 1972): 652–78; Edward Shorter, *Women's Bodies: A Social History of Women's Encounter with Health, Ill-Health, and Medicine* (New Brunswick,

NJ: Transaction Publishers, 1997), 271–73; Deborah Kuhn McGregor, *From Midwives to Medicine: The Birth of American Gynecology* (New Brunswick, NJ: Rutgers University Press, 1998).

53 Abraham Lincoln to Mary Lincoln, 2 July 1848; Jean H. Baker, "Mary Todd Lincoln: Managing Home, Husband, and Children," *Journal of the Abraham Lincoln Association* 11 (1990): 6–10; Mary Lincoln to Emilie Helm, 20 September 1857.

54 Mary Lincoln to Ozias M. Hatch, 28 February 1859, *L&L*, 53; Mary Lincoln to Eliza Stuart Steele, 23 May 1871, *L&L*, 588; Mary Lincoln to Abraham Lincoln, May 1848, Lincoln Papers, ALPL; Pratt, *Personal Finances*, 145, 147; Baringer, *Lincoln Day By Day*, 2:114; *Sangamo Journal*, 17 May 1858, 1:4; *Sangamo Journal*, 18 October 1854, 2:5; Mary E. Humphrey, "Springfield of the Lincolns," *Abraham Lincoln Association Papers* (Springfield, IL: Abraham Lincoln Association, 1930), 37.

55 Mary Lincoln to Mrs. Kasson, 20 January 1866, transcribed in Schwartz and Bauer, "Unpublished Mary Todd Lincoln," 10–11.

56 Mary Lincoln to Josiah G. Holland, 4 December 1865.

57 Benjamin P. Thomas, *Abraham Lincoln: A Biography* (New York: Alfred A. Knopf, 1952), 90–91; Baker, *Mary Todd Lincoln*, 142, 227–28; Baker, *Lincoln Marriage*.

58 Deed of Abraham Lincoln and Mary Lincoln to Robert Anderson, 18 September 1854, Sangamon County Deed Record PP, 530–31, Illinois Regional Archives Depository, University of Illinois Springfield; Donald, *Lincoln*, 197; Pratt, *Personal Finances*, 147–51; Temple, *By Square and Compass*, 88, 92–93, 272.

59 *Illinois Journal*, 23 January 1855; Pratt, *Personal Finances*, 147; *Illinois Journal*, 25 January 1855, 29 January 1855, 2 February 1855; Baringer, *Lincoln Day by Day*, 2:114; Emerson, *Giant in the Shadows*, 21.

60 Lyman Trumbull served in the U.S. Senate from 1855 to 1872. As the chairman of the Senate Judiciary Committee in 1864, he was a co-author of the Thirteenth Amendment abolishing slavery in the United States. *Biographical Directory of the United States Congress 1774–2005* (Washington, DC: Government Printing Office, 2005), 2064; Michael Vorenberg, *Final Freedom: The Civil War, the Abolition of Slavery, and the Thirteenth Amendment* (New York: Cambridge University Press, 2001), 53–61.

61 Baker, *Mary Todd Lincoln*, 148–49; List of Members of the Illinois Legislature in 1855, c. January 1855, Bradley University, Peoria, IL; List of Members of the Illinois Legislature in 1855, c. January 1855, Lincoln College Museum, Lincoln, IL; Abraham Lincoln to Elihu Washburn, 9 February 1855, Lincoln Papers, ALPL; *L&L*, 44; Mary Lincoln to David Davis, 12 September 1865, Lincoln Collection, ALPL; Mary Lincoln to Elizabeth Blair Lee, 11 July 1865, *L&L*, 258–59.

62 Mary Stuart to Bettie Stuart, 3 April 1856, Milton Hay Collection, ALPL; Temple, *By Square and Compass*, 88, 92–93; *New York Daily Tribune*, 25 May 1860, 6:4.

63 Mary Lincoln to Emilie Helm, 16 February 1857, *L&L*, 48–49.

64 Mary Lincoln to Emilie Helm, 20 September 1857; *Illinois State Journal*, 24 July 1854, 3:2; *Illinois State Journal*, 26 August 1854, 3:1; *Illinois State Journal*, 15 January 1857, 3:4; *Illinois State Journal*, 23 January 1857, 3:5; *Illinois State Journal*, 29 January 1857, 2:5.

65 Mary Lincoln to Emilie Helm, 16 February 1857; Office of the U.S. Census, Eighth Census of the United States (1860), Sangamon Co., IL, 131; Temple, *By Square and Compass*, 102; Angle, "Here I Have Lived," 176–77, 188; *Illinois State Journal*, 16 February 1855, 3:1; *Illinois State Journal*, 29 September 1857, 3:1.

66 *LPAL*; William E. Gienapp, *The Origins of the Republican Party, 1852–1856* (New York: Oxford University Press, 1987), 286–89; 1850 Census, Sangamon Co., IL, 120; 1860 Census, Sangamon Co., IL, 140; Mary Lincoln to Sally Orne, 12 December 1869, *L&L*, 533–34; Emerson, *Giant in the Shadows*, 25.

67 *Illinois State Journal*, 13 January 1857, 16 February 1857; Theodore Calvin Pease, ed., *The Diary of Orville Hickman Browning*, 2 vols. (Springfield, IL: Illinois State Historical Library, 1925), 1:273.

68 Mary Lincoln to Emilie Helm, 16 February 1857; Pease, *Diary of Orville Hickman Browning*, 1:274.

69 *Daily Democratic Press* (Chicago, IL), 2 March 1857; Pratt, *Personal Finances*, 148–49; Gernon, *Lincolns in Chicago; Illinois Central Railroad v. McLean County, Illinois, and Parke* and *Lincoln v. Illinois Central Railroad*, both in *LPAL*; Mary Lincoln to Emilie Helm, 20 September 1857; Daniel W. Stowell, Susan Krause, John A. Lupton, Stacy Pratt McDermott, Christopher A. Schnell, Dennis E. Suttles, and Kelley B. Clausing, eds., *The Papers of Abraham Lincoln: Legal Documents and Cases*, 4 vols. (Charlottesville: University of Virginia Press, 2008), 3:308–83.

70 *Daily Illinois State Journal* (Springfield), 18 June 1858, 2:2–4; *Daily Illinois State Journal*, 16 July 1858, 2:2–3; *Daily Illinois State Journal*, 7 July 1858, 3:1; *Chicago Daily Press and Tribune* (IL), 12 July 1858, 1:2–6; Abraham Lincoln to Stephen A. Douglas, 24 July 1858, and Stephen A. Douglas to Abraham Lincoln, 24 July 1858, both in Abraham Lincoln Papers, LC; Baker, *Mary Todd Lincoln*, 153–55; Harold Holzer, ed., *The Lincoln-Douglas Debates: The First Complete: Unexpurgated Text* (New York: Harper Collins, 1993), 322–23; Mary Lincoln to Hannah Shearer, 24 April 1859, *L&L*, 54–56; Lincoln-Douglas Debates Scrapbook, 1858, Alfred Whital Stern Collection of Lincolniana, LC; Robert W. Johannsen, *Stephen A. Douglas* (Urbana: University of Illinois Press, 1997); Robert W. Johannsen, ed., *The Lincoln-Douglas Debates of 1858* (New York: Oxford University Press, 1965).

71 Mary Lincoln to Hannah Shearer, 28 August 1859, *L&L*, 57–58.

72 Mary Lincoln to Hannah Shearer, 1 January 1860, *L&L*, 61–62; Emerson, *Giant in the Shadows*, 38–41; Abraham Lincoln to George C. Latham, 22 July 1860, Gilder Lehrman Collection, New York, NY; Pease, *Diary of Orville Hickman Browning*, 1:348, 367, 370; Mary Lincoln to Ozias M. Hatch, 3 October 1859, Lincoln Collection, ALPL; Carl Sandburg and Paul M. Angle, *Mary Lincoln, Wife and Widow* (New York: Harcourt, Brace & Co., 1932), 202; Mary Lincoln to Ozias M. Hatch, 28 February 1859; *Chicago Press & Tribune*, 19 July 1859.

73 Mary Lincoln to Hannah Shearer, 1 January 1860.

74 1860 Census, 146.

75 Mary Lincoln to Hannah Shearer, 26 June 1859.

76 Mary Lincoln to Hannah Shearer, 2 October 1859, *L&L*, 59–62.

77 Mary Lincoln to Emilie Helm, 23 November 1856, *L&L*, 45–48 (this document is transcribed it its entirety in the Documents section); Wayne C. Temple, "'I am So Fond of Sightseeing': Mary Lincoln's Travels up to 1865," in Williams and Burkhimer, *Mary Lincoln Enigma*, 180.

78 Abraham Lincoln to Mary Lincoln, 4 March 1860, Lincoln Collection, ALPL.

79 *Speech of Abraham Lincoln in New York* (Springfield: Daily Illinois State Journal, 1860); Harold Holzer, *Lincoln at Cooper Union: The Speech That Made Abraham Lincoln President* (New York: Simon & Schuster, 2004).

80 *Chicago Press & Tribune*, 10 May 1860, 1:2; *Illinois Daily State Journal*, 21 May 1860, 2:1; *New York Daily Tribune* (NY), 25 May 1860, 6:4.

81 Angle, "*Here I Have Lived*," 236–37; *Daily Illinois State Journal*, 19 May 1860, 3:2.

82 *New York Daily Tribune*, 25 May 1860, 6:4; *Illinois Daily State Journal*, 21 May 1860, 2:1.

83 *New York Daily Tribune*, 25 May 1860, 6:4.

84 Ibid.

85 Clipping from the *Springfield Republican* enclosed in George Ashmun to Abraham Lincoln, 23 May 1860, Abraham Lincoln Papers, LC.

86 James A. Briggs to Abraham Lincoln, 25 May 1860, Abraham Lincoln Papers, LC; Holzer, *Lincoln at Cooper Union*, 9–10.

CHAPTER **4**

MRS. PRESIDENT LINCOLN

The campaign to be the "lady president" proved an exhilarating and exhausting one for Mary Lincoln. Her husband held meetings in an office at the state house and maintained very steady correspondence, but his primary task was to lay low in Springfield while others campaigned for him. Busy from the start, Mary was pressed into service to entertain a constant procession of guests, serve tea and sometimes meals to Republican Party operatives and help Lincoln read and answer the overwhelming influx of mail. However, even with all the attention and the distractions of the nomination weekend, Mary was ever the protective mother. Apparently, Mark Delahay, one of the many Republicans to visit the Lincolns, had arrived with two campaign flags that very much interested the little Lincoln boys. Delahay may have promised one flag but had carried them both away at the end of his visit. On May 25, Mary Lincoln sent a friendly but deliberate note to Delahay. "One of my boys, appears to claim prior possession of the smallest flag, is inconsolable for its absence," she wrote. "As I believe it is too small to do you any service, and as he is so urgent to have it again . . . I will ask you to send it to us, the first opportunity you may have, especially as he claims it, and I feel it is as necessary to keep one's word with a child, as with a grown person."[1]

During the coming six months, the quiet security of the Lincoln home and the comfortable routine of the family's life in Springfield gave way to an unpredictable incessant bustle. One of the major changes in the Lincoln family routine was the fact that the husband and father of the house was home all summer and fall, as presidential candidates did not campaign for themselves as they do today. However, Lincoln's time was mostly occupied with meetings at his office and in the Lincoln parlor. Mary's sisters and their husbands and a few close Lincoln family friends like Orville Hickman

Browning and the Duboises provided Mary with familiar faces and comfortable companionships. The Lincoln family home became a public venue for party negotiations and planning, as Republican Party members visited regularly throughout the summer and fall. In addition, the numerous political rallies contributed to the deluge of people wishing to have an audience with the candidate. There were serenades in the yard, and Mary helped her husband host supporters, photographers, job seekers, artists and newspaper editors.[2] The campaign brought out strangers from all over the Northern states, but it also reconnected the Lincolns with old friends and some of Mary's Kentucky relatives. One such connection was with Mary's cousin, the former Annie Parker, now the wife of prominent Republican attorney and judge William M. Dickson of Cincinnati. Dickson wrote to Lincoln to offer some political advice on Ohio prospects for the Republican Party, and at the bottom of the letter, Annie penned a personal note to Mary. "Let me congratulate you upon the success of your husband, whom I have always loved so much," she wrote. "You are an ambitious little woman and for many reasons I am delighted with your success ... Hurrah for old Abe!!! We will do what we can to make him President ... I am on this side of the line & can say what I please for my heart is with old Abe on the slavery question. Keep cool cousin Mary for you might be disappointed."[3]

Keeping cool was becoming more difficult as the weeks passed. Despite the friendly notes from relatives and friends, Mary was still feeling unsettled. "I am quite unnerved just now," she wrote her friend Adeline Judd, "and we have so much company ... Our oldest boy, has been absent, almost a year, a long year, & at times I feel wild to see him."[4] Her family and home in Springfield that had rooted her in body and in spirit was in a period of dramatic transition, and Mary's letters to her women friends reveal her uneasiness. By October, the anticipation of the impending election was getting the best of her. "You used to be worried, that I took politics so cooly[.] [Y]ou would not do so, were you to see me now," she wrote to her old friend and former neighbor Hannah Shearer. "Fortunately, the time is rapidly drawing to a close, a little more than two weeks, will decide the contest. I scarcely know, how I would bear up, under defeat ... You must think of us on election day, our friends will feel quite as anxious for us, as we do for ourselves."[5] On the one hand, Mary was enjoying the public attention and the prospects of the presidency, but on the other hand, she was clearly feeling some panic about the disruption that the campaign brought to her family.

On election Tuesday, November 6, 1860, Mary was at home and Lincoln spent most of the day at his state house office. Around three o'clock in the afternoon, Lincoln walked to the courthouse, where a crowd cheered for him while he cut his own name from a ballot and voted a straight Republican Party ticket. It was a more festive election day than was usual in Springfield, with throngs of people milling about at the capitol building, roving bands playing and discharges of a cannon. In the wee hours of the next morning, Lincoln settled in at the telegraph office to collect election returns. The ladies of Springfield hosted an early morning event, serving coffee to the voters and singing songs. Mary was their guest of honor, and Lincoln made a brief appearance, which resulted in "the wildest climax of feminine ecstasy," reported the *New York Tribune*. The election results continued to pour in, and in the early afternoon on Wednesday, Lincoln's victory was certain. The deep political divisions in the country and the four-way race for the presidency had given him the edge in the Northern states, and though he garnered only 40 percent of the popular vote, he commanded the necessary electoral votes to win. Lincoln went home to share the news with Mary, who no longer had to fear how she might have born a defeat. Her husband had just become president-elect of the United States, and she would be his First Lady.[6]

If the pace of life had been chaotic during the campaign, Mary must have been ever the more exhilarated and exhausted by the chaos that ensued following the election. There were even more visitors, the incoming mail increased and now Lincoln and his wife had to prepare their family for a move to Washington, the latter of which would fall primarily on her. However, first, there was an important visit to Chicago. The Lincolns left Springfield together on November 21, 1860, traveling by train to Chicago for a meeting with Hannibal Hamlin, Lincoln's vice-president-elect. A cheering crowd gathered at the train depot in Springfield to see off the Lincolns; the train made quick stops at Lincoln, Bloomington and Lexington, where Lincoln made brief remarks to more cheering crowds at those railroad stations. Upon their arrival in Chicago, the Lincolns checked in at the Tremont House; toured the Republican Party's convention wigwam, which was about to be torn down; and attended church services the next day at the St. James Church. Wherever Lincoln went, cheering crowds greeted him, and newspapers provided story after story about the candidate's politics and his personal background. Mary and the boys were the subjects of much public interest as well. In November, Mary, Willie and Tad posed for a photograph in the Springfield photography shop of Preston Butler. The next month, a wood-cut image of this photograph appeared in *Frank Leslie's Illustrated Newspaper*. All of this attention after the election gave Mary a real taste of what it meant to be famous. Now prominent politicians, wealthy business leaders, reporters, office seekers, artists, bearers of gifts and others were demanding the attentions of both Mr. and Mrs. Lincoln. With the conflicting emotions of excitement and trepidation swirled in with the public attention her presence garnered everywhere, it is not surprising that Mary Lincoln was feeling unsettled.[7]

From school out East, Robert Lincoln was curious about how his mother was handling the attention. "I see by the papers that you have been to

Chicago. Aren't you beginning to get a little tired of this constant uproar?" he wrote her in early December. "There was a Republican levee and supper at Cambridge to which I was invited. I did not go for I anticipated what really happened. I was sitting in my room about 6:30 when two boys came in and handed me an admission ticket, on the back of which the fellow had written asking me to come over as they were calling for me. I wrote him a note excusing myself. He must be the biggest fool in the world not to know I did not want to go over, when if I did I would be expected to make a speech!"[8] While Robert Lincoln was trying to hide from all of the attention, his mother embraced it. Although, she probably should have taken the lead from this wise son whom she herself had raised. Yet, the shopping trips to Chicago and New York to outfit herself with new dresses and accessories were thrilling to her, and the specialized attention that merchants lavished on her intensified the experience. Mary had always been prone to shopping and the purchase of clothing and adornments that set her apart from her contemporaries in Springfield. In 1859, for example, she had spent $196.55 for clothing, and the cost of one dress that year was the equivalent of two months of income for a typical family in Springfield. In addition to the shopping and celebrity status, some of the country's most powerful and wealthy citizens came to Springfield to call on the Lincolns. The visitors Mary hosted in her own home included famed abolitionist congressman Joshua R. Giddings of Ohio, Missouri politicians Edward Bates and Francis Blair Jr. (a graduate of Transylvania University in Mary's hometown), New York political boss Thurlow Weed and U.S. Senator Simon Cameron of Pennsylvania. High-end shopping, travel on private railcars, posing for photographs and hosting such political dignitaries would have been intoxicating for most small-town, middle-class wives. However, for Mary Lincoln it was particularly so. To be pursued and flattered by wealthy and influential people emboldened her opinionated nature and encouraged her stylish flair, and both would ultimately lend fuel for the fiery critique that some observers would unleash on her once she arrived in Washington.[9]

On January 10, Mary left Springfield with her brother-in-law Clark Smith and former New Hampshire congressman Amos Tuck, who had been in Springfield to see Lincoln. They were traveling to New York, where Mary wanted to purchase clothing that would be appropriate for a president's wife. She was likely an easy mark for the shopkeepers, who showered her with compliments and extended credit for her purchases. It would be her first in a series of New York shopping trips during the coming four years. Robert Lincoln met his mother in New York, and the two traveled to Buffalo on their way home to Springfield. At Buffalo, they discovered that they had no pass for the State Line Railroad. Mary took a seat, and Robert went into the railroad office to speak to the superintendent. "My name is Bob Lincoln; I'm a son of Old Abe," he said. Continuing, he added, "the old woman is in the cars raising h-ll about her passes—I wish you would go and attend to her."[10] The superintendent then provided Bob and his mother complimentary passage. The story reflects Mary's growing sense of entitlement, even before her husband's inauguration as president.

The Lincolns spent the month of January making arrangements for their departure from Springfield. They rented their home, sold many of their belongings and made arrangements for their animals. On January 30, Lincoln traveled to Charleston, Illinois, to visit his stepmother and other relatives. Just days before their departure from Springfield, the Lincolns held a public reception at their home on February 6, 1861. From seven o'clock until well past midnight, they were "thronged by thousands" of visitors. Wearing a white moire-antique silk gown with full trail and small French lace collar, a string of pearls and a simple head dress, Mary received the guests, who then passed into the parlor to pay respects to President-Elect Lincoln.[11] The St. Louis *Missouri Democrat* reported from the event that Mary was "a lady of fine figure and accomplished address" and "well calculated to grace and do honor to the White House." Also taking note of her sisters, the same newspaper commented: "When looking upon the lovely group of the Todd family, how proud old Kentucky would have felt if she could have been present to witness the position in which her son and daughters were placed."[12] Perhaps Mary Lincoln wondered how her own father, Robert Todd, would have felt about the success of his third daughter's husband. As she stood there with her sisters greeting the guests, perhaps she even closed her eyes for a moment and wished that her father who so loved politics had lived long enough to enjoy with her its ultimate prize.

Mary's old friend Mercy Conkling and her husband, James Conkling, were in attendance, as were all of the Lincolns' closest friends. The next day, in a letter to her son Clinton, who was a close friend of Robert Lincoln, Mercy described the scene: "Such a crowd, I seldom, or ever saw at a private house. It took about twenty minutes to get in the hall door. And then it required no little management to, make your way out." Then she went on to share a vignette about Robert that she knew her son would appreciate: "While I was standing near Mr. L. he [Robert] came up, and in his humorous style, gave his hand to his father, saying: 'Good evening, Mr. Lincoln!' In reply his father gave him a gentle slap in the face."[13] The story illustrates the affectionate teasing that characterized the Lincoln children's relationships with their father. Two days after the reception, the Lincoln family moved out of their home on Eighth and Jackson Streets. When they closed the door with the brass plate engraved "A. Lincoln" and stepped down the front steps, leaving the house behind them, there were likely tears and bittersweet feelings. This comfortable beige house with green shutters had been their family home for seventeen years; it was where three Lincoln boys had been born and where one had died. We can only speculate as to the emotions each of the five members of the Lincoln family felt at that moment. However, they all believed that the parting was not to be a permanent one; Lincoln purchased a $3,200 insurance policy on the house and outbuildings to insure the home in their absence. The family checked in at the Chenery House, where they would stay until the departure of the inaugural train to Washington. Over the next two days, the Lincolns said their painful good-byes to their family, to their friends and to their hometown.[14]

The most difficult good-bye came at 7:30 a.m. on Monday, February 11, when an emotional Abraham Lincoln delivered brief remarks at the Great Western Railroad Depot. "No one, not in my situation, can appreciate my feeling of sadness, at this parting," he said. "To this place, and the kindness of these people, I owe every thing."[15] No doubt, the parting was an emotional one for Mary and the boys as well. After the speech, Lincoln and Robert boarded the presidential car on his inaugural trip to Washington. Mary, Willie and Tad met up with the president and the party in Indianapolis the next day, on Lincoln's fifty-second birthday. No doubt to Mary's liking, the presidential railroad car was elegant and represented the latest fashion, with light tapestry carpeting, dark furniture and accents replete with Victorian motifs. The walls were covered in plush red fabric and rich blue silk banners with thirty-four silver stars. The interior was elaborate and rich in color and featured varied patriotic images, like silver stars on the banners, silk national flags and patriotic streamers.[16]

Along the journey to Washington, there were stops through Indiana, Ohio, Pennsylvania, New York, New Jersey and Maryland; in each place, the train was greeted with cheering crowds who desired a few words from the president-elect. At some of the stops, Lincoln and his entourage left the train to attend various rallies and events. In other locations, the train rolled into a station, and Lincoln would appear on the platform of the rear car and wave and deliver quick remarks. At the quicker stops, there were sometimes calls from the crowd to see Mrs. Lincoln and the boys as well. On a couple of occasions, Mary joined her husband on the platform, and Lincoln shared a joke that revealed much about his witty personality but also something of his comfortable relationship with his wife. In Ashtabula in northern Ohio, Lincoln answered calls to see Mrs. Lincoln by remarking that he should hardly hope to induce her to appear, as he had always found it very difficult to make her do what she did not want to.[17] Sons Willie and Tad enjoyed the long train ride. Willie delighted in greeting visitors who boarded at various stops by asking them if they wanted to see Old Abe, and then pointing to people who were not, in fact, his father. In Columbus, where the train was greeted by a crowd of 60,000 people, the Lincoln entourage visited the Ohio State

House, where Lincoln delivered remarks and greeted citizens. After a dinner and an appearance at a military ball in the president-elect's honor, the Lincoln family stayed as the overnight guests of Governor William Dennison at his residence. The Lincolns were the guests of former President Millard Fillmore at his mansion in Buffalo, New York, even though the former president had opposed Lincoln's election to the presidency. In Albany, the Lincolns stayed with New York's Republican governor Edwin Morgan.[18] At another stop in Pennsylvania, a large and enthusiastic crowd greeted Lincoln, who appeared and said he was too unwell to say much to them. However, this time, answering demands for an appearance by Mrs. Lincoln, he brought her out and said that he had concluded to give them "the long and the short of it!" Upon this humorous remark regarding the fourteen-inch disparity in the couple's heights, the crowd again cheered and waved enthusiastically as the trail pulled away.[19]

In twelve days, the inaugural train passed through more than fifty cities in seven states. The Lincolns met with former president Millard Fillmore, dined with governors, attended receptions hosted by politicians and others hosted by their wives, shook the hands of hundreds of well-wishers and spent time with Vice President-Elect Hannibal Hamlin. In New York City, Mrs. Lincoln smoothed her husband's hair and kissed him as the couple stepped off of the train to join a procession of eleven carriages of the presidential party. The procession passed 250,000 people along the route on their way to the Astor House, where Mary hosted a reception and the family spent the night. Along the cross-country journey, Mary and the boys witnessed a snowstorm in Cleveland, went on a tour of showman P.T. Barnum's museum in New York and enjoyed a band concert and fireworks in Philadelphia. Because of threats on Abraham Lincoln's life, his security detail deemed it unsafe for him to go to the hostile city of Baltimore, so a small group broke off from the main party and took Lincoln ahead to Washington on another train. The family and the remainder of the party continued on the inaugural train as planned. Mary was terrified at the prospect of being separated from her husband, but the presence of her close friend Hannah Shearer and her husband, who had boarded the train in Pennsylvania, was a comfort. As soon as Lincoln arrived safely in Washington, he sent a telegram to his frantic wife. Mary arrived in Washington twelve hours after her husband and rode to Willard's Hotel with William Seward and Illinois congressman Elihu Washburne.[20]

That night, the Lincolns settled into their rooms, likely collapsing in their beds for a good night's sleep. For the next several days, the family occupied two bedrooms and two parlors at the hotel, where they held meetings and receptions and entertained guests, many of whom stayed for dinner, drank liquor and smoked cigars. There was no rest from the procession of visitors and plans and arrangements for the inauguration, their first official dinner in the White House and the Inaugural Ball. Lincoln had a presidential cabinet to assemble and a national crisis to face, but for Mary, one of the most important aspects of the preparations was her wardrobe. Once Lincoln was inaugurated, there would be frequent public receptions, state dinners and diplomatic visitations, and Mary was determined to show the public that she was worthy of the role despite her western origins. That had been precisely the purpose for her New York shopping trip, and she had with her many fine fabrics and items purchased in Springfield, Chicago and New York. However, she needed to employ a dressmaker who would clothe her like Republican royalty. With the help of her female relatives who were in Washington with the Lincolns—sisters Elizabeth Edwards and Margaret Kellogg and her cousin Elizabeth Grimsley—Mary found her dressmaker. Elizabeth Keckley, a renowned seamstress and former slave, had worked for Senator Jefferson Davis's wife until his resignation from the Senate the month before and the family's return to the South. Keckley also made dresses for Mrs. Stephen A. Douglas, Mrs. Gideon Welles and Mrs. Edwin Stanton, so Mary placed her wardrobe in expert hands. However, the employment of Elizabeth Keckley provided a value that far exceeded her talents with the sewing needle. Elizabeth Keckley would become Mary Lincoln's first and most important female friend in Washington.[21]

In the early afternoon on Monday, March 4, Mary watched as Justice Roger B. Taney of the U.S. Supreme Court delivered the oath of office to her husband, inaugurating him as the sixteenth president of the United States. As she listened, Abraham Lincoln delivered his first inaugural address on the portico of the U.S. Capitol, its unfinished dome looming above a crowd of some 30,000 people. That evening, surrounded by a hoard of Todd family relatives, mostly from Springfield, Mary Lincoln made her first public appearance as First Lady. She was wearing a low-cut blue silk gown trimmed in French Alençon lace, her favorite pearls, some new diamonds and a blue ostrich feather in her hair. As etiquette required the president and his wife to enter the gala separately, Mary's escort was a very special old friend from Illinois, Senator Stephen A. Douglas; it was with the "Little Giant" that she enjoyed her first dance as First Lady. The two might have been old friends, but the gesture was politically symbolic as well, as it demonstrated the Union loyalties of her husband's old political rival. Mary was far more at home in this social and genteel environment than her husband, who fussed with his dress gloves all night and retired at midnight. Mary and her relatives remained into the early morning hours, enjoying the sumptuous buffet provided by Washington's most celebrated caterers, more dancing and, no doubt, interesting and lively conversation on this triumphant occasion.[22]

The new president's wife received many positive reviews of her first public performance as First Lady. The *New York Times* declared her "the belle of the evening" and noted that all of her party "dressed exquisitely, and in perfect taste."[23] During her time in the White House, Mary would host hundreds of events and entertain thousands of guests. Whether she was presiding over an extravagant event for prominent and politically important people, serving tea to close friends or meeting private, ordinary citizens in a reception line, Mary Lincoln dressed like she believed a First Lady should dress. In the spring and summer of 1861, she and Elizabeth Keckley worked together to create sixteen dresses, and there would be more outfits created and more accessories accumulated in the coming years. Mary presided over the White House receptions with the poise and charm she learned as a girl in Kentucky. Much like our modern media reporting on a First Lady's attire, the Civil War newspapers carried frequent reports of Mary Lincoln's outfits. Right next to reports from the battlefields, newspapers provided descriptions of her clothing. As fashion is very much in the eye of the beholder, it is not at all surprising that Mary's fashion sense played to very mixed reviews. Some observers found her dresses and accessories elegant and appropriate, while others criticized her tastes and chastised her for dressing too youthfully for her age. Perhaps those critics were not aware of the fact that Mary was a woman who shamelessly fibbed about her age and, thus, dressed according to the spirit of the "younger" woman within her mind and her soul.[24]

In hiring a dressmaker, Mary had already taken the necessary steps to ensure that she would be well outfitted for all of the necessary public engagements she would attend. However, Mary Lincoln's concerns for refined presentations to the public of herself extended to her environment as well. Upon waking up in the White House the day after the inauguration, she found "miserably furnished rooms," assessed the dingy décor as lacking in refinement and found much of the mansion in some degree of disrepair, having suffered neglect from previous occupants. The house was also infested with insects and rodents and was a dusty old place. Mary wanted to dress like Republican royalty, but she also wanted the residence and public areas of the president's house to be fitting of Republican royalty as well. Indeed, the White House, which sat on twenty-two wooded acres, was somewhat drab and musty. Yet it did possess many positive characteristics from the start. When the Lincolns arrived, it had a fresh coat of exterior paint and some modern amenities. There were toilets and running water in the family quarters, gas lighting throughout the mansion and a furnace that minimized the need for stoking fireplaces.[25] Mary found the White House conservatory, installed by President James Buchanan, "delightful." She wrote a friend, "We have the most beautiful flowers & grounds imaginable."[26] Another perk of the White House was the proximity of the family quarters to President Lincoln's working spaces, which provided opportunities for family interactions even in the face of Lincoln's heavy burdens and unrelenting schedule. For each presidential administration, Congress provided a $20,000 appropriation for redecorating and furnishing the president's home as well as $6,000 annual budget for repairs and upkeep on the building. There was much to appreciate within the White House and on the grounds as well, but Mary wasted no time in purchasing furnishings and updating the décor to make it a brighter more elegant place for the family and for visitors.[27]

As Mary set out to create a home for her family in Washington, the anxiety of the national crisis did not escape her. "Thousands of soldiers are guarding us, and if there is safety in numbers, we have every reason, to feel secure," she wrote a Springfield friend. "We can only hope for peace!"[28] She could play no direct role in effecting that peace, but she could provide a quiet, comfortable and beautiful oasis for her increasingly distracted and worried husband. Robert had returned to his classes at Harvard, but Mary also had her two small boys to make comfortable and keep safe from the chaos outside of the White House. On April 13, Fort Sumter in the Charleston Harbor fell to Confederate forces, and Virginia seceded from the Union four days later. The war was underway, and Mary appears to have assuaged some of her fears by focusing primarily on her household responsibilities and diligently attending to official duties during those first months. Most of her Springfield family went home in the days following the inauguration, but her cousin Elizabeth Grimsley stayed on, providing an important tether for Mary, as her insecurities about the national crisis escalated with the secession of Arkansas and Tennessee and the movement of federal troops. Making a start on expending that $20,000 for the White House was one way to set the fears aside, at least for a time. In mid-May, she and Elizabeth journeyed to New York, Philadelphia and Boston to make purchases both for the family and for the White House. It was the first of many such trips, and criticisms about her spending were swift in making headlines. Many observers believed that the spending was indecent coinciding as it did with the tremendous financial burdens facing the country in equipping an army to save the Union. However, Mary had no qualms, or if she did she never expressed them.[29]

Among a long list of purchases Mary Lincoln made for the White House was a $900 carriage, furniture, a rosewood grand piano, draperies, luxurious carpets and close to $7,000 on wallpaper. On May 24, 1861, in one shopping trip to one store in New York she chose $952.48 worth of rugs and fabrics. She also purchased personal items, like expensive shawls and jewelry. Sometimes such items came to her in the form of gifts, but she was personally responsible for the payment of most. Merchants flattered the First Lady, who in some cases overpaid for items so as not to appear simple or cheap; they were quick to provide credit, which no doubt resulted in an inability on her part to keep track of the purchases she was making. There was a $2,500 carpet for the East Room, a 700-piece set of glassware, exorbitant expenditures for two sets of china (one for the White House and one for the family), a chandelier and a grand piano. One class of her purchases was for the Executive Mansion's library, and these were expenses her husband wholeheartedly approved. Mary had charge of a $250 appropriation for books, and she chose a wide variety, including a history of England, a history of birds, a set of Shakespeare's work and a book of Indian tales.[30] Mary also oversaw expensive repairs in the house and on the grounds, ordered extensive cleaning and demanded various improvements in the mansion. Eventually, she overspent the appropriation more than $6,000.[31] In her personal spending, Mary was more frugal. For example, she haggled with a milliner over the costs of ribbons and headdresses. In addition, she insisted that the Lincolns spend little of the presidential salary, and they succeeded by living on less than $7,000 of Lincoln's annual $25,000 salary each year. However, in the end, she saw her personal shopping as a business expense. This was quite remarkable for three reasons. First, Mary's wardrobe was a personal expense and came out of the family's budget. Second, during this historical time period, presidential administrations were responsible for expenses incurred for White House entertainment and state dinners. When the Lincolns fed or provided drinks for guests, they footed the bill. The party they hosted in February 1862 cost the Lincolns $1,000. Third, during his presidency, Lincoln invested more than $54,000 in federal treasury bonds, which moneys the government used to finance the war.[32]

Many historians have examined the evidence and convicted Mary of fraud and dishonesty in the accounting of the expenditures she made for the White House. Others have interpreted the spending on furnishings and clothing as evidence of Mary's growing mental instabilities. There is no historical doubt about the fact that Mary spent lavishly for herself and for the White House. She wore very expensive, handmade gowns, adorned herself with extravagant accessories and purchased many unnecessary luxury items for the White House. This biography does not deny these facts nor does it condone her actions. However, a lengthy discussion of Mary Lincoln's expenditures and actions related to them, an investigation of the possible psychological motives for them or casting judgment on her because of them is for other authors in other books. It would be dishonest to ignore the topic entirely, especially given the significance that so many historians have given it. However, for the purposes of this relatively brief segment on Mary Lincoln's life in the White House, the purchases are important for two simple reasons. First, they tell us something about Mary Lincoln's personality. They reveal her love of fashion and material possessions and her frivolous nature. She enjoyed clothes, jewelry and fine interiors her entire life, and what she enjoyed did not change just because the country was at war. Mary also made attempts to improve the attire of her husband, no doubt playing a role in his purchase of a handcrafted Brooks Brothers coat, for example. All across the United States, people still attended the theatre, enjoyed live music, danced, sang and wore fancy clothes. Life continued in spite of the horrors on the battlefields. As a middle-class woman, Mary was also trying to make herself worthy of Washington society, many of whose women spent far more money on clothing, luxury items and entertaining than Mary did. Second, the purchases frame the significance of the domestic sphere for Mary Lincoln. She was making a home, being a homemaker, albeit it on a much grander and more public scale than had been the case in Springfield. While she certainly had more resources in Washington than she had back in Illinois, her goals were really no different. From her perspective as a wife and First Lady, she was reflecting her vision of her husband's stature, and she was working to create a domestic and public space she believed reflected the importance of the president of the United States.[33]

Lincoln did not always agree with his wife's purchases, but he personally signed off on many of them. Mary endured public criticism for her shopping, but there was no direct official investigation of her expenditures. There were political concerns however, that Mrs. Lincoln's debts would cause reelection problems for her husband. However, few who visited the thirty-one-room mansion and attended the public events held there would have argued that they had not made a difference in the appearance of the president's residence. Mary understood that in maintaining an appropriate and functioning White House in the midst of a war—hosting state dinners and holding public receptions in a stately and sophisticated environment—she was helping to send a message of a functioning government to the nation. Mary's most important duty as hostess of the White House was to plan and preside over these functions. Making good impressions on diplomatic visitors and, most importantly, the voting public audiences who attended the levees was a requirement of this responsibility. In the late summer of 1861, for example, Prince Jerome Napoleon, the nephew of Napoleon III, visited Washington. Mary threw a big dinner party for him and his entourage. Although the spoiled prince was not that impressed with the American fare, the American press compared Mary Lincoln to Queen Victoria and Empress Eugénie. The Washington *Evening Star* commented that "the fine supervisory taste of Mrs. Lincoln was apparent in all its appointments as well as in the beauty of the floral embellishments, &c, of the table, and of the reception and other rooms."[34] In addition, during the winter and spring seasons, thousands of citizens attended the twice-weekly public receptions that took place in the East Room, where Mary had installed that glorious carpet. The receptions had become a tradition of the American Republican government, and even with the Civil War underway, the Lincolns kept up this tradition because they deemed it an important one.[35]

The newly decorated White House was a retreat in the midst of a dirty, unhealthy and increasingly dangerous city during the Civil War. In 1861, only one street in all of Washington City was paved. During the wet winter months, the mud was at least a foot deep, and during the summer, dust and dirt blew through windows and doors. The Washington Canal ran just south of the White House, and while it allowed commercial transport into the city, it was often slow-flowing and a stagnant breeding ground for mosquitoes. To make matters worse, the city's poor residents swam and bathed in the canal. The city had no drainage and sewage systems, and, as a result, the canal became a cesspool of the city's debris, including dead animals and human waste. The stench from the canal wafted through the White House. All of these factors made the city an unhealthy one, especially during rainy seasons. "I am feeling very far from well," Mary wrote her cousin Lizzie Grimsley in the fall of 1861. "September and early in Oct—are always considered unhealthy months here—my racked frame certainly bears evidence to that fact."[36] During the Civil War, the Lincoln family suffered from various ailments born in the fetid waters, like scarlet fever, malaria, measles and typhoid fever. Wealthy residents vacated the city during some seasons to escape the stench and the airborne and waterborne sicknesses that plagued nineteenth-century Washington. Periodically, Mary and the boys would escape the city for health reasons, and the Lincoln family spent summers at the Soldiers' Home, a cottage three miles from the White House.[37]

When the Lincoln family arrived in Washington, it was a city of more than 65,000 people, and with the coming of the war, the population ballooned to 200,000. The city's substandard infrastructure could not cope with the influx of people, including the nearly 40,000 fugitive slaves and emancipated blacks who arrived during the war. Health issues related to poor sanitation and increasing numbers of residents were one problem, but security of the capital and its government posed more immediate concerns. When Virginia seceded from the Union in mid-April 1861, the capital was directly adjacent to a Confederate state, and that geographic position of Washington put it at constant risk throughout the war. Baltimore, just forty miles to the northeast, was full of secessionists and pro-Southern sympathizers as well. Washington's police force and the military's Provost Guard worked tirelessly to maintain civil order, and the latter held military and civilian jurisdiction and employed efforts to rid the city of people disloyal to the Union. However, the overpopulation, Confederate threats within and just outside of the city and the very real fear of military invasion made the capital a volatile environment. Thousands of federal troops occupied the city throughout the war, and much of the time it looked more like a military encampment than a city. Through a telescope from the White House, Confederate flags could be seen flying above buildings in Alexandria, just six miles south of the capital. There was an ever-present fear of Confederate incursions, and with the unfinished Capitol dome, patent office and Washington obelisk combined with the ubiquitous soldiers on the streets, Washington must have had a disquieting gloom about it.[38]

Abraham and Mary Lincoln had brought their two young boys to an unhealthy and dangerous city and placed them in proximity to a terrible war, and so they were determined to let them be children. Both Mary and her husband spoiled them, let them run wild and showered them with presents. The boys also received gifts from the public and attracted a great deal of attention. The Lincolns employed a tutor, but they did not make scholarly lessons a priority. Tad preferred to run, and Willie joined in, as the boys played war games, pulled pranks on White House staff, interrupted cabinet meetings and raised a new menagerie of pets. With Bud and Holly Taft, the sons of a Washington judge, they used the White House roof as a fort, and with other children in the neighborhood, they drilled on the White House grounds like soldiers. In addition, the real soldiers stationed on the grounds were favorite playmates for the boys. When the Lincolns moved into the White House, Willie and Tad received from Secretary of State William Seward two kittens, which were their inaugural animals. Following those kittens were a dog named Jip, two goats named Nanny and Nanko and a pony. When Tad was away on trips with his mother, he worried about the animals he had left at the White House. In April 1864, Lincoln telegraphed Mary in New York with news for her and for their son. "The draft will go to you. Tell Tad the goats and father are very well, especially the goats."[39]

Though Robert, who was eighteen in 1861, was away for most of the time the Lincoln family was in the White House, his younger brothers idolized him, and he enjoyed his visits with them. "Our boy Robert, is with us, whom you may remember," wrote his mother in 1862. "We consider it a 'pleasant time' for us, when his vacations, roll around, he is very companionable, and I shall dread when he has to return to Cambridge."[40] The younger boys were best friends. Mary later reflected that "Their love for each other, was charming to behold."[41] All three of the Lincoln boys were fond of each other, but they had their own unique personalities. Robert was serious and independent, handsome and mature. Willie, who was eleven in 1861, was an intelligent, articulate and kind boy with a generous spirit. He treated his younger brother, Tad, like a pet and cared deeply for him. Tad, who was eight, was a loving boy, playful and mischievous. He likely had a learning disability, and he suffered from a speech impediment that was exacerbated by horribly misaligned teeth. His physical problems, however, did not ruin his fun, and they only further endeared him to his parents. During the war, Tad fancied himself a little soldier, and Secretary of War Edwin Stanton commissioned him a lieutenant for fun. Once commissioned, Tad ordered muskets and drilled the White House staff, much to the annoyance of his brother Robert, who complained to their father. However, to no avail, as Lincoln was amused.[42]

Both of Tad's parents were happy to indulge their young soldier, providing Tad with a full Union blue uniform, a toy cannon and a pistol. "Let 'Tad' have a little gun that he can not hurt himself with," Lincoln wrote to Captain John Dahlgren in October 1862.[43] Seven months later, Lincoln wrote to the Washington Arsenal about a gun. "Let Tad have the pistol, big enough to snap caps—but no cartridges or powder."[44] A month later, Lincoln was second-guessing his indulgence of the gun. He telegraphed Mary, who was in Philadelphia with Tad, "Think you better put 'Tads' pistol away. I had an ugly dream about him."[45] Lincoln also solicited military gifts for Tad from his cabinet members. During a celebratory week at the end of the war, Lincoln sent one note to Secretary of War Edwin Stanton—"Tad wants some flags. Can he be accommodated"—and another to Secretary of the Navy Gideon Welles: "Let Master Tad have a Navy sword." Clearly, the youngest Lincoln boys were a little spoiled.[46]

Despite the Civil War and their busy parents, the Lincolns' young sons were priorities for them. Lincoln sometimes brought them along when he reviewed troops, and he would take time out of a cabinet meeting when the boys burst into the room, much to the annoyance of some cabinet members. Tad was with Lincoln when he toured Richmond in April 1865. The boys accompanied Mary on several of her shopping trips. Robert and Tad sometimes accompanied Mary on her hospital visits to sit with sick or injured soldiers. Willie would often sit with his mother in her room to read and to study, while Tad would be playing in his father's office. The boys also frequently attended the theatre and concerts with their parents or with other adults. The Lincolns loved their children, but they also enjoyed other children as well. Friends of the boys were always welcome in the White House, and sometimes they invited other children to events or on trips. In August 1861, for example, Mary suggested to her friend that she bring her own boys for a visit. "We would be pleased to have them with us, and I am determined to bring you all home with me. The boys would enjoy it here."[47] In some ways, Abraham and Mary Lincoln were trying to give the younger boys a normal childhood, but they could not shield them from the war and, therefore, did not really try. They indulged Tad's war games and took the boys to the army hospitals, where the suffering the war wrought was on public display. Because Robert was older and eligible for military service, Mary wanted to keep him at Harvard and out of the army; but ultimately, he put on a Union uniform late in the war and served as an aide-de-camp for General Ulysses S. Grant.[48]

The sorrows of the war affected most families in some direct way, and the Lincoln boys were no exception. On May 24, 1861, before the first major battle of the Civil War, family friend Elmer Ellsworth was killed in the act of removing a Confederate flag from a building in Alexandria, Virginia. Ellsworth had studied law in Lincoln's office in Springfield and had come to Washington with him on the inaugural train. It was an emotional loss for the Lincoln family, as his body lay in state in the East Room of the White House before his military funeral. Five months later, the war would take another important person in the lives of the Lincoln family. On October 21, 1861, Edward D. Baker, who had been the namesake of the Lincolns' second son, was killed in the Battle of Ball's Bluff. The entire family grieved, and a family story records a poem penned by Willie Lincoln about their lost friend. It began, "There was no patriot like Baker, so noble and so true."[49]

Those personal losses for the Lincoln family would not be the last, and no one—not politicians nor military commanders nor even soothsayers—could have predicted the human losses that would come for the entire war-torn country. In the winter of 1861–62, as the war escalated and casualties began to mount, it was inconceivable that they would ultimately result in more than 600,000 deaths and more than 500,000 wounded.[50] During the course of the war, Mary understood the pressures her husband faced. She decided that she and her husband and the government could use an entertaining distraction from all of the worries and fears. At 9 p.m. on Wednesday, February 5, some 500 or 600 beautifully attired guests—including cabinet members, senators, congressmen, and governors and their wives—began arriving at the White House for a gala. Close friend Senator Orville Browning and his daughter joined the Lincolns in the promenade. The Washington *Evening Star* poked some fun at the event but reported that Mrs. Lincoln was "tastefully, elegantly dressed . . . in white satin, with black lace flounces."[51] The Marine Band played for the guests, and included in their repertoire was a new piece entitled the Mary Lincoln Polka. The food and patriotic-themed sugar art was displayed at midnight, and many guests remained until three o'clock in the morning. However, what was supposed to be a pleasant diversion from the war for the guests and for the Lincolns turned out to be an unpleasant obligation that divided the time and attentions of the presidential couple between their guests and a dangerously sick little boy in the family's quarters upstairs.[52]

The unhealthy city had crept into the White House, and Willie and Tad Lincoln had developed typhoid fever. By the evening of the gala, Willie's condition had worsened, and his fever raged as the White House guests danced into the night. Elizabeth Keckley helped Mary dress, arranged her hair and coaxed her down the stairs. The Lincolns spent the evening running between their guests and their son's bedside. For the next two weeks, Tad was recovering, but Willie's suffering increased. The bacterial disease caused violent stomach cramps and diarrhea and left him dehydrated. His suffering no doubt brought back sad memories of the suffering of little Eddy Lincoln and terrified his mother, who refused to leave his side. Willie's friend Bud Taft spent hours with him as well, staying in the White House with the Lincolns during Willie's illness. While simple medicines available today would have saved the boy, there was no help for him in 1862. On February 20, Willie Lincoln died, and his death carved huge holes out of the hearts of his parents and his brothers, who had loved him so well. "The body of little Willie Lincoln was visited to-day by a number of the friends of the family," wrote the *New York Herald*. "The body was laid out in a plain suit of brown clothes, with a blossom of mignonette on his left breast . . . The funeral will take place at two o'clock to-morrow afternoon. The youngest son of President Lincoln is considerably better to-day."[53]

Lincoln's tremendous responsibilities forced him to fight through his grief, although John Nicolay, one of the president's personal secretaries, reported later that upon sharing the devastating news, the president burst into tears. Robert came immediately from Harvard to grieve with his family, and Mary's sister Elizabeth Edwards arrived from Springfield. Lincoln and Tad, who was still ill, were immediate and great comforts to each other, but Mary Lincoln was inconsolable. She took to her bed and cried for days. Eddy's death had been a terrible blow to her, but Willie's death was far more difficult. Perhaps the context of the war and those pressures and fears that crowded her life resulted in a more protracted grief. Perhaps she was suffering from depression or had a mental breakdown of some sort that contributed to her extreme emotional difficulties. Whatever the reason, Mary's suffering at the loss of her second child was unbearable for her. It was during this time of grief that Mary became interested in spiritualism, which was a popular fad of her day. It appealed to Mary's interest in avant-garde trends, but it also played to her emotional longing for Willie. The Lincolns' friend Orville Browning reported in his diary that Mary sought out a spiritualist, who offered "wonderful revelations of her little son Willie."[54] Mary met with three spiritualists, who told her what she wanted to hear: that Willie was with her even though he was gone. The spiritualists provided comfort for some grieving Victorian women, and the First Lady was a willing practitioner of their methods, holding as many as eight séances in the White House. It is easy to dismiss Mary's interest in spiritualism as ridiculous, but in the 1860s, it was a popular movement, albeit not a respectable one, that drew in many middle-class women who were open to the power of its promises. However, whereas most women dabbled privately and quietly, Mrs. Lincoln's public position as First Lady put her involvement with the spiritualists on a public stage and opened her up to additional criticisms.[55]

If the spiritualists gave her some peace, they did not quiet her sorrows in her correspondence. "We have met with so overwhelming an affliction in the death of our beloved Willie[,] a being too precious for earth, that I am so completely unnerved, that I can scarcely command myself to write," she wrote in May.[56] Being unnerved was becoming a regular condition for Mary, and her letters illustrate her sadness. For months after Willie's death, her correspondence was filled with woeful lamentations regarding his untimely passing. In July, the Lincoln family, including Robert, moved out to the Soldiers' Home, which offered Mary a great deal of peace. "In the loss of our idolised boy, we naturally have suffered such intense grief, that a removal from the scene of our misery was found very necessary. Yet, in this sweet spot, that his bright nature, would have so well loved, he is not with us, and the anguish of the thought, oftentimes, for days overcomes me. How often, I feel rebellious, and almost believe that our Heavenly Father, has forsaken us, in removing, so lovely a child from us! Yet I know, a great sin, is committed when I feel thus."[57] Mary understood that her entire family was suffering, and being together at the president's summer home was therapeutic for them all.

Since the Lincoln family had arrived in Washington, the war and the president's political concerns and the unusual circumstances of living a public life interfered with the ability of Abraham and Mary Lincoln to maintain a happy, healthy marriage. Additional factors contributed to the stress. Lincoln's private secretaries clashed with Mary and competed for the president's attentions, Secretary of War Edwin Stanton scolded her for interfering with political appointments, and Mary's expenditures for the White House angered her husband. Mary's emotional difficulties, fears and grief following Willie's death put further stress on the overburdened president. Lincoln's own depression, his occasional emotional detachment and his inability to be a comfort to his grieving wife contributed to Mary's difficulties with her husband. Mary understood the distractions of her "noble & good husband" but once wrote, "I consider myself fortunate, if at eleven o'clock, I once more find myself, in my pleasant room & very especially, if my tired & weary Husband, is there, resting in the lounge to receive me—to chat over the occurrences of the day."[58]

However, despite the stresses on their lives and on their marriage and despite the war, they enjoyed some happy times in the White House and out at the Soldiers' Home. In addition, there were private dinners, regular carriage rides and concerts at the White House, at least until Mary suspended them after Willie's death. Their shared loved of theatre offered an important outlet for both of them and allowed them to steal some time together. For both Abraham and Mary Lincoln, attending the theatre provided an enjoyable diversion from the pressures of the White House. During the Civil War, they attended dozens of theatre productions at various theatres across Washington and delighted in such performances as Giuseppe Verdi's opera *Trovatore*, a performance by British burlesque actress Matilda Vining Wood portraying "Pocahontas" and Shakespeare's *Othello*. The Lincoln children enjoyed these diversions as well. On April 11, 1863, the Lincolns took Tad to Grover's Theatre to enjoy a benefit performance of Shakespeare's *Macbeth*, which raised over $2,000 for the relief of soldiers.[59]

The Lincolns had been married twenty years, and some of the romance had definitely faded away. There was a more business-like quality to their correspondence during this time period, yet there was some evidence of tenderness. When Mary and Tad went to Philadelphia in June 1863, the time when Lincoln had had that dream about Tad and his pistol, Mary telegraphed back, "Taddie & myself are well dreams to the contrary."[60] Lincoln telegraphed in response, "Your three despatches received. I am very well; and am glad to know that you & 'Tad' are so."[61] When either of the Lincolns traveled, they sent messages as to their safe arrivals, and while much of the content of their messages simply relayed news, there was concern for each other as well.

During their marriage, Lincoln often commented about Mary's figure and complimented her on her attire and appearance. This attention indicated a physical interest in his wife; her figure pleased him. More evidence of their intimacy appeared in one letter Mary wrote to her husband discussing her gynecological issues. "I had one of my severe attacks, if it had not been for Lizzie Keckley, I do not know what I should have done," she wrote. "Some of these periods, will launch me away."[62] Her frank language with Lincoln indicates a comfort level with him that would not be in evidence had there been no intimacy between them. Of course, there is no hard historical evidence regarding the physical nature of their marriage. However, one of the soldiers who guarded the president at the Soldiers' Home reported to a later biographer that he once discovered the president in bed with his wife. In addition, there was enough perceived intimacy between the couple to spur some rumors in the press that the First Lady was pregnant, which of course she was not. The couple managed some intimate moments, and they worried over each other's health and safety as well. Even in their difficult trials during the Civil War, there was love and care between Abraham and Mary Lincoln. To Mary, he was "always—lover—husband—father & all all to me."[63] Despite all of the pressures on Lincoln and the almost total lack of personal time available to him, he made it a habit to take regular carriage rides with his wife. This time that they took for each other offered them both a respite from the war, but more importantly, it allowed them quiet, sweet time as a loving couple.[64]

However, while the Lincolns were husband and wife during the Civil War, their personal concerns were far less important than the public concerns. As the war progressed, and the lines in Abraham Lincoln's face cut deeper, Mary was trying to make sense of the war and involve herself in the war effort as well. At the beginning of the war, she had reviewed troops with her husband, but as the war progressed, she spent more time in Washington's military hospitals. She did not work as a nurse, but she sat with wounded and sick soldiers and kept them company, wrote letters home for them and brought them fruit, flowers or books to read. On one occasion, she sat with a solder named James Agen and penned a letter for him to his mother. "I am sitting by the side of your soldier boy," she wrote. "He has been quite sick, but is getting well. He tells me to say to you that he is all right. With respect for the mother of the young soldier, Mrs. Abraham Lincoln."[65] Mary made two visits to Agen, but apparently he was so ill that he did not know who she was until his mother showed him the First Lady's letter when he returned home. After Willie died, Tad accompanied Mary on more of her hospital visits, and she also frequently went with friends. In April 1863, she invited Col. Thomas Sweney. "About 1 o'clock to day," she wrote, "Taddie & myself are going in the carriage about a mile & half out to carry some flowers to the sick soldiers, if you are disengaged, will you go with us. Taddie, as usual is appropriating you, for a ride on horseback this afternoon to the Navy Yard. It is sometimes, unfortunate, to be a favorite, with so exacting a young man."[66] Mary also solicited donations and purchased special fruits or other items for soldiers as well. In August 1862, she donated $1,000 for troops and spent $200 of it to purchase lemons and oranges. On another occasion, she raised money to provide a Christmas dinner at Douglas Hospital, and when she received liquor as a gift at the White House, she often brought it with her on her trips to see the soldiers. In February 1864, she donated to the Sanitary Fair "two splendid vases of flowers," which were sold for $50 each to benefit the soldiers. Mary seemed to enjoy these efforts, and she was disappointed when poor health or other duties interfered with her visits to the hospitals. "Owing to an intensely severe headache . . . I fear, that I shall be prevented from visiting the Hospitals today," she wrote Mary Jane Welles, who was a frequent companion on these trips.[67]

In Washington, Mary maintained a few close relationships with women, like Mrs. Welles, but it was male companionship she most often sought in her parlor at the White House. Often, she played hostess to various prominent men in what became known as the Blue Room Salon. Over tea Mary would discuss the war, politics and literature with her guests. Senators Charles Sumner, Daniel Sickles and Ira Harris were frequent visitors, and Mary enjoyed hearing their news and sharing with them her fears and opinions about the war. From the Soldiers' Home, she wrote to Sickles in the fall of 1862,

"When we are within hearing, as we on this elevation have been, for the last two or three days, of the roaring cannon, we can but pause & think. Yet, as to Washington, yielding to the Rebels, a just Heaven would prevent that! ... Mr. L. has so much to excite his mind, with fears for the Army, that I am quite considerate in expressing my doubts & fears to him concerning passing events."[68] These men played a surrogate role for Mary in the absence of her husband. Favorite among her salon attendees was Senator Sumner, for whom Mary developed a great deal of respect. Sumner became an important political ally to the president and a trusted and close personal friend to him and to Mrs. Lincoln. After Willie's death, Mary was in the throes of grief, and Lincoln was unable to help her. Thinking a close friend might make a difference, Lincoln sent for Sumner. "Mrs L. needs your help," he wrote. "Can you come?"[69] Sumner engaged Mary's mind and offered a warm friendship, filling a gap in her life created by her husband's heavy burdens.

While Sumner was Mary Lincoln's most important male friend, Elizabeth Keckley was the woman on whom she most relied. Lizzie, as Mary affectionately called her, was more than a talented dressmaker. She was a caring nurse when Mary was ill, she was a cheerful personal assistant and traveling companion and, most importantly, she was an intimate confidante. The two women were almost inseparable companions, especially on particularly dark days. For example, when Mary kept vigil at Willie's deathbed, Lizzie watched over Mary. Keckley's only son had died early in the war, and a mother's grief now bonded them further. Mary's friendships with Keckley and Sumner provided critical emotional connections for her and were of significant importance to the quality of her life in Washington. However, these relationships also exposed Mary to a different view of the war. She had arrived in Washington a devout Unionist, but her friendships with Sumner, an anti-slavery politician, and Keckley, a former slave, made her sympathetic to the Radical Republicans and the plight of freed slaves, particularly those in the city of Washington. Keckley worked tirelessly during the war for the benefit of 1,800 slaves freed in the District of Columbia and the thousands who flocked into Washington City during the war. By 1863, there were 15,000 freed slaves in the city, and most of them lacked basic necessities. Mary's political discussions with Sumner about slavery and emancipation and her discussions with Lizzie about the human costs of slavery and the stories of suffering of freed slaves in Washington affected Mary's own understanding about the war and of freedom. She would come to believe in the historical importance of the Emancipation Proclamation and see the war as a war for freedom. She would also later boast that she always urged her husband "to be an extreme Republican."[70]

In 1862, Mary Lincoln asked her husband to take $200 from a $1,000 fund for soldiers. She wanted to give the money to Keckley to purchase much needed supplies for free blacks. Mary wrote to her husband, describing that the contrabands in the city were "suffering intensely, many without bed covering & having to use any bits of carpeting to cover themselves. Many dying of want." She added, "The cause of humanity requires it."[71] While Mary and Lizzie were in New York in November 1862, Mary helped her friend connect with prominent and wealthy individuals in the city to aid in her campaign to raise funds. In 1864, Mary introduced to Sumner two black visitors who had come to Washington from Philadelphia to see him because, as she noted, "they would call to see you, whom all the oppressed colored race, have so much cause, to honor."[72] She ended the note by pausing to acknowledge the recent death of abolitionist and Illinois congressman Owen Lovejoy. "Our friend, whom we all so loved & esteemed, has so suddenly & unexpectedly passed away—Mr Lovejoy! An all wise power, directs these dispensations, yet it appears to our weak & oftentimes erring judgments, 'He should have died hereafter.'"[73] Back in 1856, Mary Lincoln had apologized for her husband's support of John C. Fremont, the first candidate of the anti-slavery Republicans, and she had endeavored to convince her Kentucky relatives that her husband was not an abolitionist.[74] Here she was in 1864 lamenting the passing of one of the nation's most outspoken abolitionists, who was also the brother of the martyred abolitionist Elijah P. Lovejoy. This Southern girl, turned Northern woman was not only a staunch Unionist but also now anti-slavery in her thinking. She believed that her husband's Emancipation Proclamation had lifted "the great evil" that had cursed the country and would be for her sons "a rich & precious legacy."[75]

Mary Lincoln had arrived in Washington with the Republican ideals of her husband, and it is not surprising given her relationships with Radical Republicans and a black seamstress to whom she became so attached, that her thinking about race and slavery evolved. However, Mary deserves some of the credit for her growing enlightenment as well. After Lincoln's inauguration in 1861, Mary Lincoln had thrown herself into her domestic role as First Lady, but she had also thrown herself into politics. Although her influence was limited as a woman and greatly tempered by her husband's hands-on approach to all aspects of his administration, Mary raised her voice and, from her perspective at least, played a role. Unlike First Ladies before her, most of whom lived reclusive lives and shied away from public events while their husbands were in office, Mary was a very public First Lady. She was much more like Eleanor Roosevelt, who would live in the White House seventy years after her, than her contemporaries Jane Pierce, Abigail Fillmore and Eliza Johnson. From 1861 to 1865, she wrote dozens of letters supporting the appointments of friends and loyal Republicans as sutlers, West Point cadets, and even cabinet members. She supported the petitions of people she believed had suffered an injustice, she offered letters of introduction and she advocated the release of a woman held in Sing Sing Prison on a murder charge. In 1861, she asked a favor of Montgomery Meigs, who had just become U.S. quartermaster general. She asked him "to purchase 500 or 1000 young Ky horses, belonging to an especial friend of mine in Ky. a strong Union man. It would be a particular pleasure to me to have, as Kentucky is my native state, some horses from there on the battle field."[76] Mary Lincoln also shared gifts she received with political supporters and friends, like raspberries with Ozias Hatch and figs with Rev. Phineas Gurley, always interested in sharing the benefits of her political station with loyal and true fellow Republicans.[77]

In her interactions with visitors in the White House and on her trips to New York, Philadelphia and Boston, Mary shared her opinions on all of these matters in person as well. She was a successful advocate in some cases, and in others, the recipients of her advice cast it aside. When the president was available to listen, Mary shared her opinions with him as well. In 1862, the Union Army was stalled, and increasingly some observers were blaming George B. McClellan for inaction. Lincoln had been growing increasingly frustrated with McClellan's unwillingness to pursue the enemy. Perturbed, Lincoln sent a telegram to the general on October 24: "I have just read your despatch about sore tongued and fatigued horses. Will you pardon me for asking what the horses of your army have done since the battle of Antietam that fatigue anything?"[78] Shortly after that note, Mary went to New York. A letter she sent her husband on November 2, 1862, illustrates Mary's engagement with the political issues facing him, her interactions with people beyond the White House and her willingness to share her views with the president. "Strangers come up from W[ashington]. & tell me you are well, which satisfies me very much. Your name is on every lip and many prayers and good wishes are hourly sent up, for your welfare, and McClellan & his slowness are as vehemently discussed . . . Many say, they would almost worship you, if you would put a fighting General, in the place of McClellan."[79] On November 5, Lincoln replaced McClellan with Ambrose E. Burnside as the Commander of the Army of the Potomac. Mary Lincoln likely had nothing at all to do with pushing her husband to action on McClellan; however, it is likely that Mary took some of the credit for herself. Most importantly to note here is that Mary was intellectually engaged, that she was comfortable in her opinions and that the influence that she attempted to wield was founded in her belief in her husband, his administration, the goals of the Union and the correctness of her own convictions. Her role here was not historically important, but it was personally important to Mary Lincoln.[80]

Despite Mary's loyalty to her husband, the Republican Party, the Union and the Emancipation Proclamation, Mary Lincoln' family ties to the

Confederacy posed problems for the Lincoln presidency. Before her marriage, Emilie Todd had lived for a time with the Lincolns in Springfield, and Emilie was very close to both her sister and to her brother-in-law. Before the war, Emilie had married Benjamin Helm, a Kentucky lawyer and legislator. In April 1861, Lincoln hoped to keep Helm in the Union and offered him a position as a paymaster in the Union Army. The following month, Kentucky proclaimed its neutrality, but Helm declined the appointment and raised a Kentucky regiment for the Confederate Army. On September 21, 1863, Helm, then a Confederate brigadier general, was killed in the Battle of Chickamauga in Georgia. Mary was in New York, and Lincoln telegraphed her with the news. Mary's favorite little sister was now a widow behind Confederate lines in Georgia, and Helm's death in a Confederate uniform brought the brutal sectional divisions of the war right to the Lincoln family's doorstep. On October 15, Lincoln issued a pass to his mother-in-law Betsey Todd to go south to retrieve Emilie and her children and bring them safely back to Kentucky. After the group was stopped in Richmond and questioned by federal troops, Lincoln sent word to allow Emilie to come on to Washington, while Betsey took the other children and returned to Lexington. As was the case with many families during the Civil War, blood ties and family concerns muddied the boundaries of sectional loyalty and made for heart-wrenching conflicts between one's human connections and one's political beliefs.[81]

The Todd family epitomized the deep divisions that many families faced. At the beginning of the war, Mary Lincoln had three Union sisters in Springfield—Elizabeth Edwards, Frances Wallace and Ann Smith—and Lincoln appointed his brother-in-law William Wallace as a paymaster in the Union Army. Brother Levi was in Kentucky during the war and supported the Union, but his struggles with alcoholism kept him from military service. Mary's half-brothers George, Sam, David and Alexander all joined the Confederate Army, and half-sisters Martha and Emilie were married to Confederate officers. Martha and another half-sister Elodie were in Selma, Alabama, when the war began, and both attended the inauguration of Jefferson Davis as president of the Confederacy. Half-sister Margaret lived in Cincinnati, and she and her merchant husband, Charles H. Kellogg, attended Lincoln's inauguration. However, Kellogg had strong Southern sympathies from the start and took suspicious trips south during the war despite the fact that Lincoln had made him a captain and commissary of subsistence for the Union Army.[82] In 1862, Sam Todd died at Shiloh, and Alexander Todd died while serving as an aide-de-camp for Ben Helm. David Todd's command of a military prison erupted in national scandal when it came to light that he was ordering the abuse of prisoners of war. Mary's stepmother remained in Lexington during the war, but she followed the lead of her biological sons and became a staunch Confederate.[83]

Politically, Mary could not have been more different from her Southern siblings. Her political and sectional loyalties at the beginning of the war were crystal clear. She was the wife of the Republican Union president, but she was also a Northern Republican woman who was outraged by the Southern point of view. In a business letter to a New York tailor in October 1861, she shared her opinion about secession: "In the hour of peace, the kind words of a friend are always acceptable, how much more so, when a 'man's foes, are those of their own household,' when treason and rebellion, threaten our beloved land, our freedom & rights are invaded and every sacred right, is trampled upon!" Even more passionately, she continued, "Clouds and darkness surround us, yet Heaven is just, and the day of triumph will surely come, when justice & truth will be vindicated. Our wrongs will be made right, and we will once more, taste the blessings of freedom, of which the degraded rebels would deprive us."[84] To Mary, those Confederate brothers of hers were such degraded rebels, and she bore little sympathy for the deaths of Sam and Alexander because she believed they had made the wrong choice at the start of the war. She briefly mourned for "little Aleck" who she had cuddled and adored when he was a baby, but she defiantly remarked to a friend that "they would kill my husband if they could, and destroy our Government— the dearest of all things to us."[85] Later in her life when a newspaper article connected her to those Confederate brothers and accused her of Southern sympathies all over again, she was enraged. Writing to Elizabeth Keckley, she wrote of the reporters making such claims: "If they had been friendly with me they might have said they were half brothers of Mrs. L., whom she had not known since they were infants; and as she left Kentucky at an early age her sympathies were entirely Republican—that her feelings were entirely with the North during the war, and always."[86]

While Mary blamed her brothers for being Confederates, it was harder for her and for her husband to blame Emilie for her Confederate connections. When Emilie and her four-year-old daughter arrived in Washington in early December, it is likely that the Lincolns were happy to see her again and were entertaining thoughts of allowing her to stay. John Hay noted in his diary, "I visited with Mrs. L. Her sister, Mrs. Gen. Helm is with her just arrived from Secessia."[87] Hay's sarcasm exposed his own opinion about Emilie's arrival, but more prominent voices chimed in Lincoln's ear. On December 14, former senator and close Lincoln family friend Orville Browning met with Lincoln and was shocked when Lincoln revealed the news of this Southern visitor and his wish to keep that news quiet. No doubt, the widow of a Confederate general in the Union president's residence would certainly raise eyebrows. Mary's Blue Room Salon friend Daniel Sickles was horrified by her presence. He was a Union major general who had lost his leg in the Battle of Gettysburg that July, and he told the president and First Lady that they should not have a rebel in their home. Senator Ira Harris was also dismayed, and apparently Emilie angrily told him and Sickles that if she had twenty sons that they would be fighting against their Union sons.[88] Any criticism that Mrs. Lincoln was a Confederate spy or was sympathetic to the Confederacy because of her Southern upbringing and Confederate family was absurd. The situation was certainly politically awkward for Lincoln, but Emily's presence had greatly lifted the spirits of his grieving wife, who finally put away her mourning clothes. However, Lincoln told Emilie that she could not stay unless she agreed to take the Oath of Amnesty of 1863, which pardoned Confederates in exchange for their sworn allegiance to the Union. Lincoln wrote out an oath for Emilie to sign, but she refused and left for Kentucky. If Emilie had not been so outspoken in her Southern sympathies and had signed the oath, the Lincolns would probably have allowed her and all three of her children to stay with them in Washington indefinitely. A year later, Emilie was struggling to provide for herself and her children, and she wrote to Lincoln for assistance. Her Confederate pride got the better of her, however, when she blamed him and Mary for the death of their brother Levi Todd, who had died in 1864 from alcoholism and not from a Union bullet. "He died from utter want and destitution as a letter sent to Sister Mary by Kitty gives particulars," she wrote, "another sad victim to the powers of more favored relations." From there she went on to ask for permission to ship cotton, and if she had not lessened her chances for an affirmative response with her opening salvo, she certainly sealed the deal with her final parting shot: "I also would remind you that your Minnie bullets[89] have made us what we are & I feel I have that additional claim upon you."[90] Upon the arrival of that letter to her husband, Emilie Helm's relationship with her older sister Mary ended. Now Emilie was as much a degraded rebel as her brothers who took up arms against the Union.[91]

As the war had progressed, Mary was feeling increasingly isolated, and emotional insecurities and physical health problems plagued her. When her husband and son were out of her sight, her worry bordered on panic. She would leave for a trip and immediately send a message to her husband demanding to hear news from home. On a trip to New York in December, she sent four telegrams that depict some of the panic she was feeling. On December 4, she wrote: "Reached here last evening very tired & severe headache. Better this morning hope to hear you are doing well expect a telegraph to-day."[92] Lincoln responded that all was well, but on December 6, she sent two separate telegrams. In one to Lincoln, she wrote: "Do let me know immediately how Taddie and yourself are." In another to the White House doorkeeper, she demanded, "Let me know immediately exactly how Mr. Lincoln and Taddie are."[93] Lincoln responded, "All doing well."[94] Yet, Mary Lincoln seemed unable to calm her nerves.

In addition, Mary Lincoln's severe headaches increased as the war progressed. She had suffered from migraine headaches most of her adult life. However, whereas in the early period of the war she worked through them, after Willie's death they seemed to interfere more with her ability to accomplish her daily activities. Robert Lincoln speculated that a head injury may have contributed to the increased frequency of Mary's headaches. In July 1863, while riding in a carriage out near the Soldiers' Home, the driver's seat was dislodged, and Mary was left alone in the runaway carriage. The horses bolted, and fearing for her life, Mary leapt from her seat and landed hard on the road, hitting her head. She suffered a bleeding wound on the back of her head, which became infected. Lincoln was so preoccupied with reports from the Battle of Gettysburg, that he spent little time fussing over Mary's injury and wired for Robert to come sit with his mother. It is likely that she had suffered a concussion, and she took nearly three weeks to fully recover. Robert believed that the accident had lasting effects on his mother's emotional health. Likewise, the accident may have also precipitated her heightened fears for the safety of the president.[95] Whatever the reasons for her increased headaches, they continued to plague her. In May 1864, she wrote to Mary Jane Welles: "I was quite unable during several hours yesterday to leave my bed, owing to an intensely severe headache."[96] This was the same letter in which she sent along her regrets that her headache would keep her from her daily visit to the military hospitals. In July, another debilitating headache was the result of a long drive in the heat of the summer day.[97] Yet the headaches were just one sorrow amid a cacophony of unpleasant realities that combined to diminish her ability to cope. It was the headaches; the death of her beloved Willie; the fears for Robert, Tad and her husband; the loss of friends on the battlefields; and the estrangements from family and former friends who had chosen the Confederacy over her husband and the Union. Other causes were the pressures of a public life, the unending misinterpretation of her motives and the noise of the chaotic world around her that was ringing in her head.

Mary Lincoln was war weary. Abraham Lincoln was war weary. The entire country was war weary. Yet, as 1865 dawned, the future was brightening. Some events had passed to lift the hearts and spirits of the president and First Lady. First and foremost had been Lincoln's reelection back in November. For that glorious occasion, Mary argued, afforded her the right "to smile & be cheerful, over the triumph our party has won."[98] However, also of enormous consequence was Sherman's March to the Sea cutting the Confederacy in half, the fall of Charleston, Lincoln's inauguration and plan "to bind up the nation's wounds"[99] and the passage of the Thirteenth Amendment to forever abolish the institution of slavery. Mary had been suffering with her own state of mental and physical unhealthiness, but she recognized the toll that the war had taken on her husband. Mary had watched the worry lines on the president's face deepen, and she knew that the Civil War, the long workdays, the sleepless nights and the human toll for which he felt responsible had aged him. Shortly after the inauguration in March 1865, she wrote to Sumner: "The President & myself are about leaving for 'City Point' and I cannot but devoutly hope, that change of air & rest may have a beneficial effect on my good Husband's health."[100] March was a whirlwind of good news for the Lincoln administration and the Union, and the end of the March brought the Appomattox campaign. On April 3, Richmond and Petersburg in Virginia were occupied by Union troops, and word came to the White House that brought Mary something she had forgotten how to feel: happiness. Excited, she dashed off a note to Senator Sumner: "The Sec of War, has just left & says that Richmond was evacuated last night & is ours! This is almost too much happiness, to be realized! I can say no more—except that Grant is pursuing the enemy."[101]

On April 4, Abraham Lincoln and Tad traveled from City Point, where they had been for several days, to Richmond to tour the Confederate capital. From there, Lincoln was keeping Mary abreast of the news. On that day, she wrote to a friend, "I receive telegrams from my Husband every two or three hours. He has improved in health VERY GREATLY—And after 3 days of exposure to rebel shots my darling Boy [Tad] is well and happy."[102] The next day, Mary, Elizabeth Keckley, the marquis de Chambrun of France, Charles Sumner and Senator James Harlan of Iowa, along with his wife and daughter Mary, boarded the steamship *Monohasset* to meet the president and Tad at City Point. For the next four days, the group stayed on the steamboat *River Queen* and toured Richmond and Petersburg, reviewed troops and enjoyed a military band concert on board. As the *River Queen* headed back to Washington on Sunday, April 9, the party discussed literature, and Lincoln recited Shakespeare much to the party's delight. That afternoon, Confederate general Robert E. Lee surrendered to Union general Ulysses S. Grant at Appomattox Court House in Virginia. When the president's party arrived in Washington at 6 p.m. that evening, people were celebrating in the streets, bonfires were burning, music was playing and the city was alive in celebration. After four long years of bloody civil strife and unimaginable suffering, the war was finally over. After four long years of losing a little more each day of her husband as he shouldered the burdens of that war, Mary must have felt an incredible wave of exhilaration and relief at the news of Lee's surrender.[103]

Upon their return to the capital, the president was immediately engaged in business, meeting with his cabinet and with General Grant and making plans for the transition to peace. However, the president's mood, and the mood of everyone in Washington, was lifted by the news of the Confederate surrender, and the celebratory scene on the White House grounds and throughout Washington reflected the changing mood of the Union as well. On Good Friday, April 14, on what would be the last day of her husband's life, Mary Lincoln enjoyed a private lunch with her husband at two in the afternoon. Lincoln then suggested a long carriage ride alone. Reflecting on that happy afternoon, Mary later wrote: "Having a realizing sense, that the unnatural rebellion, was near its close, & being most of the time, away from W[ashington], where he had endured such conflicts of mind, within the last four years, feeling so encouraged, he freely gave vent to his cheerfulness. Down the Potomac, he was almost boyish, in his mirth & reminded me, of his original nature, what I had always remembered of him, on our own home—free from care, surrounded by those he loved so well & by whom, he was so idolized. The Friday, I never saw him so supremely cheerful—his manner was even playful. At three o'clock, in the afternoon, he drove out with me in the open carriage, in starting, I asked him, if any one, should accompany us, he immediately replied—'No—I prefer to ride by ourselves to day.' During the drive he was so gay, that I said to him, laughingly, 'Dear Husband, you almost startle me by your great cheerfulness,' he replied, 'and well I may feel so, Mary, I consider this day, the war, has come to a close—and then added, 'We must both, be more cheerful in the future—between the war & the loss of our darling Willie—we have both, been very miserable.'"[104]

NOTES

1 Mary Lincoln to Mark Delahay, 25 May 1860, *L&L*, 63–64; Mary Lincoln to Amos Tuck, 4 June 1860, and Mary Lincoln to Dyer Burgess, 29 October 1860, both in Lincoln Collection, ALPL.

2 Frederick H. Meserve, *The Photographs of Abraham Lincoln* (New York: privately printed, 1911), 53; Rufus R. Wilson, *Lincoln in Portraiture* (New York: Press of the Pioneer, 1935), 104; Theodore Calvin Pease, ed., *The Diary of Orville Hickman Browning*, 2 vols. (Springfield, IL: Illinois State Historical Library, 1925), 1:416, 422; *New York Herald* (NY), 13 August 1860, 5:2–3; William E. Baringer, ed., *Lincoln Day By Day: A Chronology, 1809–1865*, 3 vols. (Washington, DC: Lincoln Sesquicentennial Commission, 1960), 2:280–96, passim; William H. Herndon to Lyman Trumbull, 19 June 1860, Lyman Trumbull Papers, LC; *New York Herald*, 13 August 1860, 5:2–3; *Illinois State Journal* (Springfield), 18 July 1860, 3:2.

3 William M. Dickson to Abraham Lincoln and Annie Parker Dickson to Mary Lincoln, 21 May 1860, Abraham Lincoln Papers, LC.

4 Mary Lincoln to Adeline Judd, 13 June 1860, *L&L*, 64–65.

5 Mary Lincoln to Hannah Shearer, 20 October 1860, *L&L*, 65–66.

6 *New York Tribune* (NY), 7 November 1860, 5:4; *New York Tribune*, 8 November 1860, 8:2; A. James Fuller, *The Election of 1860 Reconsidered* (Kent, OH: Kent State University Press, 2012).

7 *New York Daily Tribune* (NY), 23 November 1860, 5:1; *Lexington Weekly Globe* (IL), 22 November 1860, 3:2; Gage, Brother & Drake to Abraham Lincoln, 19 May 1860, and George W. Gage to Abraham Lincoln, 24 November 1860, both in Abraham Lincoln Papers, LC; *Chicago Daily Journal* (IL), 22 November 1860 and 26 November 1860; *Chicago Press & Tribune* (IL), 24 November 1860; Blain Brooks Gernon, *The Lincolns in Chicago* (Chicago: Ancarthe Publishers, 1934), 44; Harold Holzer, "'I Look Too Stern': Mary Lincoln and Her Image in the Graphic Arts," in Frank J. Williams and Michael Burkhimer, eds., *The Mary Lincoln Enigma: Historians on America's Most*

Controversial First Lady (Carbondale: Southern Illinois University Press, 2012), 313; *Frank Leslie's Illustrated Newspaper*, 15 December 1860, 1.

8 Robert Lincoln to Mary Lincoln, 2 December 1860, in Katherine Helm, *The True Story of Mary, Wife of Lincoln* (New York: Harper & Brothers, 1928), 153–55.

9 *Illinois State Journal* (Springfield), 26 November 1860, 2:1; *Illinois State Journal* (Springfield), 27 November 1860, 2:4; *Illinois State Journal*, 14 December 1860, 3:2; Robert Lincoln to Mary Lincoln 2 December 1860; *New York Herald*, 9 December 1860, 17 December 1860, 21 December 1860, and 7 January 1861; *New York Tribune*, 25 December 1860; *L&L*, 69; *Biographical Directory of United States Congress, 1774–2005* (Washington, DC: Government Printing Office, 2005), 664; Jean H. Baker, *Mary Todd Lincoln: A Biography* (New York: W. W. Norton & Co., 1987; reprint, New York: W. W. Norton & Co., 2008), 156.

10 Helm, *True Story of Mary*, 153; *L&L*; *Baltimore Sun* (MD), 22 February 1861.

11 Ruth Painter Randall, *Mary Lincoln: Biography of a Marriage* (Boston: Little, Brown & Co., 1953), 194–95; *Illinois State Journal*, 31 January 1861, 2:1; Helm, *True Story of Mary*, 155–56; Henry B. Rankin, *Intimate Character Sketches of Abraham Lincoln* (Philadelphia: Lippincott, 1924), 255–56.

12 Reminiscence of a correspondent to the St. Louis *Missouri Democrat*, transcribed in Jesse W. Weik, *The Real Lincoln: A Portrait* (Boston: Houghton Mifflin Co., 1922), 304.

13 Mercy Conkling to Clinton Conkling, 12 February 1861, transcribed in Harry E. Pratt, ed., *Concerning Mr. Lincoln: In Which Abraham Lincoln Is Pictured as He Appeared to Letter Writers of His Time* (Springfield, IL: Abraham Lincoln Association, 1944), 49.

14 Rankin, *Intimate Character Sketches of Abraham Lincoln*, 258–59; Harry E. Pratt, *Personal Finances of Abraham Lincoln, Personal Finances of Abraham Lincoln* (Springfield, IL: Abraham Lincoln Association, 1943), 175.

15 Abraham Lincoln's Farewell Address at Springfield, Illinois, 11 February 1861, Abraham Lincoln Papers, LC.

16 Randall, *Biography of a Marriage*, 195, 202–203; David Herbert Donald, *Lincoln* (New York: Simon & Schuster, 1995), 273.

17 Report of Remarks in Ashtabula, Ohio, *Ashtabula Weekly Telegraph* (OH), 16 February 1861, 2:1.

18 *New York Tribune*, 14 February 1861; *New York Herald*, 14 February 1861, 5:1–2, and 19 February 1861; *Baltimore Sun*, 15 February 1861; Paul Finkleman, *Millard Fillmore* (New York: Times Books, 2012), 135.

19 Summary of Abraham Lincoln's Remarks at Leaman Place, Pennsylvania, *Daily Evening Express* (Lancaster, PA), 22 February 1861, 3:5; *Evening Star* (Washington, DC), 14 February 1861; Donald, *Lincoln*, 275.

20 Baringer, *Lincoln Day by Day*, 11–22, passim; *New York Times* (NY), 20 February 1861 and 21 February 1861; *New York World* (NY), 21 February 1861 and 25 February 1861; *Philadelphia Inquirer* (PA), 22 February 1861; *Baltimore Sun*, 25 February 1861 and 2 March 1861; Jay Monaghan, *Abraham Lincoln Deals with Foreign Affairs: A Diplomat in Carpet Slippers* (New York: Bobbs-Merrill, 1945; reprint, Lincoln: University of Nebraska Press, 1997), 30; *New York Herald*, 23 February 1861; *National Intelligencer* (Washington, DC), 26 February 1861; Ida M. Tarbell, *The Life of Abraham Lincoln*, Sangamon ed., 4 vols. (New York: Lincoln History Society, 1924), 3:42; Mary Lincoln to Hannah Shearer, 28 March 1861, *L&L*, 1–82.

21 Willard's Register, Manuscripts Division, LC; Jean H. Baker, *The Lincoln Marriage: Beyond the Battle of Quotations*, 38th Annual Robert Fortenbaugh Memorial Lecture (Gettysburg, PA: Gettysburg College, 1999), 178; Donna McCreary, "Fashion Plate or Fashion Trendsetter," in Williams and Burkhimer, *Mary Lincoln Enigma*, 204–5; Elizabeth Keckley, *Behind the Scenes in the Lincoln White House: Memoirs of an African-American Seamstress* (Mineola, NY: Dover Publications, 2006), 30, 35; William J. Cooper, *Jefferson Davis, American* (New York: Alfred A. Knopf, 2000), 3.

22 Baker, *Mary Todd Lincoln*, 178–79; McCreary, "Fashion Plate or Fashion Trendsetter," 201; Margaret Leech, *Reveille in Washington 1860–1865* (New York: Harper, 1941), 46; *New York Times*, 5 March 1861, 1:5; Kenneth J. Winkle, *Abraham and Mary Lincoln* (Carbondale: Southern Illinois University, 2012), 92; Robert W. Johannsen, *Stephen A. Douglas* (New York: Oxford University Press, 1973; reprint, Urbana: University of Illinois Press, 1997), 843–45.

23 *New York Times*, 5 March 1861, 1:5

24 Baker, *Mary Todd Lincoln*, 192, 198–99; McCreary, "Fashion Plate or Fashion Trendsetter," 191, 202–207.

25 Mary Lincoln to Elizabeth Grimsley, 29 September 1861, *L&L*, 104–6; Kenneth J. Winkle, *Lincoln's Citadel: The Civil War in Washington, DC* (New York: W. W. Norton, 2014), 124.

26 Mary Lincoln to Hannah Shearer, 28 March 1861; Mary Lincoln to Hannah Shearer, 11 July 1861, *L&L*, 93–95.

27 Winkle, *Lincoln's Citadel*, 115–16; Mary Lincoln to Elizabeth Grimsley, 29 September 1861; Baker, *Mary Todd Lincoln*, 182, 189.

28 Mary Lincoln to Mrs. Samuel H. Melvin, 27 April 1861, *L&L*, 85–86.

29 *L&L*, 87; "What Mrs. Lincoln Bought for the White House," *Lincoln Lore* 1492 (June 1962); Bill of Sale of Alexander T. Stewart & Co. to Mary Lincoln, 25 May 1861, Record Group 217: Records of the Accounting Officers of the Department of the Treasury, National Archives Building, College Park, MD.

30 Pratt, *Personal Finances*, 180–81; Abraham Lincoln to Benjamin B. French, 26 August 1862, in Roy P. Basler, *The Collected Works of Abraham Lincoln*, 8 vols. (New Brunswick, NJ: Rutgers University Press, 1853), 5:394; Baker, *Mary Todd Lincoln*, 194; Winkle, *Abraham and Mary Lincoln*, 97.

31 Bill of Sale of Alexander T. Stewart & Co. to Mary Lincoln, 25 May 1861; Winkle, *Lincoln's Citadel*, 116; *L&L*, 87–89; Baker, *Mary Todd Lincoln*, 190; Thomas F. Schwartz and Kim M. Bauer, "Unpublished Mary Todd Lincoln," *Journal of the Abraham Lincoln Association* 17 (Summer 1996): 11.

32 Pratt, *Personal Finances*, 124–28; Baker, *Mary Todd Lincoln*, 192, 198, 207; Abraham Lincoln to Salmon P. Chase, 10 June 1864, Lincoln Collection, ALPL.

33 *L&L*, 84–85. James M. McPherson, *Battle Cry Freedom: The Civil War Era* (New York: Oxford University Press, 2003); Edward L. Ayers, *In the Presence of Mine Enemies: War in the Heart of America, 1859–1863* (New York: W. W. Norton, 2003); Paul A. Cimbala and Randall M. Miller, eds., *An Uncommon Time: The Civil War and the Northern Home Front* (New York: Fordham University Press, 2002). Lincoln's Brooks Brothers coat is in the collections of the Ford's Theatre, National Park Service, in Washington, D.C.

    Kenneth J. Winkle, who has written very balanced narratives of Mary Lincoln, provides a succinct analysis of Mary Lincoln's spending and the political problems they posed for her husband in *Lincoln's Citadel*, 206–8.

34 *Evening Star*, 6 August 1861, 2:1. The article also mentioned the attire of Mrs. Lincoln, who was wearing "a very elegant white grenadine over white silk, and with a long train; and her cousin Elizabeth Grimsley, who was wearing "a salmon tulle dress, with exquisite flowers, (natural)." Bill of Sale of William H. Carryl & Bro. to Abraham Lincoln, with endorsement by Abraham Lincoln, 29 May 1861, and Abraham Lincoln to Salmon P. Chase, 15 June 1861, both in vault, RG 217: Withdrawn Documents, National Archives, College Park, MD.

35 Baker, *Mary Todd Lincoln*, 198–200.

36 Mary Lincoln to Elizabeth Grimsely, 29 September 1861, *L&L*, 104–6.

37 Winkle, *Lincoln's Citadel*, 123–24; Matthew Pinsker, *Lincoln's Sanctuary: Abraham Lincoln and the Soldiers' Home* (New York: Oxford University Press, 2003), 2–4, 13.

38 Winkle, *Lincoln's Citadel*, xiv, 188, 195; Ernest B. Furgurson, *Freedom Rising: Washington in the Civil War* (New York: Alfred A. Knopf, 2004), 12, 77, 85, 241.

39 Abraham Lincoln to Mary Lincoln, 28 April 1864, Record Group 107, Entry 34: Records of the Secretary of War, 1798–1889, Telegrams Sent and Received by the War Department Central Telegraph Office, 1861–1882, National Archives Building, Washington, DC; Phillip Shaw Paludan, *The Presidency of Abraham Lincoln* (Lawrence: University of Kansas Press, 1994), 168; Peter McConnell to Abraham Lincoln, 28 March 1864, Abraham Lincoln Papers, LC; Donald, *Lincoln*, 309–10, 428; Mary Lincoln to Andrew Johnson, 29 April 1865, *L&L*, 226; Randall, *Biography of a Marriage*, 277; Wayne C. Temple, "'I am So Fond of Sightseeing': Mary Lincoln's Travels up to 1865," in Williams and Burkhimer, *Mary Lincoln Enigma*, 140–81.

40 Mary Lincoln to Mrs. Charles Eames, 26 July 1862, *L&L*, 130–31.

41 Mary Lincoln to Francis Bicknell Carpenter, 8 December 1865, *L&L*, 297–300.

42 Donald, *Lincoln*, 159; Jason Emerson, *Giant in the Shadows* (Carbondale: Southern Illinois University Press, 2012), 86; Michael Burlingame, *The Inner World of Abraham Lincoln* (Urbana; University of Illinois Press, 1994), 64.

43 Abraham Lincoln to John A. Dahlgren, 14 October 1862, Lincoln Collection, ALPL.

44 Abraham Lincoln to Unknown, 5 May 1863, in Roy P. Basler, ed., *The Collected Works of Abraham Lincoln, First Supplement, 1832–1865* (New Brunswick, NJ: Rutgers University Press, 1974), 187.

45 Abraham Lincoln to Mary Lincoln, 9 June 1863, Lincoln Collection, ALPL.

46 Abraham Lincoln to Edwin M. Stanton, 10 April 1865, in Basler, *Collected Works of Abraham Lincoln*, 8:395; Abraham Lincoln to Gideon Welles, 10 April 1865, Lincoln Collection, Wayne County Public Library, Fort Wayne, IN.

47 Mary Lincoln to Hannah Shearer, 1 August 1861, *L&L*, 95–96; Mary Lincoln to "Mrs. Blair," 20 November 1863, *L&L*, 158; Donald, *Lincoln*, 428, 433, 576; Abraham Lincoln to Mary Lincoln, 24 June 1864, vault, RG 107, Entry 34: Records of the Secretary of War, Record Series Originating During the Period 1789–1889, Telegrams, Telegrams Sent and Received by the War Department Central Telegraph Office, 1861–1882, National Archives Building, Washington, DC; Emerson, *Giant in the Shadows*, 86; *L&L*, 93, 120.

48 Emerson, *Giant in the Shadows*, 90; Baker, *Mary Todd Lincoln*, 224–25.

49 Donald, *Lincoln*, 306; *L&L*, 92; *Directory of United States Congress*, 597; Helm, *True Story of Mary*, 191–92; Keckley, *Behind the Scenes*, 41–42.

50 Paludan, *Presidency of Abraham Lincoln*, 66.

51 *Evening Star*, 6 February 1862, 2:1.

52 *Evening Star*, 6 February 1862, 2:1; Baker, *Mary Todd Lincoln*, 205–7.

53 *New York Herald*, 24 February 1862, 5:2; Keckley, *Behind the Scenes*, 42–43; Donald, *Lincoln*, 336–38; Randall, *Biography of a Marriage*, 283–84; Glenna Schroeder Lein, *Lincoln and Medicine* (Carbondale: Southern Illinois University Press, 2012), 21–25.

54 Pease, *Diary of Orville Hickman Browning*, 1:607–8.

55 Randall, *Biography of a Marriage*, 283; Baker, *Mary Todd Lincoln*, 208–9, 220–21; Keckley, 42–43; Donald, *Lincoln*, 336–38; Mary Lincoln to Mrs. Charles Eames, 26 July 1862, *L&L*, 130–31; Ann Braud, *Radical Spirits: Spiritualism and Women's Rights in the Nineteenth Century* (Bloomington: Indiana University Press, 2001); *L&L*, 122–23.

56 Mary Lincoln to Julia Ann Sprigg, 29 May 1862, *L&L*, 127–28.

57 Mary Lincoln to Mrs. Charles Eames, 26 July 1862, *L&L*, 130–31.

58 Mary Lincoln to Mercy Conkling, 19 November 1864, Lincoln Collection, ALPL.

59 Edward Steers Jr., *Blood on the Moon: The Assassination of Abraham Lincoln* (Lexington: University of Kentucky Press, 2001), 106; *Evening Star*, 23 January 1862, 2:5; *Evening Star*, 24 January 1862, 2:1; *Evening Star*, 13 April 1863, 1:4, 2:1; *Evening Star*, 6 October 1863, 1:3; *Evening Star*, 7 October 1863; *Evening Star*, 17 October 1863, 1:4, 3:1; *Evening Star*, 19 October 1863, 2:2; *New York*, 9 October 1863, 7:2.

60 Mary Lincoln to Abraham Lincoln, 11 June 1863, vol. 10, 325, RG 107, Entry 34: Records of the Secretary of War, Record Series Originating During the Period 1789–1889, Telegrams, Telegrams Sent and Received by the War Department Central Telegraph Office, 1861–1882, National Archives Building, Washington, DC.

61 Abraham Lincoln to Mary Lincoln, 11 June 1863, Lincoln Collection, ALPL; Mary Lincoln to Charles Sumner, 23 March 1865, *L&L*, 209–10.

62 Mary Lincoln to Abraham Lincoln, 2 November 1862, Abraham Lincoln Papers, LC (this document is transcribed in its entirely in the Documents section); Baker, *Mary Todd Lincoln*, 230.

63 Mary Lincoln to Sally Orne, 12 December 1869, *L&L*, 533–34.

64 Donald, *Lincoln*, 429; Paludan, *Presidency of Abraham Lincoln*, 106–7; David Donald, *"We Are Lincoln Men": Abraham Lincoln and His Friends* (New York: Simon & Schuster, 2003), 195–99; Mary Lincoln to Abram Wakeman, 30 January 1865, *L&L*, 200; Pinsker, *Lincoln's Sanctuary*, 107; Catherine Clinton, *Mrs. Lincoln: A Life* (New York: Harper Collins, 2009), 189; Baker, *Mary Todd Lincoln*, 227–28, 242; Keckley, *Behind the Scenes*, 43; Winkle, *Abraham and Mary Lincoln*, 114.

65 Mary Lincoln to Mrs. Agen, 10 August 1864, *L&L*, 179.

66 Mary Lincoln to Thomas W. Sweney, April 1863, *L&L*, 149–50; *L&L*, 176.

67 Mary Lincoln to Mary Jane Welles, 27 May 1864, *L&L*, 176; Baker, *Mary Todd Lincoln*, 185–86; Abraham Lincoln to Hiram Barney, 16 August 1862, Lincoln Collection, Brown University, Providence, RI; Winkle, *Lincoln's Citadel*, 376; *Daily National Republican* (Washington, DC), 18 December 1862, 3:3; *Daily National Republican*, 10 February 1864, 2:4; *New York Tribune*, 13 August 1862; Helm, *True Story of Mary*, 204.

68 Mary Lincoln to Daniel E. Sickles, 31 September 1862, *L&L*, 133–34; Baker, *Mary Todd Lincoln*, 231; Keckley, *Behind the Scenes*, 61.

69 Abraham Lincoln to Charles Sumner, 24 February 1862, Shapell Manuscript Foundation, Los Angeles, CA; *L&L*, 185; Randall, *Biography of a Marriage*, 355–56.

70 Mary Lincoln to Elizabeth Keckley, 29 October 1867, in Keckley, *Behind the Scenes*, 42–43, 146; Mary Lincoln to Abraham Lincoln, 2 November 1862; Mary Lincoln to Abraham Lincoln, 3 November 1862, Abraham Lincoln Papers, LC; Baker, *Mary Todd Lincoln*, 230–31.

Mary Lincoln was very critical of Andrew Johnson's presidency, believing that he was not committed to advancing policies of freedom that she was so proud of her husband for beginning. Mary Lincoln to Sally Orne, 15 March 1866, *L&L*, 345–46; Mary Lincoln to Charles Sumner, 2 April 1866, *L&L*, 348–49; Mary Lincoln to Charles Sumner, 10 April 1866, *L&L*, 355–56; Mary Lincoln to Elizabeth Keckley, 15 November 1867, *L&L*, 453–55.

71 Mary Lincoln to Abraham Lincoln, 3 November 1862; Furgurson, *Freedom Rising*, 255–60.

72 Mary Lincoln to Charles Sumner, 5 April 1864, *L&L*, 174.

73 Ibid.

74 Mary Lincoln to Emilie Helm, 23 November 1856, *L&L*, 45–48 (this document is transcribed in its entirety in the Documents section).

75 Mary Lincoln to Charles Sumner, 10 April 1866; Randall, *Biography of a Marriage*, 299.

76 Mary Lincoln to Montgomery Meigs, 4 October 1861, ALPL; Allida Black, *First Ladies of the United States of America* (Washington, DC: White House Historical Association, 2013).

77 *L&L*, 91–211, passim.

78 Abraham Lincoln to George B. McClellan, 24 October 1862, Lincoln Collection, ALPL.

79 Mary Lincoln to Abraham Lincoln, 2 November 1862, Abraham Lincoln Papers, LC.

80 John C. Waugh, *Lincoln and McClellan: The Troubled Partnership between a President and His General* (New York: Palgrave Macmillan, 2010); Michael Burkhimer, "The Reports of the Lincolns' Political Partnership Have Been Greatly Exaggerated," in Williams and Burkhimer, *Mary Lincoln Enigma*, 229.

81 Abraham Lincoln to Mary Lincoln, 24 September 1863, Lincoln Collection, ALPL; Abraham Lincoln to Simon Cameron, 16 April 1861, box 7, Simon Cameron Papers, Manuscript Division, LC; E. M. Bruce to Abraham Lincoln, 6 October 1863, Abraham Lincoln Papers, LC; Abraham Lincoln to Lyman B. Todd, 15 October 1863, Lincoln Collection, Brown University, Providence, RI; Stephen Berry, *House of Abraham: Lincoln and the Todds, a Family Divided by War* (Boston: Houghton Mifflin Co., 2007), 146, 150–54; Joshua H. Leet and Karen M. Leet, *Civil War Lexington, Kentucky: Bluegrass Breeding Ground of Power* (Charleston, SC: The History Press, 2011), 68–74.

82 Berry, *House of Abraham*, vi–vii; Mark E. Neely Jr., "The Secret Treason of Abraham Lincoln's Brother-in-Law," *Journal of the Abraham Lincoln Association* 17 (Winter 1996): 39–43; Charles H. Kellogg to Caleb B. Smith, 2 October 1861, Abraham Lincoln Papers, LC.

83 Berry, *House of Abraham*, 85–89, 183–84; Baker, *Mary Todd Lincoln*, 354. For an excellent study of the various ways in which sectional loyalties made an impact on human relationships, see Amy Murrell Taylor, *The Divided Family in Civil War America* (Chapel Hill: University of North Carolina Press, 2009).

84 Mary Lincoln to James Gordon Bennett, 25 October 1861, *L&L*, 110–11.

85 *L&L*, 155; Baker, *Mary Todd Lincoln*, 223.

86 Mary Lincoln to Elizabeth Keckley, 29 October 1867, in Keckley, *Behind the Scenes*, 146.

87 Michael Burlingame and John R. Turner Ettlinger, eds., *Inside Lincoln's White House: The Complete Civil War Diary of John Hay* (Carbondale: Southern Illinois University Press, 1997), 128.

88 Pease, *Diary of Orville Hickman Browning*, 1:651; Donald, *Lincoln*, 475; Winkle, *Abraham and Mary Lincoln*, 103–4.

89 Minié balls were rifle bullets used during the Civil War that were particularly damaging to flesh and bone.

90 Emily Helm to Abraham Lincoln, 30 October 1864, and Unsigned Amnesty Oath of Emily T. Helm, 14 December 1863, both in Abraham Lincoln Papers, LC.

91 Baker, *Mary Todd Lincoln*, 225–26.

92 Mary Lincoln to Abraham Lincoln, 4 December 1863, vol. 11, 218, Record Group 107, Entry 34: Records of the Secretary of War, 1798–1889, Telegrams Sent and Received by the War Department Central Telegraph Office, 1861–1882, National Archives Building, Washington, DC.

93 Helm, *True Story of Mary*, 234.

94 Abraham Lincoln to Mary Lincoln, 7 December 1863, Lincoln Collection, ALPL.

95 Pinsker, *Lincoln's Sanctuary*, 102–5.

96 Mary Lincoln to Mary Jane Welles, 27 May 1864, *L&L*, 176.

97 Mary Lincoln to George D. Ramsay, 20 July 1864, *L&L*, 177; Pease, *Diary of Orville Hickman Browning*, 1:594.

98 Mary Lincoln to Mercy Conkling, 19 November 1864, Lincoln Collection, ALPL.

99 Abraham Lincoln's Second Inaugural Address, 4 March 1865, Abraham Lincoln Papers, LC.

100 Mary Lincoln to Charles Sumner, 23 March 1865, *L&L*, 209–10.

101 Mary Lincoln to Charles Sumner, 3 April 1865, *L&L*, 212.

102 Mary Lincoln to Abram Wakeman, 4 April 1865, *L&L*, 212–13.

103 Baker, *Mary Todd Lincoln*, 241; Keckley, *Behind the Scenes*, 69–73; Adolphe de Pineton, marquis de Chambrun, *Impressions of Lincoln and the Civil War: A Foreigner's Account* (New York: Random House, 1952), 73–77; *Washington Star*, 10 April 1865; William H. Crook, "Lincoln's Last Day: New Facts Now Told for the First Time. Compiled and written down by Margarita S. Gerry," *Harper's Monthly Magazine* 115 (September 1907): 523.

104 Mary Lincoln to Francis Bicknell Carpenter, 15 November 1865, *L&L*, 283–85.

CHAPTER **5**

THE WIDOW LINCOLN

On the evening of April 14, 1865, Tad Lincoln left the White House with Alfonso Dunn, a favorite White House doorman, and the two set off to Grover's Theatre to see a production of *Aladdin! Or His Wonderful Lamp*. After their long carriage ride that afternoon, the president and his wife took an impromptu tour onboard the ironclad monitor *Montauk*, which was tied in port at the Washington Naval Yard. After the tour, the president and First Lady prepared themselves for an evening at Ford's Theatre. Lincoln had a late meeting with the Speaker of the U.S. House of Representatives, Schuyler Colfax, which delayed the departure of the presidential carriage from the White House until sometime after 8 p.m. The carriage stopped to pick up the Lincolns' theatre guests—the young Major Henry Rathbone and his fiancée Clara Harris—and the presidential party arrived at the theatre at about 8:30 p.m., thirty minutes or so late for the start of the performance. After settling into their box seats, the Lincolns were laughing and enjoying the comedy, as was the audience of some 1,700 people. Mary leaned into her husband affectionately, and he took her hand in his.[1] Mary may have taken a moment in the theatre box that night to briefly reflect on the happy events of the past week and to count blessings. The Union Army had defeated the "degraded rebels," and the "unholy rebellion" was over. Her "devoted and loving husband" was at her side. Peace had come to the nation. Peace would restore her husband's health. Peace would calm her own fears and give her hope for a happy future. However, now there was John Wilkes Booth and the sound of a gunshot. She screamed, and then, for the distraught First Lady, everything went dark.[2]

From the moment that the assassin's bullet penetrated the president's brain, Mary was seized with blinding anguish. When Lincoln was situated on a bed in a private home across the street from the theatre, Mary was desperate to revive him, kissing him and begging him to answer her. Finally, taken from the room so the doctors could attend to Lincoln and keep at bay their own grief, Mary wrung her hands uncontrollably and wailed inconsolably. Those present to her grief could not long bear witness to it, and for most of the night, she sat alone in the parlor waiting for her husband to die. Calls for Tad, who had learned of the shooting while still at Grover's Theatre, and Elizabeth Keckley were unsuccessful. However, once Robert Lincoln and the Rev. Phineas Gurley arrived, each periodically checked in on her, and her friend Elizabeth Dixon appeared around midnight to attend directly to her needs. Sometime after dawn on April 15, 1865, she saw for the last time her husband as his rasping breaths signaled the end. Mary was again overcome by emotion, and Robert and Mrs. Dixon removed her from the president, who died at 7:22 a.m. Abraham Lincoln now belonged to the ages and no longer to Mary, and the grief of her loss drew a dark cloak over her heart, her spirit and her mind.[3]

Likely in a state of shock that rendered her powerless to function, it is possible she remembered nothing of the events and chaos of the previous night, nor the details of her husband's death that morning. For the first two weeks after the horrific events of April 14 and 15, Mary grieved in a tiny private bedroom in the White House, unable to be in any familiar space in the presidential living quarters. The shock of witnessing such a violent and devastating attack would have unhinged even the strongest of people, but the depth and severity of Mary's grief illustrated the sad reality of her delicate psyche. "From the hour we were so deeply stricken," Mary would later write, "I was carried into one apartment, at the White H. laid on a bed of illness & many days & nights of almost positive derangement."[4] As Washington friends and allies of the Lincoln administration called on Mary to pay their respects directly to her, she refused to see them. She could only bear the presence of her sons and a handful of close friends: Elizabeth Keckley, Mary Jane Welles, Elizabeth Lee, Sally Orne and Anson G. Henry. She also received calls from Charles Sumner and Edwin M. Stanton. Mary never viewed her husband's body lying in state in the White House, and she did not watch some 25,000 mourners march through the mansion to pay their respects to the slain president. Mary did not attend the funeral service officiated by the Rev. Phineas Gurley, in the East Room on Wednesday, April 19. "Mrs. Lincoln did not enter the East Room," wrote the *Evening Star*, "being too ill from nervous prostration and an incipient fever, brought on by the awful excitement and sorrow to which she has been subjected."[5] Robert and Tad attended with their uncles, Ninian W. Edwards and Clark Smith, who had arrived from Springfield. In the fog of grief, Mary was probably involved with the decision to return Lincoln's body to Springfield, but she may not have been aware of the elaborate plans for a funeral train that would carry her husband's body home through six states and traversing 1,700 miles. Most sadly, perhaps, she was unable to comfort her sons, because she was incapable of even helping herself. Robert was devastated by the loss of his father, but he was strong and attended to the needs of his mother. He was also old enough to face the grief on his own terms, and he leaned heavily on his father's private secretaries, John Nicolay and John Hay. However, poor Taddie, confronted with the loss of his hero and his father, needed his mother, but as had been the case when Willie Lincoln had died, Mary failed to set aside her grief and guide her youngest boy through his.[6]

While the neglect of her own sons, whom she loved and adored, was a telling sign as to Mrs. Lincoln's mental fragility, the vandalism of the White House following the president's death was another. Mary had invested a great deal of energy and enthusiasm toward the redecorating of the White House. She had endured harsh criticism for her efforts, but it was one of her proud achievements as First Lady to bring some refinement to the dingy, old White House. However, while consumed by her own grief and locked away in her room, unscrupulous White House staff and visitors carried away souvenirs, big and small, and left a path of destruction behind them. Whether motivated by greed or the personal desire to own something of the martyred president, they emptied the closets and cupboards, stealing away pieces of china and crystal, removing furniture and slashing the carpets and draperies for pieces of textiles that belonged to President Lincoln's home. Mary was oblivious to the damage. Afterward, some would accuse her of stealing items from the White House, but a congressional investigation revealed no wrongdoing. There was no evidence that she took anything other than her clothing and the gifts that she and her family had received during their time in Washington, which, at the time, was perfectly acceptable.[7] The gifts had been particularly dear to her husband, "more precious than gold," according to Mary. They were gifts of limited financial value but of great sentiment, like wax figurines, country quilts and rough-hewn chairs made by the hands of patriotic old women and veterans who respected the president. It was these gifts that filled some of the twenty trunks and fifty boxes that she would pack and take with her when she was well enough to leave Washington.[8]

On April 29, two weeks to the day after the death of her husband, Mary penned what was probably one of the first letters of her widowhood. She was still far from well, but when she was finally able to sit up and put her mind to a task, she was compelled to carry out some late business for her husband. In so doing, she wrote to the new president Andrew Johnson, asking him to bestow a job in the newly created Freedmen's Bureau on a former White House tutor of the Lincoln boys. The job would fulfil a promise that her husband had made before his death. "I am most desirous that the promise should be fulfilled," she wrote.[9] In the next few weeks, Mary engaged in a routine of correspondence and preparations for her departure from the White House and return to Illinois. During this time, she wrote additional letters to President Johnson, making such requests as the appointment of a young Massachusetts man who wanted to enter West Point Military Academy and another urging the new president to retain one of the Lincolns' White House doorkeepers.[10] Bestowing gifts and relics on friends of Lincoln seemed to bring her comfort and, like the letters of recommendation, gave her something useful on which to focus her attention. "The memory of the cherished friends of my Husband & myself, will always be most gratefully remembered," she wrote to Charles Sumner on May 11.[11] In another letter just three days later, she offered the senator a likeness of noted English social reformer John Bright, a possession that her husband had prized. She also shared her excitement about an important political development: "The news of the capture of [Jefferson] Davis, almost overpowers me! In my crushing sorrow, I have found myself almost doubting the goodness of the Almighty!"[12]

The second letter illustrates that by the middle of May, one month after her husband's death, Mary was emerging from the darkness that had blanketed her on the night that the assassin's bullet stole away her husband. She was reading the newspapers again, taking more visitors, planning for her future and preparing to vacate the White House. Packing and going through her husband's personal items seemed to bring her some peace. Andrew Johnson had not called on her or written her a personal letter of condolence, but he respected the time she needed to collect herself. He had not pressured her to vacate the White House, choosing instead to work from an office in a nearby government building. However, finally, on May 23, clad from head to toe in heavy black mourning clothes, Mary Lincoln left the White House and Washington. She had decided against returning to Springfield, and on an afternoon train, she headed to Chicago instead. Her sons, Elizabeth Keckley and two White House guards were with her.[13]

At least one person disagreed with Mary's determination to make Chicago her new home. David Davis, Mr. Lincoln's dear friend whom he had appointed to the U.S. Supreme Court in 1862, became the administrator of Abraham Lincoln's estate. Lincoln had left no will, and Robert Lincoln asked Davis to come to Washington to manage the Lincoln family's affairs. Davis was a comfortable and logical choice for Mary and for Robert because he was a trusted family friend. Davis advised Mary that she should return to her Springfield home and live comfortably on her third of Lincoln's estate.[14] Mary balked at the suggestion, complaining to Simon Cameron that "after the many years of happiness there, with my idolized husband—to place me in the home, deprived of his presence and the darling boy, we lost in

Washington, it would not require a day, for me to lose my entire reason. I am distracted enough, as it is, with remembrances, but I will spare myself & my poor sons additional grief."[15] She went on say that her husband had promised that they would not return to a home that would remind them of Willie. "Therefore," she continued, "in settling in C. I am only carrying out the intentions of my lamented husband."[16] Mary was angry that Judge Davis would force her back to Springfield, and she promised that she would live in poverty in Chicago rather than return to Springfield to live comfortably. Chicago was her determined choice, and it made sense for a number of reasons. It was familiar, as she had spent much time there; and the family had many friends in the city. It was a large and exciting city, and Mary loved city life. In addition, since Robert would not return to Harvard, Chicago would provide the best opportunities for studying the law, as the city was replete with accomplished and well-respected attorneys.[17]

In 1865, Chicago boasted more than 200,000 residents, half of whom were foreign born. It was a rising metropolis with diverse commercial interests, paved streets and city rail service. Lake Michigan and the dredged Chicago Harbor, the Chicago River and the Illinois & Michigan Canal provided the city with important commercial and transportation advantages for growth and development as well as access to goods from across the country and around the world. Seven major railroads connected the city with every mid-sized town across Illinois—like Rockford, Peoria and, most importantly, Springfield, the state capital—and beyond the state as well. The city was becoming the grain and livestock "emporium of the world." There were routes to St. Louis and further points to the west and south, to Milwaukee and up the western shore of Lake Michigan and to Indianapolis and further points to the east. From Chicago, a person could travel quite easily by rail or steamboat to New York City in just two days. By 1865, Chicago was well on its way to becoming the most important midwestern city, connecting the eastern and western parts of the country. Much of the urban population still lived in frame houses with wood shingles, and although the city was experiencing rapid development and modernization, many residents kept animals and maintained barns and wood outbuildings within the city limits. Downtown buildings in the 1860s ranged from four to six stories tall and were mostly built of pine. The juxtaposition of small frame houses and barns with gleaming new buildings demonstrated the rapid transformation of Chicago at this time. The stunning Crosby's Opera House opened the year the Lincoln family arrived. Located on Washington Street, between State and Dearborn Streets, the Italianate structure with a mansard roof reflected the architectural direction of the city and anchored an upscale area of retail establishments and hotels. The cultural opportunities available in Chicago, along with the modern amenities, access to a variety of goods and services, opportunities for Robert and the comfort of being familiar, all made Chicago a good choice for the Lincoln family. In addition, Springfield was an easy train trip south, so they would be able to visit the graves of Lincoln, Eddy and Willie and stay connected to extended relatives living there.[18]

When Mary and her sons arrived in Chicago, they checked into the familiar Tremont House. "We arrived here some days since . . . Life & the future looked to me, wretchedly desolate when we left W[ashington] realizing as I now do, that I am alone, my all, my Husband gone from me, the agony is insupportable," she wrote a friend. "If I was not aware, that my precious Boys, depended upon me, for their happiness, I would pray our Heavenly Father, to remove me from a world, where I have been so bitter a sufferer. To rejoin my Husband, who loved me so devotedly & whom I idolized, would be bliss indeed."[19] If not for her boys, indeed. Robert was indispensable to his mother in these early weeks. He looked after her when she suffered from one of her headaches, he ran errands, he was a companion and quasi-parent to Tad and he took on other responsibilities for the family. When they were settled into the hotel, Robert went in search of a more affordable residence and a place to escape the city for the upcoming summer months. He chose the less expensive Hyde Park Hotel south of the city limits. Robert was not thrilled with the location, as he was longing for the busy life he had enjoyed in Cambridge as a college student, but the quiet neighborhood seemed a pleasant and peaceful place for the family to gain some footing. Hyde Park, a lush and green oasis away from the noise and congestion of the city, was one of the first suburbs in Chicago. Designed as an exclusive village and summer resort for Chicago's wealthiest citizens, it was located eight miles south of the city. In 1865, Hyde Park was connected to downtown Chicago by rail and had nearly 1,000 permanent residents. Senator Lyman Trumbull and Judge J. Young Scammon, both friends of Mr. Lincoln, were two of Hyde Park's first residents.[20]

The location appealed to Mary because she believed the shore of Lake Michigan would improve her health. The Hyde Park Hotel was new with "rooms exquisitely clean & even luxuriously fitted up . . . cars passing every hour of the day," wrote Mary to a friend.[21] She also noted that the location was such that Robert was able to easily travel to and from the city. To attend to the needs of his mother and little brother, Robert had decided to trade law school at Harvard for an apprenticeship, and that year began his studies with J. Young Scammon's law firm, one of the most respected in Chicago. "We occupy three very pleasant rooms," Mary wrote another friend, "& how gladly we would welcome, our Eastern friends, to see us, those who have known & loved my darling Husband, are very dear to us."[22] There were signs in those letters that Mary might be adjusting to life without her husband, and despite the heavy mourning dresses and black bonnets, she wanted to socialize with old friends. At least she said she wished to see them. Within days of the Lincoln family's arrival at Hyde Park, news from Springfield reawakened the strong-willed fighter in her. Faithful to her deceased husband's wishes, she had chosen Oak Ridge Cemetery just north of Springfield for his burial. Oak Ridge provided the quiet, park-like setting that Lincoln had told her he desired. The cemetery had received Lincoln's casket on May 4, 1865, and deposited it in the public receiving tomb. Later that month, the National Lincoln Monument Association formed in Springfield with the express purpose to construct a permanent tomb and monument for the deceased president. The news that shocked and angered Mrs. Lincoln was that the monument committee was planning to erect a memorial within the city of Springfield and not over the remains of the president at Oak Ridge Cemetery. Robert Lincoln was displeased as well. Adding to their displeasure was the association leadership of Jesse K. Dubois, the former Lincoln family neighbor and dear friend, and childhood friend of Robert, Clinton Conkling, who was the son of Mary's old friend Mercy and her husband, James C. Conkling. The sitting Illinois governor, Richard J. Oglesby, was the president of the association, and it was to him that Mary made her disapproval known: "I feel that it is due to candor and fairness that I should notify your Monument association, that unless I receive within the next ten days an official assurance that the Monument will be erected over the Tomb in Oak Ridge Cemetery, in accordance with my oft expressed wishes, I shall yield my consent, to the request of the National Monument association in Washington & that of numerous other friends in the Eastern states & have the sacred remains deposited, in the vault, prepared for [President] Washington, under the Dome of the National Capitol, at as early a period as practicable."[23]

In another short note sent to the association, Mary also demanded that only the remains of her husband, herself and her sons could be buried in the vault that would be constructed at Oak Ridge. Mary did not want her husband buried in Washington, but clearly she was up to the threat and ready for the association to call her bluff. It is not that the prominent citizens of Springfield had a grudge against the privately owned Oak Ridge Cemetery. In fact, Jesse Dubois himself had delivered a rousing dedication speech touting its beauty and repose when it had opened for business in 1860. Apparently, however, the association had already expended some $5,300 toward the building of a monument on public land just west of downtown Springfield (where the current state capitol sits today). The Springfield *Daily Journal*, the newspaper that had always been a friend to Abraham Lincoln, published a notice about the association's intentions to reject Mrs. Lincoln's demands and to send a representative to Chicago to negotiate with her. "The people of Illinois, who loved Mr. Lincoln so well, will be slow and sorry to believe that Mrs. L. can seriously entertain the idea of sending the honored remains back to Washington," wrote the *Journal*. The paper also noted that Mrs. Lincoln's threats would not sway the association, which believed that building the monument on private property would endanger fundraising efforts. The representatives met Robert in Chicago, but when Robert brought them to the Hyde Park Hotel, Mary refused to see them. "My determination," she decried, "is unalterable."[24]

On June 11, Mary wrote Governor Oglesby again: "My wish to have the Monument, placed over my Husband's remains, will meet the approval of the whole civilized world, & if not carried out, and a favorable answer, given me by the 15th of this month, I will certainly do as I have said. It is very painful to me, to be treated in this manner, by some of those I considered my friends, such conduct, will not add, very much, to the honor of our state," she admonished. "I enclose you a scrap, sent from Springfield, to the paper to-day doubtless emanating, from the fertile pen [of] E.L. Baker."[25] Mary was in full form, even calling out the *Journal*'s editor, who was also married to the daughter of her oldest sister Elizabeth. Mary was taking on all of the prominent Springfield citizens who were once her friends. They had attempted to dismiss her wishes and the wishes of her husband and oldest son, and she stood her ground and won the fight. Abraham Lincoln would be buried in Oak Ridge Cemetery, and the association would construct a memorial over the burial vault with room for herself and her sons. The battle, however, had done nothing to endear her to members of the old Springfield Coterie.

Mary may not have cared to keep many of those old friends from Springfield, but she certainly could have used them from time to time to dispel her loneliness and provide an anchor for her. One of the most unfortunate consequences of Mary's circumstances was her diminishing circle of friends. The Hyde Park Hotel afforded Mary some quiet. She enjoyed her walks in the "beautiful park, adjoining the place," but it also should have offered her companionship. The hotel was a favorite refuge of some of Chicago's best families. "Although persons, drive out every day, to see me, I receive but very few; I am too miserable, to pass through, such an ordeal, as yet. Day by day I miss, my beloved husband more & more, how I am, to pass through life, without him who loved us so dearly, it is impossible for me to say," she wrote Mary Jane Welles in July 1865.[26] Her letters that first summer were often filled with these deep lamentations, and she increasingly sanctified her husband and wallowed in her sorrow. "Alas, alas, my burden of sorrow, is too heavy, for me to bear, why, have we been so terribly afflicted," she asked one friend.[27] Lincoln was her "idolized" husband, her "beloved and devoted" husband and her "lamented" husband. Victorian hyperbole of sorrows were not so unexpected three months after Lincoln's death, but months turned into years, and still Mary's letters were laced with mournful prose. Mary's grief consumed her, and as it consumed her, it became a burden for those around her as well. As time progressed, fewer and fewer of her correspondents were women, and the female network that had sustained her during her many years in Springfield as a wife and mother with a frequently absent husband was nowhere to be found. While grieving was expected, especially given the national and historic circumstances of that grief, it drove intimate friends away.

Mary Lincoln had the intellect, aptitude and financial means to make her transition to widowhood a graceful and successful one, and she had the capacity not only to survive but also to blossom again. Being in Chicago, a big city that she loved, among so many friends from the past should have given her a foundation for making a new life for herself. However, her emotions and fears intervened, and she embarked on a course of increasing isolation. The vivacious, outspoken and social Mary was gone. It was as if the heavy mourning crepe with which she clothed herself snuffed out the light within her chest. When friends came to call on her in those early days in Chicago, she turned most of them away. She could have solicited the emotional support of her Springfield relatives, especially her sisters, but she refused. She could have engaged in charitable works as an extension of her interactions with soldiers during the war, but she did not. She could have taken advantage of the numerous opportunities in Chicago for theatre and the arts, which she had always enjoyed, but there is no evidence that she did that either. Instead, she chose to live as a recluse. "As you may well suppose, I have led a life, of most rigid seclusion, since I left Washington," she admitted to a friend. "Chicago, is a very pleasant city & we have many charming acquaintances here, the few, whom I have been sufficiently composed to receive."[28] Mary took her meals in her room and rarely ventured outside, even though the beauty of her surroundings and the elegant porch that engulfed the hotel should have offered a tranquil and more social environment in which to cope with her grief. "My friends thought, I would be more quiet here during the summer months than in the City. My great grief has left my nerves in a very weak state," she wrote to Senator Sumner in July. "I have not been able to summon sufficient courage, to receive but very few, of my friends, who, with all the world, surely, sympathize in my unutterable distress of mind."[29] Descriptions of her grief and sorrow dominated her letters. Mary seemed determined to be lonely and miserable, or she was suffering from depression or other mental health issues that kept her from being happy. "I still remain closeted in my rooms, take an occasional walk, in the park & as usual see no one," she wrote Dr. Henry in July 1865.[30]

"If it were not for my two remaining sons, I would pray the Father, to take me too hence," she wrote Alexander Williamson, who had been the family's White House tutor. "Taddie has a lovely nature & I have not the least trouble in managing him, he is all love & gentleness. Robert, in our day of sorrow and adversity, manifests himself as he really is, a youth of great nobleness."[31] While Mary was suffering, there is no doubt she loved her sons, and she did what she could to be a mother to them. Robert fell into a routine of commuting to the city each day to study law, returning in the evening for dinner and time with Tad. During this time, the two remaining Lincoln sons grew closer. Tad looked up to "Brother Bob" as a father figure, and Robert adored his little brother and embraced his new role in Tad's life. Because his parents had let him run wild in the White House, Tad was still unable to read when they arrived in Chicago, although he was twelve years old. Mary began tutoring him at home, and then in the fall of 1865, she and Robert enrolled him in school, where he began to make some academic progress, despite his serious speech impediment. Mary took Tad to see a dentist, who fitted Tad with a device to straighten his teeth; however, it was a speech tutor that was finally able to address the boy's speech difficulties.[32] Mary's letters during this time in Chicago were filled with anecdotes about her sons. She was proud of them and loved them, and clearly, without them she would have experienced no joy at all.

If joy was not forthcoming for Mary, worry was immediate and profoundly in abundance. "Three of us on earth, & three in Heaven," Tad often said during this transitional phase.[33] Mary felt the reality of her reduced little family quite keenly, and during her first three years of her life without Abraham Lincoln, two primary concerns occupied and sometimes overwhelmed her. First, she desired to establish a home that would provide the emotional and financial security that she so desperately wanted. In Springfield, Mary had focused on creating and maintaining a home for her family. In Washington, she had carved out of the drafty presidential mansion a comfortable home for her family. In Chicago, it was only natural that she was compelled to establish a home once more. Now that she had emerged from the fog of her grief, she wanted to provide a safe and appropriate home. Second, Mary was faced with the financial realities of being a widow. Securing a comfortable income for her family became a major goal for her, and worries about money weighed heavy. This predicament was common for many widows, and during a time when women of Mary's stature did not work, it could be a frightening travail. Yet, she was fairly lucky. She had some regular income from her husband's estate, she had a grown son to lean on and she was able to live on her own, albeit in reduced conditions. On top of it all, she knew that she would eventually inherit one-third of a comfortable estate. Many women in her circumstances in the mid-nineteenth century had none of these advantages and faced far more uncertain futures. Either too grief stricken or too self-absorbed, Mary was unable or unwilling to acknowledge that her lot as a widow was nowhere as desperate as it was for other women.[34]

Very soon after settling in at Hyde Park, Mary complained that it was an inappropriate residence for Abraham Lincoln's family and made obtaining a home of her own a priority. In August, she shared her complaints with Sally Orne, who was one of a small number of women with whom she was still confiding. "We are very differently situated, from what we would desire or from what should be expected, from our former station," she wrote. "We are deprived of the Comfort, of a home, where my poor sadly afflicted sons & myself, could quietly indulge in our griefs."[35] To Mary, her Hyde Park residence was temporary, and the more she remained there, the more anxious she became. Robert had arranged for the storage of all his mother's boxes in a warehouse in Chicago, and Mary had not seen most of her belongings since leaving Washington. If she had a home, she could unpack her things and get settled. Living in a hotel made her feel unsettled, much in the same way it did when she had prepared to leave Springfield in the winter of 1860. The transition was, no doubt, stressful. Buying and furnishing a house that she believed was appropriate to her status as the widow of an American president would require more than her current income could afford in Chicago, and when it appeared as though Congress would allow her only the remainder of Lincoln's presidential salary for 1865, she asked for more. In a letter to Congressman Elihu Washburne, an Illinois friend and Republican, Mary argued, "Every thing, is so fabulously high here & even if prices—come down—I could not rent, the plainest house & furnish it, with only, the additional year's salary . . . We should, in justice, to my husband's services, have $50,000. for a home & furniture & the hundred thousand to keep it up."[36] At this time, it appeared as though the Lincoln estate would be approximately $85,000, which when divided three ways would yield about $28,333 each for Mary, Robert and Tad. That figure was inadequate for acquiring a Chicago home that Mary wanted, for furnishing it and for maintaining it. Of course, David Davis reiterated to Mary that she could live in her old home in Springfield much more inexpensively, and he was correct on that point. The Lincolns owned the house in Springfield free and clear, but Mary refused to reconsider and was only more recalcitrant.[37]

In Chicago, Tad Lincoln was making friends and was enrolled in school at a private academy. Mary had brought Tad's pony from Washington, so it is possible that he was riding the pony to school or commuted with Brother Bob on the railcar. Robert Lincoln was studying law downtown and helping Mary manage the family's affairs. Both boys were adjusting, even though their mother was not. In July, Mary reluctantly sent Tad out of the city with a niece of a former Springfield friend to escape an outbreak of scarlet fever. "I am so miserable, it is painful to part with him, even for a day, yet it is best, he should be away—Taddie, has made many warm friends, in the house. I live, as secluded, as ever," she wrote her former doctor.[38] While Tad was away, Mary read the papers and kept apprised of events in Springfield and in Washington. Newspaper reports that suggested that she and the boys were financially well situated outraged her. Mary did not agree and jealously lashed out, complaining that much of her husband's estate was tied up in the Springfield house and "some wild lands in Iowa." The Lincolns did own 200 acres in Iowa, but most of the estate was tied up in government bonds. An August letter to a friend revealed the bitterness that was creeping in on Mrs. Lincoln: "Notwithstanding my great & good husband's life was sacrificed for his country, we are left, to struggle, in a manner, entirely new to us—a noble people would pronounce our manner of life, undeserved. Roving Generals have elegant mansions, showered on them, and the American people—leave the family of the Martyred President, to struggle as best they may! Strange justice this."[39] Mary was likely referring to General Grant, who received as gifts a home in Philadelphia in May 1865 and another one in Galena, Illinois, in August. No great admirer of the general, the news was galling to her.[40]

Still without a permanent home, the Lincolns moved back into the city that fall, this time into the Clifton House downtown at the corner of Wabash Avenue and Madison Street. The Clifton was a study in contrasts to the hotel in Hyde Park. It was public and noisy, and it lacked the park-like setting and refinements that Mary had enjoyed at her summer residence. It was a dreary place on a busy street, with no parks nearby to accommodate Mary's strolls, which were both enjoyable and therapeutic to her; even Robert was displeased with hotel. However, the cooler weather made the city less unhealthy, and the Clifton was far more affordable. Mary and each of her sons were drawing $1,500 each annually from the Lincoln estate, and Mary was worried more and more about money. In December, Congress passed a bill that awarded her only the unpaid portion of her husband's salary as president for 1865, an amount after taxes that totaled $22,025.34, which disappointed Mary. To add to her worries, Tad suffered a serious illness that winter, and, just as he was recovering, she embarked on a dreaded trip to Springfield for the entombment of her husband in a more secure vault in Oak Ridge Cemetery.[41] "A visit to Springfield & the Cemetery—where my beloved one's rest, last week—convinced me, that the further removed, I am, the better, it will be, for my reason, from that spot," she wrote Mary Jane Welles after Christmas.[42] If she had entertained any thoughts of moving back to Springfield, they were now erased. She reported to her friend that "the new vault, was completed in S. containing places—for my husband, myself & 4 sons—2 sons & my husband, are now far beyond the reach of care, in their glorious home."[43] The trip was a setback for Mary, as she took to her room upon her return to Chicago.

Mary Lincoln's profound grief characterized much of her widowhood, and it dominates her historical persona to us today. However, her reputation as the crazy grieving widow of one of the nation's greatest presidents is unfair, and it diminishes her life experiences from 1865 until her death in 1882. On the one hand, grief did sometimes uncontrollably consume her; it damaged her relationships and stood in the way of her happiness. While mental illness may have been a primary cause of her protracted sorrow, it also seems clear that adopting the widow's pose and hiding behind her widow's weeds for the duration of her life was a deliberate coping mechanism. It allowed her to keep a distance from people and to hold future disappointments at bay. On the other hand, she at times exhibited amazing capacity to penetrate her grief, to manage her increasingly debilitating headaches and other physical ailments and to overcome her mental health issues as well. As the remainder of the chapter will show, Mary Lincoln was a complicated woman with very human failings, but she was more than a grieving widow. As we have already seen, she successfully stared down the Springfield group that stood ready to deny her right as a widow to make decisions about her husband's memorial in their hometown. Obviously, she was still capable of fighting a battle of wills. As episodes in the rest of her life would prove—particularly her lobbying efforts for a pension, her fight against incarceration in a sanitarium and two extended trips to Europe—she was not always the suffering widow. Particularly illustrative of the two sides of the woman is her relationship with money and her sometimes maniacal fears about poverty. The emotionalism that crept into her financial activities reveals something of the darker side of her personality. However, her bold interactions with those who served as her agents and with individuals to whom she appealed for assistance offer evidence of the Mary Todd who wrote the offending newspaper article about James Shields back in 1842 and of the First Lady who advocated for political appointments during her husband's presidential administration.

Mary's letters to one correspondent are indicative of her two-sided personality on issues of money. They reveal both her frequent desperation and panic as well as expose the holes in her veiled persona of the suffering widow. Alexander Williamson had been a tutor for the Lincolns' youngest sons in the White House until 1862 when Lincoln had secured a job for him in the Treasury Department. While the details of the interaction of Mary and Williamson in the spring of 1865 after the Lincoln assassination are murky, it is entirely possible that Mary's letter to Andrew Johnson recommending Williamson for a job in the Freedmen's Bureau was part of bargain between the widow and the former tutor. From 1865 to 1868, Mary wrote more than sixty letters to Williamson. While this group of letters sometimes communicated panic regarding financial issues, they were of a very different character than the ones she penned to intimate female friends like Mary Jane Welles and Sally Orne. In the letters to Williamson, some of which were penned on the same day as mournful letters to women, Mary was calculating and direct. She was engaging Williamson as an agent for her affairs. He lobbied members of Congress on Mary's behalf, he delivered notes to creditors, he took the Lincolns' Washington carriage to New York for sale and he ran various errands related to Mary's debts. In one letter in November she wrote, "I, also enclose you all my bills . . . If, by the 1st of Dec. you return me all these bills, receipted—I will send you $50. for an overcoat for yourself & some handsome things, for your wife & daughter."[44] In this letter she even suggested that he might be able to secure funds to pay for a debt on a book from the White House library book fund that had never been expended. For months, Mary's correspondence with Williamson was a central focus of her life. He was her financial conduit to her Washington troubles, and he was someone on whom she could unload the emotional burdens of her debts. She subjected him to her misery, made demands and offered rewards and always reminded him about discretion. "Do keep, perfectly quiet, about my affairs. W[ashington] is such a gossiping place & every one—is ready to fly to Judge D[avis]—with my business."[45]

In early January 1866, Mary received a check from Washington, the payment of the remainder of her husband's salary for 1865. Congress also voted to grant her free postage for the remainder of her life, a nice perk for the prolific letter writer. Robert moved out of his mother's house and into his own rented room downtown. Now it was just her and thirteen-year-old Tad, but Mary still wanted her own home. That spring, she started a correspondence with Simon Cameron, her husband's first secretary of war. Mary was gracious and elated when Cameron agreed to solicit private funds so Mary could purchase a home. Cameron likely saw helping the widow of the martyred Republican president as a way to regain his lost political capital in the Republican Party. However, his selfish reasons for agreeing to help raise funds were of little matter to Mary. "I am sure you will use every exertion to raise the sum you named $20,000—yet if I make a suggestion, will you kindly pardon it. I wish to live plainly—yet very genteely [*sic*]—Plain 2 story frame houses here, cost the sum you have named $20,000—and if, from another quarter—you can outside of that have it increased to $25 or 30,000 I am sure you will."[46] Mary had wanted more from Congress, and now she wanted a bigger promise from Simon Cameron. Hoping that Cameron would be successful, Mary purchased a newly built, large stone house for $17,000 on the newer west side of the city near Union Park and a pretty lagoon. It was near a small enclave of Kentucky families, so that may have drawn her to the location, or, perhaps, she was seeking distance from the old Lincoln friends who mostly lived on the north side of Chicago. The home at 375 W. Washington Street between Willard (later Ann) and Elizabeth Streets boasted a "stately stone front of New York style."[47]

Mary and Tad Lincoln moved into their new home in June when construction was completed and it was finally ready. However, Mary's hopes for peace and security in a pretty and spacious new house, and the useful work of managing a household, failed to magically fulfill those hopes. Almost upon moving into the house, she realized maintaining it was likely to be impossible in the absence of additional funds. All that summer and fall, she fretted about money. Her husband's estate was still unsettled, and there was no money forthcoming from Cameron's efforts, as he had won his election to the U.S. Senate and likely lost interest in the dead president's widow. In November, Mary began to think about the possibility of relocating with Tad to Germany, where she believed it would be cheaper to live and to educate her son. However, a decision for a move like that would have to wait until Lincoln's estate was settled. During much of 1866, Mary was ill. Her headaches were ubiquitous, and, no doubt, her stress over the finances only exacerbated her poor health. In September, her health and emotional state were troubled by a trip to Springfield to meet with William H. Herndon, who Mary referred to as "Mr. L's crazy drinking law partner."[48] Herndon was collecting interviews and reminiscences from everyone who had known Lincoln throughout his lifetime and preparing for a speaking tour and the writing of a biography. On the morning of September 5, Mary sat down with Herndon at the St. Nicholas Hotel in downtown Springfield. The interview seemed innocent enough. Mary talked about her early life, about the kindness of her husband and his tenderness toward their sons, about their time in Washington and about the plans they were making for a tour of Europe following Mr. Lincoln's second term. Herndon's notes from the interview began: "Mrs. L. was born in 1823." Mary had clearly not given up that old ruse. However, mostly, she talked frankly about Lincoln's liberal nature with the children, about his developing political savvy and about his religious beliefs, or lack thereof. She also shared the fears she had harbored during the Civil War regarding her husband's safety. Mary returned to Chicago the next day and gave little thought to the meeting. Just a couple of months after the interview, however, Herndon was talking publicly about Mary. Most alarming to Victorian notions of propriety, Herndon gave a little speech in Springfield in which he argued that Abraham Lincoln's true love was Ann Rutledge, a girl he had known in New Salem and who had died young and left Lincoln heartbroken. The implication was clear. Mary Todd had not been the love of Abraham Lincoln's life.[49]

Robert Lincoln was also angry about Herndon's proclamations because he found them improper and a gross violation of privacy; he tried to shield his mother from them. However, in March 1867, Mary discovered a text of Herndon's speech in the *Chicago Tribune*. Not surprisingly, she was furious, but she kept her anger mostly under wraps. Once again, though, she believed that people were conspiring to make her miserable. Apparently, the Victorian chivalry that protected women from such public attention did not extend to the Widow Lincoln. More important to Mary in the flap over Herndon was his public declarations of her husband's lack of religion. On this point, she deeply regretted having told him that Lincoln had never joined a church.[50] In two separate letters to David Davis, she railed against Herndon. Closing one letter, she wrote, "I would not believe an assertion of Herndon's if he would take a thousand oaths, upon the Bible," she wrote. In another, she called Herndon a "dirty dog."[51] The year 1867 was not going any better for her than had 1866. Herndon's provocative actions might have been enough to ruin any progress Mary was making in adjusting to a widow's life, but the financial problems positioned an even darker cloud above her. Then there was the trial of John Surratt, son of the already hanged Mary Surratt and one of the conspirators of the Lincoln assassination, to put the horrible events of April 1865 back into Mary's delicate psyche. In June 1867, Robert and Tad Lincoln traveled to Washington to testify at the trial of John Surratt.[52] Mary felt too unwell to do so herself, and instead she traveled to Racine, Wisconsin, to investigate a school for Tad. The Lake Michigan town appealed to her, and she wrote to a new friend in Chicago, "I have a parlor & bedroom—fronting the lake & I find the air very refreshing. I may probably remain here some weeks—I am finding the rest very beneficial to me."[53] In July, Secretary of War Edwin M. Stanton telegraphed Mary to report that her sons would be able to return from Washington, as the trial was drawing to a close. Mary saw the trial as a mockery, and she complained to a friend: "What injustice and treason, is permitted in this land! Do you wonder, that I long to leave it?"[54] Two things were clear. First, she was still thinking about a possible move to Europe and was sharing that idea with friends. Second, Mary was depressed and in poor economic circumstances, at least by her standards, but she had not lost her talents for a biting critique of national affairs.

By the end of the summer, Mary's financial circumstances were no better, but at least Tad Lincoln was getting along well. He was enrolled in a fine boy's academy and was making much academic progress. At fourteen, he was growing into a man, but he was always his mother's "little troublesome sunshine."[55] He was an absolute joy to her; she never complained about the difficulties of raising such a rambunctious child with a learning disability. She missed him when he was away from her, and he truly was the best part of her widowed life. "Except for precious Tad—I would gladly welcome death," she wrote Alexander Williamson.[56] To David Davis, she bragged, "Taddie, is very gentle in character and gives trouble to no one."[57] Robert was also thriving in Chicago. By January of that year, he had completed his study of the law, and in February he was licensed to practice in Chicago. He immediately became a junior partner of Charles Scammon, the son of his mentor, and the firm of Scammon & Lincoln opened for business in March, specializing in real estate and insurance law.[58]

In August 1867, Mary abandoned her attempt to maintain a household and moved back into the Clifton House. It was humiliating, but selling or renting the house on Washington Street made more fiscal sense than living in it while unable to meet the energy bills and maintenance necessary on the big house. As she said, "Pride does not give us bread & meat."[59] By this time, Mary had hatched a plan to sell her Washington wardrobe—and why not since she seemed determined to wear widow's weeds indefinitely and no longer had need of fancy ball gowns. When Mary had left Washington in May 1865, she had left behind debts amounting to perhaps as much as $10,000. The debts related to her retail purchases during the Civil War. From the moment she had arrived in Chicago, she engaged in a crusade of sorts to rid herself of those debts, solicited funds on her behalf and called in favors from friends and prominent politicians, newspaper editors and businessmen. Some of her methods were unorthodox and violated Victorian notions of female respectability. As she told Alexander Williamson, "To meet actual necessities, I have been compelled to resort to measures, that at first, made me tremble at the thought—such as disposing of my cast off clothing, to procure mourning garments, and even home comforts."[60] She negotiated the return of more than $2,000 worth of fine jewelry to a top jeweler in Washington, Matthew Galt. She schemed to sell the presidential carriage outside of Washington, as she believed it would command more money elsewhere, because she thought that the large number of secessionists in Washington would care nothing for anything belonging to the Lincoln family.[61] Most shocking to some observers, she attempted to sell her most extravagant clothing. In the summer of 1865, she made initial enquiries to her close friend Sally Orne about selling dresses, including an inaugural gown. Mary hoped that Sally could help her identify women who might be interested in purchasing specific items.[62]

In September 1867, with several trunks in tow, Mary traveled alone from Chicago to New York City, where she met Elizabeth Keckley with the purpose of selling much of her Washington wardrobe. She traveled under the name of Mrs. Clark and introduced herself as such to the New York merchants she and Keckley visited. However, her efforts to hide her true identity failed, and when the newspapers got wind of the sale of her dresses, furs and jewelry, they lambasted her. *Frank Leslie's Illustrated Newspaper*, the same publication that had carried the sweet image of Mrs. Lincoln with her youngest sons in 1860, printed drawings of the jewelry that was up for sale. The headline of the article accompanying the drawings blared: "Mrs. Lincoln's Second-hand Clothing Sale." The New York *World* accused Mary of lying about her financial circumstances and made fun of her for engaging in such a spectacle, but withheld by request the names of three U.S. senators who called on the shop where the goods were on display. An article in the New York *Commercial Advertiser* argued that Mary had damaged her own reputation by overspending in the White House, covered up those expenses and took bribes to pay for parties. "Had Mrs. Lincoln, while in power, borne herself becomingly," the article reasoned, then she would be worthy of respect and sympathy.[63] The newspapers commenting on the sale admitted that Mr. Lincoln had not left his widow in wealthy circumstances, but that she was well enough off to refrain from the poor taste of hocking her clothes. Worse even than the humiliation of being revealed as a peddler of her own garments, some accused her of having acquired the expensive items in the first place as bribes for influence peddling within the Lincoln administration. Democrats did not miss their chance to make a complaint against the Republicans, even if it implicated the dead president. The First Lady's "unbecoming" activities in the White House—no matter what anyone thought them to be and no matter what they actually were—had tainted her reputation; that much was certain. However, what had gotten her into this debt mess was her foolish acceptance of the ready credit that merchants showered on her when she was First Lady. Now that she was just a widow, how quickly the tides had changed.[64]

Mary's attempt to raise funds through the sale of her fine clothing and accessories was a public fiasco, and it yielded no income. In fact, it cost her money in travel and expenses, and the negative press was overwhelming. Upon her return from New York, Robert was furious with her. "My mother is on one subject not mentally responsible," he wrote to Mary Harlan, the young woman he would eventually marry." "It is very hard to deal with someone who is sane on all subjects but one."[65] Mary complained that the Republican backlash was worse. "As we might have expected, the Republicans are falsifying me . . . I suppose I would be mobbed if I ventured out. What a world of anguish this is . . . You would not recognize me now. The glass shows me a pale, wretched, haggard face, and my dresses are like bags about me. All because I was doing what I felt to be my duty . . . The politicians, knowing they have deprived me of my just rights, would prefer to see me starve, rather than dispose of my things," she wrote Keckley, who had stayed in New York to follow up with the sale.[66] Mary was right; the press was far from done with her. On October 9, she wrote Keckley again: "It appears as if the fiends had let loose, for the Republican papers are tearing me to pieces in this border ruffian West. If I had committed murder in every city in this blessed Union, I could not be more traduced."[67] Mary had unleashed this fury on herself by trying to take charge of her financial affairs in the best way she knew. She did not turn over the debts to David Davis or her son Robert. Given the subterfuge of her visit to New York, it is quite clear that she did not want people to know about the debts, and she wanted to quietly dispense with them on her own. Given the public outcry against her efforts and the disparaging remarks about her womanhood that she endured once the word was out, she had certainly been no fool in her desire for discretion.

Still reeling from the dress sale fiasco, on November 10, 1867, Mary penned one of her most curt missives to Mr. Williamson: "Your note is received and you will allow me to say, that I have not the least intention of going to Europe. If I should ever do so, with my present means, it would be with the hope, that I might be more comfortable there on my small income than here. You, men have the advantage of us women, in being able to go out, in the world and earning a living . . . I am writing, with a fever on me . . . in the future, my silence by all friends, I hope, will be understood!"[68] Mary's frustration clearly indicated a recognition on her part that she was being treated differently because she was a woman. By the time Mary wrote this letter to Williamson, Robert Lincoln had already drawn some funds from his part of the Lincoln estate and David Davis was finalizing the settlement. Mary would have to read it in the papers, however, as Davis and Robert Lincoln had failed to mention it. While Mary was confused and a little miffed about the circumstances, she was certainly thrilled to finally receive her inheritance. Although Davis had not worked as quickly to settle the estate as Mary would have preferred, he had been a sound fiscal manager. In his capable hands, he had managed to increase the value of the estate to $110,974.62, quite an admirable feat in just thirty-one months. Saving Lincoln's heirs an additional $6,600, Davis had not claimed the 6 percent fee that Illinois law would have allowed him for his administration services. When Davis distributed the funds, Mary, Robert and Tad each received $36,991.54.[69] Mary now had a comfortable livelihood, and she expressed her gratitude in a letter to Davis, "Permit me to say, that in no hands save your own, could our interest have been so advantageously placed. please accept my grateful thanks for all your kindness to myself & family."[70]

No such gracious letter to Alexander Williamson survives, and it is unlikely Mary ever wrote such a missive to him. After the disbursement of her inheritance, she was no longer in need of his services; there would be only one more brief note in January 1868.[71] Mary's other agent, Elizabeth Keckley, was still in New York with Mary's dresses. By early March 1868, they had yielded no return. Settling her accounts there, Mary paid $824 to the two merchants involved with the scheme, and Keckley took possession of the dresses. Mary had tried during the early months of 1868 to contact Keckley, but the reasons for her dressmaker's silence soon became clear. In the closing months of 1867, Keckley had been working with a writer to publish her memoirs from the White House. In the spring, *Behind the Scenes, or Thirty Years a Slave, and Four Years in the White House* was published. While it was a mostly sympathetic portrayal of the Lincoln family, it breached a trust with her former employer and violated Victorian notions of decency and privacy. In the book, Keckley reported private conversations between the president and Mrs. Lincoln and included transcriptions of a set of Mary's letters to Keckley. Most galling, perhaps, in the betrayal was Keckley's estimation of Mary's debts. Mary probably felt betrayed, but she was definitely furious. "This proposition from me, does not argue a debt of $70,000! as the colored historian asserts," she bitterly complained to a friend.[72] Mary never again tried to contact Keckley, and so, she had lost another intimate female friend.[73] During this period of personal disappointment, Mary's health was very poor. She was experiencing debilitating gynecological health issues and headaches and was having so much trouble with her eyes that her physician recommended she cease all letter writing to avoid the strain. Her physician also recommended that Mary consider going abroad for her health, and by May she had decided to do just that. During the nineteenth century, it was common for people of means to move to the country, to resettle in the West, to visit mineral springs and natural areas and to travel to Europe to restore poor health. While the trend and her physician may have been the deciding factors that provided the final impetus to go, Mary was also likely eager to escape her unpopular public reputation as well. The plan was to settle in Germany, where she would put herself under the care of a physician and focus on the restoration of her health. It would also be an opportunity for Tad to obtain a European education.[74]

Before setting sail, Mary endured one last unpleasant trip to Springfield to inspect the progress at the Lincoln tomb, and then she and Tad traveled to the mineral springs in Pennsylvania, where she would spend most of the summer. The "beautiful Alleghany Mountain retreat" of Cressen Springs was a comfort to Mary, and it was from there that she wrote a friend that she was taking in the mountain breezes and gathering strength for the sea voyage ahead of her. The rest and quiet in Pennsylvania was important to her physical and mental health, but it also allowed her and Tad to make the acquaintance of Eliza Slataper, the wife of an engineer from Pittsburgh, and her son "Danie" who were staying at Cressen Springs. It was a friendship that she particularly needed as she sought to wipe clean the ugly events of the previous year. It would also spark a correspondence that would provide an emotional lifeline from Europe as well.[75] Although focused on her health and her upcoming voyage, Mary was still occupied with some important business. Still concerned about the progress of the Lincoln monument in Springfield, Mary took time to dash off a letter to Jesse Dubois, one of the members of the monument association with whom she had quarreled. Before getting to the point of her letter, however, she engaged in some pleasantries and took a moment to brag about her oldest son. "Robert grows every day, more and more like his father, & is a very beautiful character," she wrote.[76] No doubt Dubois, who had watched Robert grow up and who had been so close to her husband, would have appreciated this little note. The letter was replete with all of the social graces expected in Victorian correspondence, but the point of the note was quite clear. "I shall look to you, my dear Mr. DuBois, to see all the promises made to me, fulfilled in regard to the vault connected with the Monument."[77] It was a pretty strong clue that although Mary was leaving the United States, it did not mean she would forget about her interests in her husband's monument.

The most important event in Mary Lincoln's life that would occur before her move to Europe was the wedding of her oldest son to Mary Harlan, the daughter of a former Republican U.S. senator from Iowa. Mary was thrilled. "In regard to the proposed marriage of my son," she wrote a friend from Pennsylvania, "it is the only sunbeam in my sad future . . . I consider this marriage, a great gain—A charming daughter will be my portion & one whom my idolized husband loved & admired, since she was very young."[78] The wedding took place in Washington on Thursday evening, September 24, 1868, and it was both a blessing and a curse to her. She was happy for Robert and in love with his new wife, but being in Washington was an emotional experience for her. Upon returning to Baltimore, she became dizzy and collapsed in the dining room at Barnum's Hotel, and she required the assistance of a stranger. The trip to Europe, a dream she had maintained for most of her life, probably provided most of the emotional strength required to get past the painful reminders of the past that being in Washington had conjured.[79]

In Baltimore on October 1, 1868, Mary and Tad Lincoln, along with an assistant to attend to Mary's needs, boarded the *City of Baltimore*, a steamship in the British Inman Line. They had paid a total of $135 in gold for their fares. When they left America, the presidential campaign between popular Republican Ulysses S. Grant and Democrat and former New York governor Horatio Seymour was underway. That year, Congress had impeached Andrew Johnson, and the Fourteenth Amendment, guaranteeing citizenship and equal rights under the law, was ratified. Mary was nearly fifty years old, and Tad was fifteen when they sailed away toward a new life in Europe. They were certainly not the only Americans traveling to Europe. By 1867, more than 100 steamships were on the Atlantic. The comfort, speed and amenities available on these ships made it increasingly difficult to argue that women should not travel abroad alone. Travel of wealthy white women increased in the second half of the 1800s. There was also an increasing availability of guide books for women. For example in 1872, *Ladies Book of Etiquette and Manual of Politeness* included chapters entitled "Traveling" and "How to Behave at a Hotel."[80] In the early summer of 1867, there were an estimated

13,000 Americans living in Paris. After the Civil War, thousands of Americans, including women, traveled to Europe, as many as 50,000 in 1866 alone. Women traveled to Europe to "shop for dresses at Worth's in Paris, to mingle with nobility in England and elsewhere, and to bask in the sun and society at Swiss watering holes such as Vevey and Geneva."[81] Mary had always desired to travel to Europe, and shortly before his death, her husband had expressed his own desire to take her there. After visiting Niagara, Canada and New York in the summer of 1857, she wrote her sister: "when I saw the large steamers at the New York landing, ready for their European voyage, I felt in my heart, inclined to sigh, that poverty was my portion, how I long to go to Europe."[82] Now, here she was, on such a vessel steaming toward the port in Bremen. These "steam palaces" provided many comforts, and ship companies recognized that they must provide décor and amenities appealing to their growing number of female passengers. There were fresh flowers and refined Victorian accessories in the dining halls, furnishings in the rich aesthetic style of the era with silk upholstery and carved solid mahogany and numerous bath and toilet rooms.[83]

After two weeks at sea, Mary and Tad Lincoln arrived at Bremen, a city dating back to the eleventh century, and after a two-week stop there, they traveled on to Frankfurt. Tad enrolled in a boarding school that offered lessons in both English and German. At first he was homesick, but he was soon making friends and was comfortable in his new surroundings. Mary took one room in the Hotel D'Angleterre and found a banker, a doctor and, of course, a dressmaker. By December, a well-known designer named Popp had made her some new mourning silks. A very detailed and lengthy letter penned to her new friend Eliza Slataper revealed her contentment in her new home. In Frankfurt, there was a significant enclave of Americans in the city, and Mary adored the beautiful shops, loved espying European aristocrats who were visiting the town and appreciated the city's festive preparations for the upcoming Christmas season. Mary marveled at the rich history, architecture and art of the city. She "pined for a glass of American ice water," but she was not homesick otherwise. "Wine, of course is universally used & yet I have never seen a person the least intoxicated," she wrote Eliza. Mary was meeting people from America, interacting with continentals, focusing on her health, reading Longfellow and taking in the sites. "I like Frankfurt exceedingly," she wrote, "the true secret is, I suppose I am enjoying peace, which in my deepest, heart rending sorrow, I was not allowed, in my native land!"[84]

Frankfurt pleased her, but it was an expensive city. Tad's schooling and expenses were paid from his own share of the Lincoln estate, but Mary was funding herself and her servant, as well as seeking medical care and treatments, which included the consumption of various mineral waters. The Hotel D'Angleterre cost $30 a week, and the 6 percent interest on her inheritance was yielding just $2,500 annually. Therefore, ultimately a move to a less expensive hotel was in order, and the new one lacked carpets and other amenities. The less elegant circumstances were disappointing to Mary. By December, she was again worrying about money and began a letter-writing campaign to seek a pension from the U.S. Congress. She was hoping for an annual pension of at least $3,000. "I am a widow of a President of the United States whose life was sacrificed to his country's service," she petitioned. "In consideration of the great service my deeply lamented husband has rendered to the United States, and of the fearful loss I have sustained by his untimely death—his martyrdom, I may say—I respectfully submit to your honorable body this petition, hoping that a yearly pension may be granted me so that I may have less pecuniary care."[85] News of Mary's efforts to obtain a pension created as much of a buzz in the press as many of her past activities, and on this, public opinion was divided. One newspaper chided the Radical Republicans for voting away "seven millions of gold at the instance of a corrupt lobby, for an uninhabitable iceberg at the north pole," referring to the American purchase of Alaska, "but they cannot answer the appeal of a President's widow."[86] One letter writer to a Vermont newspaper was perturbed about the notion because Abraham Lincoln was not a soldier, and, therefore, Mary was not entitled to the pension of a soldier's widow.[87] In the end, it became too difficult for enough members of Congress to enter a vote against the wife of the dead president, and on July 14, 1870, Congress voted to bestow on Abraham Lincoln's widow a $3,000 pension.[88] The good news from America regarding the pension coincided with the outbreak of the Franco-Prussian War. Americans were leaving France and Germany in droves, and fearful of the violence, Mary and Tad packed their bags and went to England. Once there, Mary penned a gracious letter of thanks to Senator Charles Sumner, who had been a stalwart supporter of the pension bill: "Dear Mr Sumner, you are noble and good . . . Words are inadequate to express my thanks, for all your goodness to me."[89]

During her two and a half years abroad, Mary had done much of the European sightseeing she had always dreamed of doing. While she was plagued with some health problems and suffered from bouts of loneliness, she experienced much peace and happiness in Europe. Among the European cities she visited and in which she relished the deep history were Edinburgh, Glasgow, Nice, Nuremburg, Heidelberg and Oberusel, where Tad spent two months at a school after finishing his studies at the institute in Frankfurt.[90] In some ways, the letters were typical of the letters she had always written. There were still signs of profound grief in some of her letters as well as complaints about her health and acerbic opinions about American politics, but they were also laced with enthusiastic tales of her adventures, details about new friendships made and a general tone of contentment. Perhaps the most enjoyable period of her residence abroad was the seven weeks that she and Tad spent in Paris and London with her old friend and minister from Springfield, the Rev. James Smith. There was no school for Tad and no medical treatments for Mary, just time for each other and their aging American friend. Mary and her "bright little comforter Taddie" toured castles, took in the scenery, breathed in the sea air and visited historic locations, like the battlefield of Waterloo and the birthplace of the Robert Burns, the poet that she and her husband had so loved.[91]

From Europe, Mary sent lively letters to her daughter-in-law, offering advice, sharing news and professing adoration. "Do oblige me by considering me as a mother for you are very dear to me as a daughter . . . Oh! That I could be with you!" she wrote. "You should go out every day and enjoy yourself . . . Trouble comes soon enough, my dear child."[92] Mary finally had a daughter, and she wanted desperately to have a close relationship with her. Mary's doting increased when her first grandchild, Mary Todd Lincoln, was born in October 1869. The little girl became "Mamie" for short, with Robert continuing the Lincoln tradition of bestowing loving nicknames on idolized children. "I have written you about my lovely young daughter-in-law, who is just as dear to me, as if she were my own child . . . She is only 22 years old—a month or so since—and she has an infant—going on three months," Mary wrote a friend. "I cannot realize, that I am a grandmamma."[93] In Europe, Tad Lincoln had become an accomplished student, had learned proficient German and had developed European poise and grace. However, he was ready to go home. "Tad is almost wild to see Bob, you and the baby," Mary wrote her daughter-in-law in January 1871.[94] Instead of sending him home ahead of her, though, she enrolled him in a school outside of London and then went to Italy to visit Florence and Milan.[95] Finally, in May 1871, Mary and Tad Lincoln returned to Chicago.

Robert Lincoln and his wife, Mary, and baby daughter, Mamie, welcomed Mary and Tad home in late May 1871. It was a happy reunion for all, but it was short lived. Mary and Tad were exhausted, and Tad was ill. After a brief stay with Robert and his young family, Mary and Tad moved back into the Clifton House, and Mary spent her time nursing Tad. Robert spent time sitting with Tad as well, and both he and his mother were worried. Tad struggled to breathe, and only sleeping upright in a chair alleviated the congestion in his chest. His illness was "tortuous," according to Robert, and Mary must have been out of her mind with fear as she helplessly watched a third child suffer such a painful illness. By June 8, Tad was dangerously ill, and two top Chicago physicians were called to treat him. The doctors reported that Tad had water forming on his left lung, but they were hopeful. Mary had no choice but to believe them. "His youth, and vigilant care," she wrote a friend, "with the mercy of God, may ward off future trouble."[96] Hope and the mercy of God were of no use. Tad Lincoln died on July 15, 1871. He was just eighteen years old. He was buried in Springfield with his father and two brothers on July 17. Robert was there, but Mary did not attend.[97]

From Tad's death through 1876, there are very few surviving letters from Mary, and it might be argued that this fourth devastating loss had been the worst of all. "My idolized & devoted son, torn from me, when he had bloomed into such a noble, promising youth," she wrote Mrs. Slataper in October 1871.[98] Shortly after that letter, Mary was living in Robert's home on Wabash Avenue. On October 10, at around 9 p.m. on a windy evening, the Great Chicago Fire started in a backyard barn on DeKoven Street, some twenty or so blocks south and west of Robert's home. For the next thirty hours, fire burned through Chicago's main business district, leaving a path of destruction along seventy-three miles of streets, killing 300 people, leaving 100,000 people homeless and causing property damages upwards of $200 million. Robert's home was just south of the fire and was unharmed, but his office on Lake Street was destroyed. It was an emotionally and financially traumatic event for the entire city, and one that left deep scars in many people who witnessed the flames and the devastation left behind. Mary was one of them, as the image of "poor burnt out Chicago" added one more fear to her delicate psyche.[99] Still grieving and now nervous, there were the details of Taddie's estate with which to attend. In November, she wrote to David Davis: "Dear Judge, I well know, how deeply you sympathise with us, in our great great sorrow. My beloved boy, was the idol of my heart & had become my inseparable companion. My heart is entirely broken, for without his presence, the world is complete darkness."[100] She asked that Davis divide the estate equally between her and Robert despite the fact that she was entitled to two-thirds. Tad Lincoln's estate at his death consisted of $35,750 in bonds and $1,315 in cash.[101]

The next five years of Mary's life were filled with unbearable grief, depression, more public embarrassments and poor physical health. Unlike the years in Europe, there seemed to be little joy at all in her life. In May 1872, Ward Hill Lamon, Mr. Lincoln's friend and bodyguard, released a biography in which he regurgitated Herndon's theories about Ann Rutledge, railed against Mary as a bad wife and suggested the illegitimacy of Abraham Lincoln's mother and Abraham Lincoln himself.[102] "In regard to the infamous publication, to which you allude" she wrote a friend from a health resort in Wisconsin, "the vile, unprincipled and debased character of the author, are sufficient guarantees, of the truthfulness of his wicked assertions. The life of my pure, noble minded, devoted husband, requires no vindication."[103] In the months that followed, she visited one health resort after another, chasing medical therapies in Wisconsin, Canada and Florida. They offered little in the way of betterment in terms of her physical or emotional health, but they gave her something to chase. Perhaps the chase was worth something, although her last surviving son thought otherwise. The few letters that exist from this period are no different in tone or character than the ones in her earlier years. They are lucid and deliberate, and there is not one that even hints at the mental problems that led to Robert Lincoln's legal action against her in the spring of 1875. Robert believed that his mother was mentally ill, and he initiated a legal proceeding to have her declared insane, institutionalized and stripped of her rights to manage her own money.

Prior to the insanity hearing, Mary had returned from Florida from another trip seeking health remedies and the comfort of spiritualists. Once back in Chicago, she checked into the Grand Pacific Hotel, a new building constructed on the ruins following the Chicago Fire. The $45 weekly cost for room and board fit well into her now $8,000 annual budget. Apparently, she was spending much of her time and a large portion of her disposable income on shopping sprees. According to the shopkeepers who attended her, she often purchased duplicate items and was spending money on goods like curtains, for which she had no need. Following one of her shopping sprees on May 19, 1875, Mary answered a knock at her hotel room door. It was two uniformed officers and Leonard Swett, Mr. Lincoln's old political friend. They had arrived to escort her to the courthouse, where a jury would evaluate her sanity. Swett was there because he did not wish the widow of his dead friend to be taken away in handcuffs, but he agreed with Robert Lincoln that the hearing was necessary. Illinois was one of only three states that provided for a hearing for an involuntary commitment of an individual to a mental institution, which was something of an improvement over other states that required only a certified attestation of a person's derangement.[104] In a three-hour insanity hearing, witnesses testified to Mary's depression, hallucinations and paranoia. Particularly at issue were some statements she had been making about being followed, about her life being in danger and about her fears that her only surviving son might perish in a fire. Mary would find out later that Robert Lincoln had hired Pinkerton detectives to watch her, even stationing some in the lobby of the Grand Pacific Hotel. It is likely that the men she thought were following her were in fact the very detectives that her son had employed to watch her. Mary's shopping sprees, her visits to spiritualists and her obsession over money were on trial as well. The witnesses were doctors, hotel keepers, shopkeepers and her own son. His testimony was the most damning as well as the most tragic. "She has been of unsound mind since the death of father," Robert said under oath, and added that she "has been irresponsible for the past ten years."[105]

After just ten minutes of deliberation, the jury found Mary Lincoln insane and committed her to a mental institution for treatment. Upon her commitment, Robert Lincoln gained control of his mother's financial affairs.

In nineteenth-century America, eccentrics like Mary were unwelcome. It did not matter that she was spending *her* money on material possessions she probably did not need, that she was spending *her* time with spiritualists or that she was trying new health cures for *her* body. Whether Mary suffered from a mental disease that today would be diagnosed and treated is irrelevant in the context of a nineteenth-century insanity trial because such trials allowed no opportunity for mounting a defense and supported a framework in which the petitioner asking for a declaration of insanity stood to become the financial beneficiary of the defendant's incarceration.[106] The verdict stunned Mary, irreparably damaged her relationship with her only surviving son, deprived her of her grandchildren, branded her as a lunatic in the eyes of the nineteenth-century American public and diminished her character as a historical figure.[107]

Because of the financial means of the Lincoln family, Mary was taken to Bellevue Place, a sanitarium in Batavia, Illinois, instead of one of the public institutions in the state. Dr. Robert Patterson ran the sanitarium, and his methods included rest and quiet in a serene environment, nutritious food and various medicinal remedies like opium, morphine, cannabis, and whiskey-laced eggnog. Mary had no idea how long she might be incarcerated in the sanitarium, as she had received no definitive sentence. All of the historical evidence on Mary's mental health is from the statements of other people, many of whom misunderstood her or exaggerated their stories about her. There is virtually no evidence from Mary about her time in Bellevue either. What is known is that she was not happy with her incarceration, did not acknowledge that she was mentally deranged and devised a plan to gain her release. Her oldest sister, Elizabeth Edwards, agreed to allow her to move in with her in Springfield, and Mary enlisted the advocacy of lawyer activists Myra and James Bradwell. The Bradwells threatened a legal action that would question Dr. Patterson's methods and drag the issue back into the public eye, which was the last thing Robert Lincoln wanted. Robert at first tried to fight his mother's removal to Springfield but ultimately relented. On September 11, 1875, Mary left the sanitarium, and her son escorted her to the Edwards' home in Springfield.[108]

She was back on Aristocracy Hill, back where she had started her adult life nearly forty years past. For the year 1875 and the first half of 1876, there are no surviving letters to detail her life back in Springfield. However, by the accounts of others, Mary was adjusting and living a quiet and contented life, taking walks, going on carriage rides, visiting with old friends and enjoying the company of her great nephew Edward Lewis Baker Jr., the son of the editor of the *Illinois Journal* in Springfield. Elizabeth, who was once again playing a motherly role for her younger sister, reported that Mary was "delighted" with her new surroundings. After nine months resting and living a quiet life in Springfield, Mary asked for a hearing to restore her legal rights and regain control of her finances. On July 15, 1876, in a hearing kept quiet from the public, Mary's brother-in-law Ninian Edwards testified on her behalf, and the jury restored Mary to reason, declared her capable of managing her own affairs and removed Robert Lincoln as her conservator. The next day, Robert traveled to Springfield to deliver to his mother in person cash and bonds totaling $81,390.35, an increase of $8,000 from an additional investment that Robert had made in government bonds.[109] With the annual pension from the federal government and the income on her assets, she was now a relatively wealthy woman. The increase to her assets could not render moot her son's initiation of the insanity hearing, however. Three days later, she sent a scathing letter addressed to "Robert T. Lincoln." In the letter, she demanded the return of various personal items from Chicago, including "all of my paintings . . . Send me my laces, my diamonds, my jewelry," she wrote. "Two prominent clergy men, have written me, since I saw you—and mention in their letters, that they think it advisable to offer up prayers for you in Church, on account of your wickedness against me and High Heaven . . . Send me all that I have written for, you have tried your game of robbery long enough." She signed the letter "Mrs. A. Lincoln."[110]

From Mary's perspective, she could no longer stay in the United States, and now that she had control of her money, she made plans for a permanent exile in France. Her sister's house could have become her permanent home, but she felt that a life branded as a lunatic was her only fate in America. As she told her sister, "I love you, but I cannot stay."[111] She placed her finances in the hands of her husband's old friend Jacob Bunn in Springfield. Her beloved great nephew Lewis Baker escorted her to New York, and at the end of September 1876, Mary sailed to France. By the end of October, she was settled into her chosen home of Pau, a picturesque medieval village in the French Pyrenees. Most of the letters she wrote from France were to Jacob Bunn, and they reveal a clear mind and command of her financial affairs; she followed the payment of every bill, analyzed receipts and expertly handled monetary conversions to better maximize her budget. She also penned a number of affectionate letters to Lewis Baker, who was clearly a surrogate son for her. Those letters were filled with affection and great details about her health problems and sorrows. Interestingly, increasingly in this period, she signed more and more of her letters "Mrs. Abraham Lincoln," instead of "Mary Lincoln" or "Mrs. Lincoln." Perhaps this indicated a further decent into her adopted widow's pose. By October 1879, her health was in serious decline—pains in her back and side were particularly debilitating—and she was homesick for her sister's good food. However, she was not quite ready to end her exile just yet.[112]

Although she resided in hotels, she mostly lived a solitary life. Occasionally, she enjoyed the company of a select number of new friends, but as much as she loved the French language, culture and history, she found the French people "superficial." By 1880, she found them extremely obnoxious, and she shared her views with Lewis: "But it is a curiosity to see how angry, these French people can become. The most unprincipled, heartless, avaricious people, on the face of the earth. With the exception of a very few, I detest them all."[113] Mary sent gifts home to Lewis and her sisters Elizabeth and Frances, and she enjoyed receiving letters from all of them. She also sent money and clothing to Frances, who, since the death of her husband in 1867, struggled financially. The remote and quiet village of Pau was her home, but when her health allowed it, she made short visits to Paris, Vichy, Avignon and Marseilles.[114] Reading occupied much of her time. Upon arriving in France, she had purchased François Guizot's large five-volume history of France, as she desired to learn about the history of the country she had admired her entire life and now was making her home.[115] She also obtained copies of American newspapers and kept tabs on American politics. She shared many of her opinions with Lewis, and those letters reveal that she had not lost her keen talent for sarcasm and biting political commentary. When Mary read that President Rutherford Hayes had made David M. Keys his postmaster general, she wrote Lewis: "I must confess that I was surprised to find, that Hayes, has placed in his Cabinet Key, a man, who served in the Confederate Army, during the War; we have many other men in our Country, with talents & patriotism, to the true cause, not to reward a Secessionist."[116]

By the summer of 1880, the almost sixty-two-year-old Mary was too lonely and frail to maintain her exile in France any longer. A cataract in her right eye was slowly blinding her, and a fall in France had severely injured her back. She sailed from Le Harve on the *Amerique* on October 16, 1880, and Lewis met her in New York to escort her back to Springfield. She moved back into the home of Elizabeth and Ninian Edwards, again seeking the comfort of her sister. It was sister Lizzie who had always been willing to help her, even when there had been difficulties between them. It was Lizzie on whom Mary had always been able to depend in spite of the fact that the younger sister had sometimes over the years forgotten that important fact. Whether it was her poor health and eyesight or depression, Mary spent most of her time in her room, darkened by the drawn shades that shielded her from the world outside. Her physical pain and suffering crowded out the grief that had been her lot since losing Willie, and it was her medical problems that now dominated her thoughts and the conversations she had with those who visited. Two very important visitors arrived in May 1881, when Robert Lincoln and his eleven-year-old daughter Mamie came to Springfield to make amends. Robert, who was now the secretary of war under President James Garfield, had been worried for his mother's health and wanted to see her. He determined that she seemed fairly well, but just a few months later, she traveled to New York for medical assessment and treatment.[117]

Mary weighed just 100 pounds, was nearly blind and could barely walk. The New York doctor she visited offered a grim diagnosis. She had kidney disease and spinal sclerosis, and he prescribed time in a medical hotel in New York. Mary spent the winter there taking hot baths, getting massages and having electrical currents applied to her back. Full-time nursing care and treatments at the facility cost $60 weekly, and her pain was not greatly reduced.[118] "I am very feeble with my spine & limbs—now, quite unable to walk but a very few steps & my vision very greatly obscured," she wrote from New York.[119] At the end of 1881, Mary found the strength, however, to initiate an effort to have her pension increased. On January 1, 1882, her physician wrote to Illinois congressman William Springer about her medical condition: "We find Mrs. Lincoln suffering from chronic inflammation of the spinal cord, chronic disease of the kidneys, and commencing cataract of both eyes. The disorder of the spinal cord is the result of an injury received some time since . . . The nature of the spinal trouble is progressive, and will end in paralysis of the lower extremities. Connected with the spinal disease, and one of its evidences, is the reflect paralysis of the iris of the eye and the reduction of the sight to one-tenth the natural standard, together with much narrowing of the field of vision the sight will gradually grow worse. There is no possibility that there will be any permanent improvement in Mrs. Lincoln's condition, considering the nature of her disease and her age. She is now quite helpless, and unable to walk with safety, without the aid of an attendant, or indeed to help herself to any extent. She requires the continued services of a nurse and also constant medical attendance."[120] It was a grim diagnosis indeed. However, the letter did not fall on deaf ears. That same month, the U.S. Congress increased Mary's annual pension to $5,000 and awarded her $15,000 in back payments.[121] The additional money ensured that she would be able to afford whatever health care she needed. It did not, however, lessen the physical pain of her illnesses, nor change the future that promised eventual blindness and paralysis.

After accepting the sad truth that the treatments were not effective, Mary left New York and returned to Springfield, arriving on March 24, 1882. In the house on Aristocracy Hill where Mary Todd had been the center of attention of the Springfield Coterie, where she had fallen in love with a tall unknown lawyer and where she had become Mrs. Abraham Lincoln, the Widow Lincoln returned to her bedroom. All spring her health worsened, and the room became darker as her eyesight failed and her spirit weakened.

On July 15, 1882, on the eleventh anniversary of the death of Tad Lincoln, Mary Lincoln suffered a stroke, collapsed and fell into a coma. She died the next day at the age of sixty-three.[122]

Notes

1 Edward Steers Jr., *Blood on the Moon: The Assassination of Abraham Lincoln* (Lexington: University of Kentucky Press), 2001, 104–5, 270; Craig L. Symonds, *Lincoln and His Admirals: Abraham Lincoln, the U.S. Navy, and the Civil War* (New York: Oxford University Press, 2008), 365; *Washington Chronicle* (DC), 16 April 1865; *Washington Star* (DC), 14 April 1865; *L&L*, 221–22; Jean H. Baker, *Mary Todd Lincoln: A Biography* (New York: W. W. Norton & Co., 1987; reprint, New York: W. W. Norton & Co., 2008), 243.

2 Mary Lincoln to James Gordon Bennett, 25 October 1861, *L&L*, 110–11; Mary Lincoln to Charles Sumner, 14 May 1865, *L&L*, 228–29; Mary Lincoln to Sally Orne, 31 August 1865, Lincoln Collection, ALPL (this document is transcribed in its entirely in the Documents section); *Daily Illinois State Journal*, 17 July 1882, 6:1.

3 Baker, *Mary Todd Lincoln*, 245; Otto Eisenschiml, *In the Shadow of Lincoln's Death* (New York: Funk, 1940), 351; Henry J. Raymond, *The Life and Public Services of Abraham Lincoln* (New York: Derby & Miller, 1865), 783–801; Jason Emerson, *Giant in the Shadows* (Carbondale: Southern Illinois University Press, 2012), 100, 104.

4 Mary Lincoln to Mrs. Kasson, 20 January 1866, transcribed in Thomas F. Schwartz and Kim M. Bauer, "Unpublished Mary Todd Lincoln," *Journal of the Abraham Lincoln Association* 17 (Summer 1996): 10–11.

5 *Evening Star* (Washington, DC), 20 April 1865, 1:2; Baker, *Mary Todd Lincoln*, 248–49.

6 Steers, *Blood on the Moon*, 272; *L&L*, 224, 247, 271–72, 279; Catherine Clinton, *Mrs. Lincoln: A Life* (New York: Harper Collins, 2009), 248; Emerson, *Giant in the Shadows*, 108.

7 Baker, *Mary Todd Lincoln*, 248–50; Mary Lincoln to Sally Orne, 13 January 1866, *L&L*, 325–26; Elizabeth Keckley, *Behind the Scenes in the Lincoln White House: Memoirs of an African-American Seamstress* (Mineola, NY: Dover Publications, 2006), 87–88.

8 Mary Lincoln to Sally Orne, 13 January 1866; Baker, *Mary Todd Lincoln*, 253.

9 Mary Lincoln to Andrew Johnson, 29 April 1865, *L&L*, 226.

10 Mary Lincoln to Andrew Johnson, 29 April 1865; Mary Lincoln to Andrew Johnson, 3 May 1865, *L&L*, 226–27.

11 Mary Lincoln to Charles Sumner, 11 May 1865, *L&L*, 228.

12 Mary Lincoln to Charles Sumner, 14 May 1865, *L&L*, 228–29; Wayne C. Temple, "'I am So Fond of Sightseeing': Mary Lincoln's Travels up to 1865," in Frank J. Williams and Michael Burkhimer, eds., *The Mary Lincoln Enigma: Historians on America's Most Controversial First Lady* (Carbondale: Southern Illinois University Press, 2012), 182.

13 Baker, *Mary Todd Lincoln*, 253; *L&L*, 231, 235; Keckley, *Behind the Scenes*, 86.

14 Appointment of David Davis as Associate Justice of the U.S. Supreme Court, 17 October 1862, Lincoln Collection, ALPL; Harry E. Pratt, *Personal Finances of Abraham Lincoln, Personal Finances of Abraham Lincoln* (Springfield, IL: Abraham Lincoln Association, 1943), viii, 131–33.

15 Mary Lincoln to Simon Cameron, 6 April 1866, Lincoln Collection, ALPL.

16 Ibid.

17 John M. Palmer, ed., *The Bench and Bar of Illinois: Historical and Reminiscent*, 2 vols. (Chicago: Lewis Publishing Co., 1899), 1:79–124.

18 *Chicago City Directory, 1865–6* (Chicago: T. M. Halpin, 1865), 45–47; William Cronon, *Nature's Metropolis: Chicago and the Great West* (New York: W. W. Norton & Co., 1991), 69, 77, 93, 238; Robert P. Howard, *Illinois: A History of the Prairie State* (Grand Rapids, MI: William B. Eerdmans Publishing Co., 1972), 346–47.

19 Mary Lincoln to Oliver S. Halsted Jr., 29 May 1865, Lincoln Collection, ALPL.

20 Blain Brooks Gernon, *The Lincolns in Chicago* (Chicago: Ancarthe Publishers, 1934), 47; Emerson, *Giant in the Shadows*, 116–18; Donald L. Miller, *City of the Century: The Epic of Chicago and the Making of America* (New York: Simon & Schuster, 1996), 281–83.

21 Mary Lincoln to Oliver S. Halsted Jr., 29 May 1865.

22 Mary Lincoln to Harriet Howe Wilson, 8 June 1865, *L&L*, 242–43; Emerson, *Giant in the Shadows*, 116–17.

23 Mary Lincoln to Richard J. Oglesby, 5 June 1865, Lincoln Collection, ALPL; *Oak Ridge Cemetery* (Springfield, IL: Oak Ridge Cemetery Board of Managers, 1879), 7, 51.

24 Mary Lincoln to National Lincoln Monument Association, c. June 1865, *L&L*, 243; Mary Lincoln to Richard J. Oglesby, 10 June 1865, and Mary Lincoln to Richard J. Oglesby, 11 June 1865, both in Lincoln Collection, ALPL; *Illinois State Journal* (Springfield), 12 June 1865, 2:1; Baker, *Mary Todd Lincoln*, 252; Emerson, *Giant in the Shadows*, 119.

25 Mary Lincoln to Richard J. Oglesby, 11 June 1865.

26 Mary Lincoln to Mary Jane Welles, 11 July 1865, *L&L*, 256–57.

27 Mary Lincoln to Elizabeth Blair Lee, 25 August 1865, *L&L*, 267–69.

28 Mary Lincoln to Sally Orne, 31 August 1865.

29 Mary Lincoln to Charles Sumner, 4 July 1865, *L&L*, 255–56.

30 Mary Lincoln to Anson G. Henry, 17 July 1865, *L&L*, 259–62.

31 Mary Lincoln to Alexander Williamson, 15 June 1865, *L&L*, 250–51.

32 Emerson, *Giant in the Shadows*, 132–33.

33 Mary Lincoln to Elizabeth Blair Lee, 11 December 1865, *L&L*, 301–3.

34 Ida Blom, "The History of Widowhood: A Bibliographic Overview," *Journal of Family History* 16 (April 1991): 191–210.

35 Mary Lincoln to Sally Orne, 31 August 1865.

36 Mary Lincoln to Elihu Washburne, 9 December 1865, *L&L*, 300–301; Mary Lincoln to Elihu Washburne, 29 November 1865, *L&L*, 288–89; Mary Lincoln to Mary Jane Welles, 14 October 1865, *L&L*, 276–78; Mary Lincoln to Mary Jane Welles, 11 November 1865, *L&L*, 288–89.

37 Wayne C. Temple, *By Square and Compass: Saga of the Lincoln Home* (n.p.: Ashlar Press, 1984; reprint, Mahomet, IL: Mayhaven Publishing, 2000), 184; Mary Lincoln to Mary Jane Welles, 11 July 1865; Mary Lincoln to Anson G. Henry, 17 July 1865.

38 Mary Lincoln to Anson G. Henry, 26 July 1865, *L&L*, 262–64.

39 Mary Lincoln to Alexander Williamson, 17 August 1865, *L&L*, 264–65; Pratt, *Personal Finances*, 136–37; Baker, *Mary Todd Lincoln*, 254–55.

40 William S. McFeely, *Grant: A Biography* (New York: W. W. Norton & Co., 1981), 232, 263.

41 Notice: "Congress has passed a bill giving $25,000 to Mary Lincoln, widow of our late President Lincoln," *New York Tribune*, 21 December 1865, 6; Baker, *Mary Todd Lincoln*, 256–58; Pratt, *Personal Finances*, 184; "An Act for the Relief of Mrs. Mary Lincoln, widow of the late President of the United States," 21 December 1865, *Statutes at Large*, vol. 14, 577; Mary Lincoln to Alexander Williamson, 16 December 1865, *L&L*, 308–9.

42 Mary Lincoln to Mary Jane Welles, 29 December 1869, *L&L*, 315–17.

43 Ibid.

44 Mary Lincoln to Alexander Williamson, 11 November 1865, *L&L*, 280–81.

45 Mary Lincoln to Alexander Williamson, 13 December 1865, *L&L*, 305–6.

46 Mary Lincoln to Simon Cameron, 6 April 1866; Mary Lincoln to Sally Orne, 13 January 1866; Baker, *Mary Todd Lincoln*, 263; Emerson, *Giant in the Shadows*, 121.

47 Gernon, *Lincolns in Chicago*, 49–50.

48 Mary Lincoln to Henry C. Deming, 16 December 1867, *L&L*, 463–64; Mary Lincoln to David Davis, 12 August 1866, Lincoln Collection, ALPL; Mary Lincoln to Alexander Williamson, 5 November 1866, *L&L*, 394–96; Baker, *Mary Todd Lincoln*, 266.

49 Douglas L. Wilson and Rodney O. Davis, eds., *Herndon's Informants: Letters, Interviews, and Statements about Abraham Lincoln* (Urbana: University of Illinois Press, 1998), 357–61; Baker, *Mary*

Todd Lincoln, 267–68; L&L, 380; Douglas L. Wilson, "William H. Herndon and Mary Todd Lincoln," in Williams and Burkhimer, Mary Lincoln Enigma, 112–39; David Donald, Lincoln's Herndon (New York: Alfred A. Knopf, 1948), 185–87.

50 Emerson, Giant in the Shadows, 143–44; Baker, Mary Todd Lincoln, 268–69; L&L, 412–13.

51 Mary Lincoln to David Davis, 4 March 1867, and Mary Lincoln to David Davis, 6 March 1867, both in Lincoln Collection, ALPL.

52 Emerson, Giant in the Shadows, 129; Andrew C. A. Jampoler, The Last Conspirator: John Surratt's Flight from the Gallows (Annapolis, MD: Naval Institute Press, 2008).

53 Mary Lincoln to Elizabeth Emerson Atwater, 30 June 1867, L&L, 425–26; Mary Lincoln to David Davis, 30 June 1867, Lincoln Collection, ALPL.

54 Mary Lincoln to Elizabeth Emerson Atwater, 13 July 1867, Lincoln Collection, ALPL.
     After two years of imprisonment, Jefferson Davis was released on $100,000 bail. The federal court eventually dropped the treason indictment against him in February 1869. Ray F. Nichols, "United States vs. Jefferson Davis," American Historical Review 31 (January 1926): 266–84.

55 Mary Lincoln to Elizabeth Emerson Atwater, 30 June 1867.

56 Mary Lincoln to Alexander Williamson, 26 May 1867, L&L, 422–23.

57 Mary Lincoln to David Davis, 17 June 1867, Lincoln Collection, ALPL.

58 Emerson, Giant in the Shadows, 124.

59 Mary Lincoln to David Davis, 6 April 1867, Lincoln Collection, ALPL.

60 Mary Lincoln to Alexander Williamston, 17 October 1866, L&L, 393.

61 Mary Lincoln to Leeds & Miner, 11 November 1865, L&L, 264–65; Mary Lincoln to Alexander Williamson, 17 August 1865; Mary Lincoln to Alexander Williamson, 9 September 1865, L&L, 272–73; Mary Lincoln to Alexander Williamson, 16 December 1865, L&L, 280–81; Mary Lincoln to Alexander Williamson, 3 January 1866, L&L, 308–9.
     The exact amount of the debts has been a longtime historical debate. In her memoir, Elizabeth Keckley reported the debts at $70,000. Jean Baker estimates them at $10,000. Keckley, Behind the Scenes, 87; Baker, Mary Todd Lincoln, 194.

62 Mary Lincoln to Sally Orne, 31 August 1865.

63 Crisis (Columbus, OH), 16 October 1867, 304.

64 Catherine Clinton, "Mrs. Lincoln Goes Shopping," New York Archives 8 (Winter 2009), 26–30; Baker, Mary Todd Lincoln, 275–76.

65 Baker, Mary Todd Lincoln, 277; Mary Lincoln to Elizabeth Keckley, 6 October 1867, L&L, 440.

66 Mary Lincoln to Elizabeth Keckley, 8 October 1867, in Keckley, Behind the Scenes, 142–43.

67 Mary Lincoln to Elizabeth Keckley, 9 October 1867, in Keckley, Behind the Scenes, 143.

68 Mary Lincoln to Alexander Williamson, 10 November 1867, L&L, 452–53.

69 Baker, Mary Todd Lincoln, 279; Pratt, Personal Finances, viii, 134, 141.

70 Mary Lincoln to David Davis, 18 November 1867, Lincoln Collection, ALPL.

71 Mary Lincoln to Alexander Williamson, 9 January 1868, L&L, 467.

72 Mary Lincoln to Rhoda White, 2 May 1868, L&L, 475–77.

73 L&L, 472.

74 Mary Lincoln to Alexander Williamston, 9 January 1868, L&L, 467; Mary Lincoln to Rhoda White, 2 May 1868; Mary Lincoln to Jesse K. Dubois, 19 June 1868, L&L, 477; Mary Lincoln to Rhoda White, 19 August 1868, L&L, 481–82.

75 Mary Lincoln to Martha Stafford, 18 July 1868, L&L, 475–77; Mary Lincoln to Jesse K. Dubois, 19 June 1868; Mary Lincoln to Rhoda White, 18 July 1868, Lincoln Collection, ALPL; L&L, 474.

76 Mary Lincoln to Jesse K. Dubois, 26 July 1868, transcribed in Schwartz and Bauer, "Unpublished Mary Todd Lincoln," 14–15.

77 Ibid.

78 Mary Lincoln to Rhoda White, 27 August 1868, L&L, 482.

79 Mary Lincoln to Eliza Slataper, 21 September 1868, L&L, 483–84; Mary Lincoln to Eliza Slataper, 27 September 1865, L&L, 485–86.

80 Charles Robert Vernon Gibbs, *Passenger Liners of the Western Ocean: A Record of Atlantic Steam and Motor Passenger Vessels from 1838 to the Present Day* (New York: John De Graff, 1957), 112–24. Mary Suzanne Schriber, ed., *Telling Travels: Selected Writings by Nineteenth-Century American Women Abroad* (DeKalb: Northern Illinois University Press, 1995), xiv–xv, xviii; Mary Lincoln to Eliza Slataper, *L&L*, 483–84.

81 Schriber, *Telling Travels*, xii; David McCullough, *The Greater Journey: Americans in Paris* (New York: Simon & Schuster, 2011), 264.

82 Mary Lincoln to Emilie Helm, 16 February 1857, *L&L*, 48–49.

83 Schriber, *Telling Travels*, xiv–xv.

84 Mary Lincoln to Eliza Slataper, 13 December 1868, *L&L*, 493–96; David Blackbourn, *The Long Nineteenth Century: A History of Germany, 1780–1918* (New York: Oxford University Press, 1998); *L&L*, 489.

85 Mary Lincoln to the U.S. Senate, December 1868, *L&L*, 493; Mary Lincoln to George S. Boutwell, 4 December 1868, *L&L*, 491–92; Mary Lincoln to Nathaniel P. Banks, 4 December 1868, *L&L*, 492–93; Baker, *Mary Todd Lincoln*, 294.

86 *Patriot* (Harrisburg, PA), 4 February 1869, 2.

87 *Argus and Patriot* (Montpelier, VT), clipping, c. February 1869, 6.

88 "An Act Granting a Pension to Mary Lincoln," approved 14 July 1870, *Statutes at Large*, vol. 16, 653.

89 Mary Lincoln to Charles Sumner, 7 September 1870, *L&L*, 576–77.

90 Mary Lincoln to Eliza Slataper, 17 February 1869, Lincoln Collection, ALPL; Mary Lincoln to Mary Harlan Lincoln, 19 May 1870, *L&L*, 559; Wayne C. Temple, "I am So Fond of Sightseeing," in Williams and Burkhimer, *Mary Lincoln Enigma*, 140–85.

91 Mary Lincoln to Eliza Slataper, 21 August 1869, *L&L*, 512–13; Mary Lincoln to Rhoda White, 30 August 1869, *L&L*, 515–17; Mary Lincoln to Sally Orne, 18 October 1869, *L&L*, 519.

92 Mary Lincoln to Mary Harlan Lincoln, 22 March 1869, *L&L*, 504–6.

93 Mary Lincoln to Rhoda White, 20 December 1869, *L&L*, 536; Emerson, *Giant in the Shadows*, 151.

94 Mary Lincoln to Mary Harlan Lincoln, 26 January 1871, *L&L*, 582–83.

95 Mary Lincoln to Eliza Slataper, 7 November 1870, Lincoln Collection, ALPL; Mary Lincoln to Mary Harlan Lincoln, 12 February 1871.

96 Mary Lincoln to Rhoda White, 8 June 1871, *L&L*, 590; Gernon, *Lincolns in Chicago*, 57; Mary Lincoln to Rhoda White, 21 May 1871, *L&L*, 587–88; Mary Lincoln to Eliza Stuart Steele, 23 May 1871, *L&L*, 588–89.

97 Emerson, *Giant in the Shadows*, 153.

98 Mary Lincoln to Eliza Slataper, 4 October 1871, *L&L*, 596.

99 Miller, *City of the Century*, 146, 159; Emerson, *Giant in the Shadows*, 155; Mary Lincoln to Norman Williams, 8 August 1872, *L&L*, 599–600: Ross Miller, *The Great Chicago Fire* (Urbana: University of Illinois Press, 2000).

100 Mary Lincoln to David Davis, 9 November 1871, Lincoln Collection, ALPL.

101 Pratt, *Personal Finances*, 184.

102 Ward Hill Lamon, *The Life of Abraham Lincoln: His Birth to His Inauguration as President* (Boston: James R. Osgood and Co., 1872).

103 Mary Lincoln to James H. Knowlton, 3 August 1872, *L&L*, 598–99.

104 Baker, *Mary Todd Lincoln*, 315–16.

105 Jason Emerson, "'I Miss Bob, So Much,' Mary Lincoln's Relationship with Her Oldest Son," in Williams and Burkhimer, *Mary Lincoln Enigma*, 269–71; Jason Emerson, *The Madness of Mary Lincoln* (Carbondale: Southern Illinois University Press, 2007); Jason Emerson, *Mary Lincoln's Insanity Case: A Documentary History* (Champaign: University of Illinois Press, 2012).

106 Baker, *Mary Todd Lincoln*, 315–32; Myra Samuels Himelhock and Arthur H. Shaffer, "Elizabeth Packard: Nineteenth Century Crusader for the Rights of Mental Patients," *Journal of American Studies* 13 (December 1979): 343–75.

The best source for study and understanding of the insanity hearing of Mary Lincoln is Mark E. Neely Jr. and R. Gerald McMurtry, *The Insanity File: The Case of Mary Todd Lincoln* (Carbondale: Southern Illinois University Press, 1986).

107 "Mrs. Lincoln's Lunacy," *Indianapolis Sentinel* (IN), 21 May 1875, 4–5; "Mrs. Lincoln's Derangement," *New York Evangelist*, 27 May 1875, 8; "The Case of Mrs. Lincoln," *Patriot*, 24 May 1875, 4; "A Sad Revelation," *Kalamazoo Gazette* (MI), 28 May 1875, 2; James S. Brust, M.D., "A Psychiatrist Looks at Mary Lincoln," in Williams and Burkhimer, *Mary Lincoln Enigma*, 237–58.

108 Baker, *Mary Todd Lincoln*, 327–41; Emerson, *Giant in the Shadows*, 171–77.

109 Emerson, *Giant in the Shadows*, 177–82; *L&L*, 611–12, 616–17; Baker, *Mary Todd Lincoln*, 348–49.

110 Mary Lincoln to Robert Todd Lincoln, 19 June 1876, *L&L*, 615–16.

111 *L&L*, 617.

112 Mary Lincoln to Edward Lewis Baker Jr., 4 October 1879, *L&L*, 690–91 (this letter is transcribed in its entirety in the Documents section); Mary Lincoln to Edward Lewis Baker Jr., 12 June 1880, *L&L*, 698–700.

113 Mary Lincoln to Edward Lewis Baker Jr., 12 June 1880, *L&L*, 698–700.

114 Mary Lincoln to Elizabeth Edwards, 19 March 1877, *L&L*, 626–27; Mary Lincoln to Edward Lewis Baker Jr., 22 June 1879, *L&L*, 682–84; Roger Magraw, *France, 1815–1914: The Bourgeois Century* (New York: Oxford University Press, 1986).

115 Mary Lincoln to Edward Lewis Baker Jr., 17 October 1876, Lincoln Collection, ALPL.

116 Mary Lincoln to Edward Lewis Baker Jr., 11 April 1877, Lincoln Collection, ALPL.

117 *L&L*, 706.

118 Mary Lincoln to Josephine Remann Edwards, 23 October 1881, *L&L*, 708–9; Baker, *Mary Todd Lincoln*, 366.

119 Mary Lincoln to Noyes W. Miner, 3 January 1882, *L&L* 710–11.

120 "Mrs. Lincoln's Condition," *Cincinnati Commercial Tribune*, 16 January 1882, 1:2.

121 Baker, *Mary Todd Lincoln*, 368.

122 As well as her other ailments, Mary Lincoln had likely been suffering from diabetes. Glenna Schroeder Lein, *Lincoln and Medicine* (Carbondale: Southern Illinois University Press, 2012), 87–88; Baker, *Mary Todd Lincoln*, 368.

Mary Lincoln left an estate totaling $84,035. Robert Todd Lincoln was the sole heir. Pratt, *Personal Finances*, 185.

EPILOGUE

In a letter written to Robert Lincoln in August 1874, Mary Lincoln outlined her last requests. "I wish my remains to be clothed in the white silk dress . . . after my decease, I wish my remains placed beside my dear husband & Taddie's on one side of me," she wrote.[1] As well, she requested that there be a reading of the Psalm 23. As she also desired, her body was arranged for private viewing in the very parlor in which she had been married nearly forty years earlier. Her sister Elizabeth made the funeral arrangements, as Robert Lincoln traveled from Washington, D.C. Mary was dressed in her white gown and wore the wedding band that Abraham Lincoln had given her.

On Wednesday, July 19, 1882, a funeral procession left the Edwards' home just before ten in the morning and proceeded to the First Presbyterian Church for the funeral of Mary Lincoln. State and city offices and businesses were closed for the day, flags flew at half-mast and the city was draped in mourning bunting. A large crowd greeted the procession at Mary's old neighborhood church, and as the mourners passed through the doors, "a magnificent display of floral tributes" caught their gaze. One of the arrangements featured a large cross made of carnations and tea roses set in a base of carnations, violets, pansies and hollyhocks. Another was a pillow made of tea roses and carnations with an inscription "From the Citizens of Springfield." Yet another was a star of lilies displayed prominently above the pulpit, which was elegantly draped in black and white velvet. Mary would have been very pleased with the sophisticated floral displays and would have appreciated the extravagance of their designs, some of which had come from Chicago. As Beethoven's "Funeral March" played on the organ, two old friends of Abraham Lincoln—federal judge Samuel H. Treat and Col. John Williams—led the procession, as Mary's casket approached the altar in the charge of its distinguished pallbearers—sitting Illinois governor Shelby M. Cullom, Civil War general John A. McClernand, Captain John S. Bradford, Milton Hay, Jacob Bunn and James C. Conkling. The selection of Bunn and Conkling would have been particularly gratifying to Mary. Robert Lincoln and Mary's Springfield sisters and two brothers-in-law—Elizabeth and Ninian Edwards, Frances Wallace and Ann and Clark Smith—followed closely behind. Many old friends and neighbors were packed into the church that morning, as were most of the surviving members of the Springfield Todd clan, including Mary's cousin and dear friend Lizzie Grimsley.[2]

Starting from the inscription on Mary Lincoln's wedding band, "Love is Eternal," the eulogy delivered by the Rev. James A. Reed focused on the love that Mary had shared with her beloved husband. Reed extolled the virtues of Abraham Lincoln and acknowledged the grief that his assassination had caused the nation and his widow. "It is no reflection upon either the strength of her mind or the tenderness of her heart, to say that when Abraham Lincoln died, she died," Reed said.[3] After the funeral service, the hearse delivered the coffin to Oak Ridge Cemetery, the tranquil and green space Mary Lincoln had chosen for her husband. Mary had fought and won the battle to have her husband's monument built above his tomb at Oak Ridge, and now she would join him in that restful place alongside their three sons— Eddy and Willie and Tad. Escorted by the Lincoln Guard of Honor, the pallbearers entered the catacomb and placed Mary Lincoln's casket next to the sarcophagus of her husband. "Thus did the hands of affection complete the last duty that they could perform for the dead," reported a Springfield newspaper, "and Abraham and Mary Lincoln, re-united at last in death, were left to their final sleep."[4]

Notes

1 Mary Lincoln to Robert Lincoln, August 1874, Lincoln Collection, ALPL.
2 "Laid to Rest," *Illinois State Journal* (Springfield), 20 July 1882, 1:3–4; "The Last of Earth," *Daily Illinois State Register* (Springfield), 20 July 1882, 5:3–4; "Mrs. Mary Lincoln, *Daily Inter Ocean* (Chicago), 3; Jason Emerson, *Giant in the Shadows: The Life of Robert T. Lincoln* (Carbondale: Southern Illinois University Press, 2012), 239–40.
3 *Illinois State Journal*, 20 July 1882; "United in Death," *Daily Inter Ocean* (Chicago), 20 July 1882, 1.
4 *Daily Illinois State Register*, 20 July 1882, 5:3.
   Various obituaries from around the country provided biographies of Mary Lincoln's life, offered respectful eulogies, paid homage to her husband and offered condolences to her family and friends. Some stories that appeared remarked on her grief-stricken widowhood and discussed the various controversies that surrounded her as well. Overall, there was an enormous outpouring of respect for her position as the wife of the martyred Abraham Lincoln.
   "Death of Mrs. Lincoln," *Watertown Daily Times* (NY), 17 July 1882, 2:1; "Mary Todd Lincoln," *Daily Illinois State Journal*, 17 July 1882, 6:1; "Awaiting the Burial," *Daily Illinois State Journal*, 18 July 1882, 6:1; "Rest at Last," *Illinois State Register*, 18 July 1882, 3:3; "The Funeral," *Daily*

Illinois State Journal, 19 July 1882, 6:1–2; "United in Death," *Daily Inter Ocean* (Chicago), 20 July 1882, 1; "Mrs. Lincoln," *Daily Illinois State Register*, 20 July 1882, 2:4–5; "Laid Away," *Evansville Courier and Press* (IN), 20 July 1882, 2:2; "Respect to Mrs. Lincoln," *Salt Lake Tribune* (UT), 22 July 1882, 1; "In Memory of Mrs. Lincoln, *Tombstone Epitaph Prospector* (AZ), 22 July 1882, 2; "Laid to Rest," *Philadelphia Inquirer*, 2 August 1882, 7.

DOCUMENTS

When Mary Todd moved from her hometown of Lexington, Kentucky, to Springfield, Illinois, she left her childhood behind, but her full transformation into womanhood was as yet incomplete. As she settled into a routine of sewing and other chores punctuated by the social and political events she attended, she struggled to navigate the excitement and worries of courting. As the men and women in her social group married, she questioned and examined their choices and the institution of marriage itself. At the heart of her personal analysis were her own fears about choosing an appropriate companionable husband for herself. In a letter to her friend Mercy Levering, who had left Springfield for a visit with family on the East Coast, Mary shared the latest Springfield gossip and offered some commentary of her own. The letter not only reveals something about Mary Todd's personal experiences and thoughts about marriage, but also illustrates some of the nineteenth-century historical constructs of courting and marriage, especially from the perspective of women.

Mary Lincoln to Mercy Ann Levering[1]

Springfield Decr 1840

Many, very many weary days have passed my ever dear Merce, since mine has been the pleasure of hearing from you, some weeks since I received your kind, soul cheering epistle & had I been <u>then</u> told such a length of time would have intervened ere I had availed myself of an opportunity of replying to it, I would not have given credence to the tale, yet such has been the case & I feel that I owe you many apologies & sincerely trust our future correspondence may be more punctual, my time has been much occupied of late, you will be surprised to learn, I have scarce a leisure moment to call my own, for several weeks this fall, a formidable supply of <u>sewing</u>, necessary to winter comfort, engaged our constant attention, now the scene is changed. M[r] Edwards[2] has a cousin from Alton[3] spending the winter with us, a most interesting young lady, her fascinations, have drawn a concourse of beaux & company round us, occasionly, I <u>feel as Miss Whitney</u>, we have too much of such useless commodities, you know it takes some time for habit to render us familiar with what we are not greatly accustomed to. Could you step in upon us some evenings in these "western wilds," you would be astonished at the change, <u>time</u> has wrought on the hills,[4] I would my Dearest, you now were with us, be assured your name is most frequently mentioned in our circle, <u>words of mine</u> are not necessary to assure you of the loss I have sustained in your society. on my return from Missouri, my time passed most heavily, I feel quite made up, in my present companion, a congenial spirit I assure you. I know you would be pleased with Matilda Edwards, a lovelier girl I never saw. M[r] <u>Speed's</u>[5] ever changing heart I suspect is about offering <u>its young</u> affections at her shrine, with some others, there is considerable acquisition in our society of <u>marriagable gentlemen</u>, unfortunately only "birds of passage," M[r] <u>Webb</u>,[6] a widower of modest merit, last winter, is our <u>principal lion</u>, dances attendance very frequently, we expect a very gay winter, evening before last my sister[7] gave a most agreeable party, upwards of a hundred graced the festive scene. I trust the period is not very distant when your presence will be among us to cheer us & morever I trust <u>our homes</u> may be near, that as in times past so may it <u>ever be</u>, that our hearts will acknowledge the same kindred ties, memory oftimes reverts to bygone days, & with the past your memory is intimately blended, well did you say "time has borne changes on its wing," Speed's "<u>grey suit</u>" has gone the way of <u>all flesh</u>, an interesting suit of <u>Harrison blues</u> have replaced his <u>sober living, Lincoln's</u>,[8] <u>lincoln green</u> have & gone to dust. M[r] Webb sports a <u>mourning p</u>[in?] by way of reminding us <u>damsels</u> that we "<u>cannot commit</u>," of the new recruits I need not mention, some few are gifted & all in our humble estimation interesting. M[r] C.[9] seems to have <u>given up</u> all, when deprived of his "own particular star," I have not met him, to have a chat since Martha Jane's marriage, I have often wished for the sake of his society & your <u>dear self</u> he would be more social. Harriet Campbell[10] appears to be enjoying all the sweets of married life, M[rs] <u>Abell</u>,[11] came down two or three weeks since, have seen but very little of her, her <u>silver tones</u>, the other evening were not quite so captain like as was their wont in former times, why is it that married folks always become so serious?

Miss Lamb, report says is to be married next week, M[r] <u>Beauman</u>[12] I caught a glimpse of a few days since, looked <u>becomingly</u> happy at the prospect of the change, that is about to await him. I am pleased she is about perpetrating the crime of matrimony, like some of our friends in this place. M J L for instance, I think she will be much happier. I suppose like the rest of us Whigs though you seem rather to doubt my faith you have been rejoicing in the recent election of Gen Harrison,[13] a cause that has excited such deep interest in the nation and one of such vital importance to our prosperity. This fall I became quite a politician, rather an unladylike profession, yet a such a crisis, whose heart could remain untouched while the energies of all were called in question? You bid me pause, in your last, on the banks of "Lionel"[14] & there glean a n[eed]ful lesson, by marking the changes, the destroying hand of time had written on all, a moments thought, would suffice to assure me that all is not, as it then was, the icy hand of winter has set its seal upon the waters, the winds of Heaven visit the spot but roughly, the same stars shine down, yet not with the same liquid, mellow light as in the olden time, some forms & memories that enhanced the place, have passed by, many weary miles are you dear Merce removed from us, the star of hope, must be our guiding star, and we must revel in the happy anticipations of a reunion, may the day be not far distant. Once more, allow me my dear friend to wish you were with us, we have a pleasant jaunt in contemplation, to Jacksonville,[15] next week there to spend a day or two, Mr Hardin[16] & Browning[17] are our leaders the van brought up by Miss E.[18] my humble self, Webb, Lincoln & two or three others whom you know not, we are watching the clouds most anxiously trusting it may snow, so we may have a sleigh ride. Will it not be pleasant?

Your Brother's family,[19] are well, and all speak of you most frequently, & wonder when you expect to wander westward, we cannot do much longer without you, your mate, misses you too much from her nest, not to marvel at the delay, do trust a friend & be more communicative in your next, feeling as you must do the great interest I take in you, would you deny me the consolation of being a sharer in your joys & sorrows, may the latter be never known to you. The State House is not quite completed, yet sufficiently so to allow the Legislature to meet within its walls. Springfield has improved astonishingly, have the addition of another bell to the Second church, it rings so long & loud, that as in days past we cannot mistake the trysting hour. I trust you do not allow your sister to sing you any more such melancholy dirges, I know by sad experience that such dolorous ditties only excites one's anxiety to see a beloved object, therefore tell her for the sympathetic feel[ings] I entertain towards you dearest, bid her cease the strain. The weather is miserably cold, & my stump of a pen keeps pace with the times, pass my imperfections lightly by as usual, I throw myself on your amiable nature, knowing that my shortcomings will be forgiven. Fanny Wallace sends much love to you, her little urchin, is almost a young lady in size.

Elizabeth has not been well of late, suffering with a cold, I still am the same ruddy <u>pineknot</u>, only not quite so great an exuberance of flesh, as it once was my lot to contend with, although quite a sufficiency. I must close, write very, very soon if you love me.

ever your attached friend
Mary

Like most couples, Abraham and Mary Lincoln experienced difficulties and hardships during their twenty-two-year marriage. They also shared love and friendship with each other, and together they adored their children. Much of the Lincoln marriage was characterized by Abraham's frequent absences from home. When he was traveling for his law practice or for politics, Mary alone tended to the needs of a growing family, sometimes for weeks at a time. One of the more lengthy separations occurred when Lincoln was serving his one term in the U.S. Congress. During that separation, Mary was comfortable in Lexington with her family, and Lincoln was enjoying his life in Washington City as a congressman. Yet they were both lonely for each other. The following two letters reveal the companionate nature of the Lincoln marriage, show the emotional connections they had with each other and their children and belie the interpretation of some historians that their union was an unhappy one.

_____

Abraham Lincoln to Mary Lincoln[20]

Washington, April 16, 1848

Dear Mary:

In this troublesome world, we are never quite satisfied. When you were here, I thought you hindered me some in attending to business; but now, having nothing but business—no variety—it has grown exceedingly tasteless to me. I hate to sit down and direct documents, and I hate to stay in this old room by myself. You know I told you in last sunday's letter, I was going to make a little speech during the week; but the week has passed away without my getting a chance to do so; and now my interest in the subject has passed away too. Your second and third letters have been received since I wrote before. Dear Eddy thinks father is "gone tapila"[21] Has any further discovery been made as to the breaking into your grand-mother's house?[22] If I were she, I would not remain there alone. You mention that your uncle John Parker is likely to be at Lexington. Dont forget to present him my very kindest regards.[23]

I went yesterday to hunt the little plaid stockings, as you wished; but found that McKnight has quit business, and Allen had not a single pair of the description you give, and only one plaid pair of any sort that I thought would fit "Eddy's dear little feet." I have a notion to make another trial to-morrow morning. If I could get them, I have an excellent chance of sending them. Mr Warrick Tunstall, of St Louis is here. He is to leave early this week, and to go by Lexington. He says he knows you, and will call to see you; and he voluntarily asked, if I had not some package to send you.

I wish you to enjoy yourself in every possible way; but is there no danger of wounding the feelings of your good father, by being so openly intimate with the Wickcliffe family?[24]

Mrs Broome has not removed yet; but she thinks of doing so to-morrow. All the house—or rather, all with whom you were on decided good terms—send their love to you. The others say nothing.

Very soon after you went away, I got what I think a very pretty set of shirt-bosom studs—modest little ones, jet, set in gold, only costing 50 cents a piece, or 1.50 for the whole.

Suppose you do not prefix the "Hon" to the address on your letters to me any more. I like the letters very much; but I would rather they should not have that upon them. It is not necessary, as I suppose you have thought, to have them to come free.

And you are entirely free from head-ache? That is good—good—considering it is the first spring you have been free from it since we were acquainted. I am afraid you will get so well, and fat, and young, as to be wanting to marry again. Tell Louisa I want her to watch you a little for me. Get weighed, and write me how much you weigh.

I did not get rid of the impression of that foolish dream about dear Bobby, till I got your letter written the same day. What did he and Eddy think of the little letters father sent them? Dont let the blessed fellows forget father.

A day or two ago Mr Strong, here in congress, said to me that Matilda would visit here within two or three weeks.[25] Suppose you write her a letter, and enclose it in one of mine; and if she comes I will deliver it to her, and if she does not, I will send it to her.

Most affectionately
A. Lincoln

Mary Lincoln to Abraham Lincoln[26]

Lexington May, 48.

My Dear Husband,

    You will think indeed, that <u>old age</u> has set <u>its seal</u>, upon my humble self, that in few or none of my letters, I can remember the day of the month, I must confess it as one of my peculiarities; I feel wearied & tried enough to know, that this is <u>Saturday night</u>, our <u>babies</u> are asleep, and as Aunt Maria B.[27] is coming in for me tomorrow morning, I think the chances will be rather dull that I should answer your last letter tomorrow. I have just received a letter from Frances W,[28] it related in an <u>especial</u> manner to <u>the box</u>, I had desired her to send, she thinks with you (as good persons generally agree) that it would cost more than it would come to, and it might be lost on the road, I rather expect she has examined the specified articles, and thinks as <u>Levi</u>[29] says, they are <u>hard bargains</u>. But it takes so many changes to do children, particularly in summer, that I thought it might save me a few stitches. I think I will write her a few lines this evening, directing her not to send them. She says Willie is just recovering from another spell of sickness, Mary or none of them were well.[30] Springfield she reports as dull as usual. Uncle S.[31] was to leave there on yesterday for Ky. Our little Eddy, has recovered from his little spell of sickness. Dear boy, I must tell you a little story about him. Boby in his wanderings to day, came across in a yard, a little kitten, <u>your hobby</u>, he says he asked a man for it, he brought it triumphantly to the house, so soon as Eddy, ^spied it^ his <u>tenderness</u>, broke forth, he made them bring it <u>water</u>, fed it with bread himself, with his <u>own dear hands</u>, he was a delighted little creature over it, in the midst of his happiness Ma[32] came in, she you must know dislikes the whole cat race, I thought in a very unfeeling manner, she ordered the servant near, to throw it out, which of <u>course</u>, was done, Ed, screaming & protesting loudly against the proceeding, <u>she</u> never appeared to mind his screams, which were long & loud, I assure you. Tis unusual for her <u>now a days</u>, to do any thing quite so striking, she is very obliging & accommodating, but if she thought any of us, were on her hands again, I believe she would be <u>worse</u> than ever. In the next moment she appeared in a good humor, I know she did not intend to offend me. By the way, she has just sent me up a glass of ice cream, for which this warm evening, I am duly grateful. The country is so delightful I am going to spend two or three weeks out there, it will doubtless benefit the children. Grandma[33] has received a letter from Uncle James Parker of Miss saying he & his family would be up by the twenty fifth of June, would remain here some little time & go on to Philadelphia to take their oldest daughter there to school, I believe it would be a good chance for me to pack up & accompany them. You know I am so fond of <u>sight seeing</u>, & I did not get to New York or Boston, or travel the lake route. But perhaps, dear husband, like the <u>irresistible Col M^c</u>,[34] cannot do without his wife next winter, and must needs take her with him again. I expect you would cry aloud against it. How much, I wish instead of writing, we were together this evening, I feel very sad away from you. Ma & myself rode out to Mr Bell's splendid place this afternoon, to return a call, the house and grounds are magnificent, Frances W would <u>have died</u> over their rare exotics. It is growing late, these summer eves are short, I expect my long <u>scrawls</u>, for truly such they are, weary you greatly; if you come on, in July or August <u>I</u> will take you to the springs. <u>Patty Webb's</u>, school in L[exington]. closes the first of July, I expect <u>Mr Webb</u>, will come on for her, I must go down about that time & carry on quite a flirtation, you know <u>we</u>, always had a <u>penchant</u> that way.[35] I must bid you good night. Do not fear the children, have forgotten you, I was only jesting. Even E.[36] eyes brighten at the mention of your name. My love to all. Truly yours

M L.

When Mary Lincoln was in Lexington in 1848, she had developed a close relationship with her stepsister Emilie, and afterward, Emilie visited the Lincoln family in Springfield. By 1856, however, there was a widening gap in political opinions between Mary and her Kentucky family. Emilie had just married Benjamin Helm, an attorney and member of the Kentucky legislature who would just four years later be fighting for the Confederacy. Mary's letter reveals her fondness for her little sister and shares typical social gossip and family news. However, it also contains a calculated defense of her husband's politics, a direct response to the increasing divisiveness of national politics as it pertained to the issue of slavery.

Mary Lincoln to Emilie Helm[37]

Springfield Nov 23rd 1856

With much pleasure, my dear Emilie, I acknowledge, the receipt of one of your ever acceptable letters, & notwithstanding many weeks have passed since writing you, I have frequently *intended* doing so, & you have been oftentimes in my thoughts. Mr E[dwards] expressed great pleasure at meeting you last summer, you know you have a very warm place in his heart. You have been such a wanderer around with your good husband, and a letter might have failed reaching you, I must try & devise some excuses—for my past silence, forgetfulness you know it could not be.

Besides, there is a *great deal* in getting out of the habit of letter writing, once I was very fond of it, nothing pleases me now better than receiving a letter from an absent friend, so remember dear E. when you desire to be particularly acceptable, sit thee down & write one of your agreeable missives & do not wait for a return of each, from a staid matron, & moreover the mother of three noisy boys.

Your Husband, I believe, like some of the rest of ours, has a great taste for politics & has taken much interest, in the late contest, which has resulted very much as I expected, not hoped.

Altho' Mr. L.[38] is, or was a *Fremont*[39] man, you must not include him with so many of those, who belong to *that party*, an *Abolitionist*. In principle he is far from it—All he desires is, that slavery, shall not be extended, let it remain, where it is—My weak woman's heart was too Southern in feeling, to sympathise with any but Fillmore,[40] I have always been a great admirer of his, he made so good a President & is so just a man & feels the *necessity* of keeping foreigners, within bounds. If some of you Kentuckians, had to deal with the "wild Irish," as we housekeepers are sometimes called upon to do, the south would certainly elect Mr Fillmore next time[41]—The democrats in our state have been defeated in their Governor,[42] so there is a crumb of comfort, for each & all—What day is so dark, that there is no ray of sunshine to penetrate the gloom? Speaking of politics, Gov's && reminds me of your questions, relative to Lydia M.[43] the hour of her patient lover's deliverance is at hand, they are to be married, privately I expect, some of us who had a handsome dress for the season, thought, it would be in *good taste* for Mrs Matteson, in consideration of their being about to leave their present habitation, to give a general reception. Lydia, has always been so retiring, that she would be very averse, to so public a display. This fall in visiting Mrs M I met with a sister of Mr McGinnis, a very pretty well bred genteel lady from Joliet—she spoke of being well acquainted with Margaret K. in Kty.[44]

Frances W. returned from her visit to Pennsylvania, two or three days since, where she had been spending the fall. Mr Edward's family are well. Mr B & Julia are still with them.[45] Miss Iles was married some three weeks since, I expect you do not remember her, which gave rise to some two or three parties.[46] Mr Scott is frequently here, rather playing the devoted to Julie Ridgeley,[47] I suspect, whether any thing serious I do not know. I expect the family would not be very averse to him. Charley R was on a visit to him, in Lex. this fall[48]—*He*, it is said, is to be married this winter to Jennie Barrett—a lovely girl, you remember her—I am very sorry to hear that our Mother,[49] is so frequently indisposed. I hope she has recovered from her lameness—Tell her when you see her that our old acquaintance O.B. Ficklin[50] took tea with us—an evening or two since, made particular enquiries about her—still as rough & uncultivated as ever altho some years since married an accomplished Georgia belle, with the *advantages* of some winter's in Washington—Ma & myself when together, spoke of our minister Dr Smith, who finding his salary of some $1600 inadequate, has resigned the church. Uncle & some *few* others are desirous of getting Dr Brown, your former pastor in Lex. within the last year, both his wife & himself, have been a great deal here, he has purchased lands, and appears rather identified with the country.[51] I must acknowledge, I have not admired him very much, his wife appears pleasant but neither I think would suit the people. Dr Smith is talented & beloved, & says he would stay if they would increase his salary, yet notwithstanding the wealthy in the church, as usual, there are many very close. But I am speaking of things that will not interest you in the least—If you do not bring *yourself* & Husband to see us very soon we will think you are not as proud of *Him*, as rumor says you should be—Do write soon, in return for this long & I fear dull letter from yours truly

Mary Lincoln

After Abraham Lincoln's election to the presidency in November 1860, there was much discussion about the makeup of his cabinet. When Mary traveled to New York to purchase clothing for her transition from being the wife of a prairie lawyer and politician in Illinois to being the wife of a president in Washington, she followed the political news as reported in the New York City newspapers. Norman B. Judd had been an important Republican Party operator and played an instrumental role in Lincoln's nomination as the party's candidate that past spring. Judd was on a short list of names for the cabinet, but he was a former Democrat, and some Republican insiders did not support him. In a letter to David Davis, who was a personal friend of Lincoln and his campaign manager, Mary demonstrated her political acumen and appealed to the Judge to apply some personal pressure on the president-elect. The letter also reveals Mary's clear understanding that antebellum society regarded it as impolitic for a woman to be so politically bold.[52]

Mary Lincoln to David Davis[53]
Confidential

New York Jany 17th

Judge Davis:

Dear Sir,

   Doubtless you will be surprised to receive a note from me, when I explain the cause, of my writing, I believe your honest, noble heart, will sympathise with me, otherwise I am assured, you will not mention ^it^. Perhaps you will think it is no affair of <u>mine</u>, yet I see it, almost daily mentioned in the Herald,[54] that <u>Judd</u> & some <u>few</u> Northern friends, are <u>urging</u> the <u>former's</u> claims to a cabinet appointment. <u>Judd</u> would cause trouble & dissatisfaction, & if Wall Street testifies correctly, his business transactions, have not always borne inspection. I heard the report, discussed at the table this morning, by persons who did not know, who was near, a party of gentlemen, evidently strong Republicans, they were laughing at the idea of <u>Judd</u>, being any way, connected with the Cabinet in <u>these times</u>, when honesty in high places is so important. Mr Lincoln's great attachment for you, is my present reason for writing. I know, a word from you, will have much effect, for the good of the country, and Mr Lincoln's future reputation, I believe you will speak to him on this subject & urge him not to give him so responsible a place. It is strange, how little delicacy those Chicago men have. I know, I can rely on what I have written to you, to be kept private. If you consider me intrusive, please excuse me, our country, just now, is above all.

Very Respectfully,
Mary Lincoln.

When Mary Lincoln arrived in Washington in February 1861, she was appalled at the physical condition of the White House and its shabby furnishings, and she immediately set out to recreate a home and public space properly befitting an American president. As there was a $20,000 congressional appropriation for such expenditures, Mary's goals in this case were not unwarranted, although she did ultimately overspend the allotment. Almost immediately upon making purchases for herself and for the White House, there was tremendous public scrutiny. Many people judged the expenditures as frivolous in the context of a government bracing for the financial burdens of the impending Civil War. This article reflected one newspaper's disdain for the Lincoln family's western roots and lambasted Mary Lincoln's taste and propriety.[55]

Excerpt of Newspaper Article in the Philadelphia *Sunday Dispatch*[56]
30 May 1861

Mrs. President Lincoln, as the ladies call her, was shopping to a considerable extent in this city in the early part of the week. She has evidently no comprehension that Jeff. Davis[57] will make good his threat to occupy the White House in July for she is expending thousands and thousands of dollars for articles of luxurious taste in the household way that it would be very preposterous for her to use out in her rural home in Illinois. The silver plate from Houghwout, and the china services from the same . . . will admirably suit the mulberry-colored livery of her footmen . . . and possibly may help very nicely to get rid of the apparently exhaustless $25,000 a year salary of Mr. Lincoln. So may the elegant black point lace shawls she bought at

Stewart's for $650 each, and the real camel's hair cashmere at $1,000 . . . Let me do Mrs. Lincoln the justice to say that she was dreadfully importuned to enter into extravagances of various kinds; but I heard her, myself, observe at Stewart's that she could not afford it, and was "determined to be very economical." One thousand dollars for a shawl was quite high as her sense of economy would permit her to go in these excessive hard times!

In the fall of 1862, Mary Lincoln traveled to New York with her son Tad and her dressmaker Elizabeth Keckley. She was beginning to emerge from the intense grief she suffered following Willie's death the previous February. The Union Army had suffered horrific losses at the Battle of Antietam, and President Lincoln was growing increasingly frustrated by General McClellan's unwillingness to pursue the Confederate Army.[58] Mary's letter to her weary husband touched on her health, updated the president on Tad's activities and furthered Keckley's effort to support the Contraband Relief Association, which was raising money to assist former slaves. Even though Mary was preoccupied with her grief, health issues and the needs of Tad, the letter reveals her continued engagement with the political issues of the day.

Mary Lincoln to Abraham Lincoln[59]

Nov2[d]

My Dear Husband

I have waited in vain to hear from you, yet as you are not <u>given</u> to letter writing, will be charitable enough to impute your silence, to the right cause. Strangers come up from W.[60] & tell me you are well, which satisfies me very much. Your name is on every lip and many prayers and good wishes are hourly sent up, for your welfare, and McClellan & his slowness are as vehemently discussed. Allowing this beautiful weather, to pass away, is disheartening the North.

Dear little Taddie is well & enjoying himself very much. Gen & M[rs] Anderson[61] & myself called on yesterday to see Gen Scott.[62] He looks well, although complaining of Rheumatism. A day or two since, I had one of my severe attacks, if it had not been for Lizzie Keckley, I do not know what I should have done. Some of <u>these periods</u>, will launch me away.[63] All the distinguished in the land, have [tried?] how polite & attentive, they could be to me, since I came up here. Many say, they would almost worship you, if you would put a fighting General, in the place of M[c]Clellan. This would be splendid weather, for an engagement. I have had two suits of clothes made for Taddie which will come to 26 dollars. Have to get some fur outside wrappings for the coachman's carriage trappings. Lizzie Keckley, wants me to loan her thirty dollars, so I will have to ask for a check of $100, which will soon be made use of, for these articles. I must send you, Taddie's tooth. I want to leave here for Boston, on Thursday & if you will send the check by Tuesday, will be much obliged.

One line to say that we are occasionally remembered will be gratefully received.

by yours very truly
M.L.

I enclose you a note from M[r] Stewart, he appears very solicitous about his young friend. M[r] S. is so strong a Union Man, & asks so few favors. if it came in your way, perhaps it would not be amiss to oblige.[64]

After Abraham Lincoln's death on April 15, 1865, Mary Lincoln received an outpouring of correspondence from private citizens and international leaders, sending condolences to her and to the nation. Queen Victoria's letter is one of public and diplomatic sympathy, but it is also one of intense, personal sentiment. The letter also provides insight about how Victorian women defined and exhibited their emotional responses to life's tragedies. Queen Victoria, who was just six months older than Mary, suffered agonizing grief after she lost her husband Albert in 1861. Mary responded to the Queen's condolences on May 21, just two days before she left the White House. She expressed her gratitude for the Queen's "tender sympathy, coming as they do, from a heart which from its own sorrow, can appreciate the intense grief I now endure."[65]

Queen Victoria of England to Mary Lincoln[66]

Osborne.

April 29. 1865.

Dear Madam

Though a Stranger to you I cannot remain silent where so terrible a Calamity has fallen upon you & your Country; and I must personally express my <u>deep</u> & <u>heartfelt</u> sympathy with you under the shocking circumstances of your present dreadful misfortune.

<u>No</u> one can better appreciate than <u>I</u> can, who am myself <u>utterly broken-hearted</u> by the loss of my own beloved Husband, who was the <u>Light</u> of my

Life, my stay, <u>my all</u>, what your sufferings must be; and I earnestly pray that you may be supported by Him to whom alone the sorely stricken can look for comfort, in this hour of heavy affliction.

With the renewed expression of true sympathy, I remain, dear Madam,

Your Sincere friend
Victoria

After her husband's death, Mary Lincoln could not bear the thought of returning to the Lincoln home in Springfield. Therefore, after she and Tad left the White House, they settled in Chicago. During the first few years of her widowhood, she lived under an oppressive veil of grief, and she constantly worried about money. Less than five months after the Lincoln assassination, Mary penned a heartbreaking letter to her close friend Sally Orne, the wife of a wealthy Philadelphia carpet dealer. While it is clear that Mary's financial worries were less dire than she perceived them to be, this letter conveys the depths of her grief and offers details of her desperate attempts to secure a sound financial future for herself and her young son.[67]

Mary Lincoln to Sally Orne[68]

Chicago Aug 31ˢᵗ

My Dear Mʳˢ Orne

Bowed down & heart broken, in my terrible bereavement, my thoughts, this last sad summer have often turned to you & I have remembered with most grateful emotions, your tender sympathy, in the first days of my overwhelming anguish. Time, does not reconcile me to the loss, of the most devoted & loving husband, a sadly afflicted woman, ever possessed, how dearly, I long, my kind friend to lay my aching head, & sorrowing heart, by the side, of this dearly loved one. When the summons comes for my departure, I will gladly welcome it, for there, the weary, are at rest.

As you may well suppose, I have led a life, of most rigid seclusion, since I left Washington. Chicago, is a very pleasant city & we have many charming acquaintances here, the few, whom I have been sufficiently composed to receive, have as a matter of course, deeply sympathized with me, in my great sorrow. I trust, some day, My dear Mrs Orne, I shall have the pleasure of seeing you here, you would be well repaid by a visit to the West. We are very differently situated, from what we would desire or from what should be expected, from our former station. We are deprived of the Comfort, <u>of a home</u>, where my poor sadly afflicted sons & myself, could <u>quietly</u> indulge in our griefs. if my darling husband had lived out, his four years, he promised me, we should pass our remaining years, in a home, we both should have enjoyed. We are left, with only $1500. a year, each, to live upon, the interest of our money, and as a matter of course, must board plainly and as genteel as possible on this sum. I mention this, by way of excusing a subject, I will mention to you. A friend of my husband's & myself, presented me last February a <u>very</u> elegant lace dress, very fine & beautiful, a lace flounce about 6 inches, in width, for the bottom of the skirt, same pattern as dress, a double lace shawl, very fine, exactly similar pattern with the request, that I would wear it, on the night of the Inauguration. For two hours, that evening, I did so, over a white silk dress, next morning, most carefully, the <u>gathers</u> were drawn from the skirt, and it was folded <u>tenderly</u> away, the flounce, was not used. I wore the article, reluctantly, as it was too elaborate for my style & too expensive for my means. My desire is, to dispose of these articles, it cost, in New York, to import them $3.500, of course, if I can get $2.500, for them, it will be a great consideration to me. If you know, of any one, who would desire, such a dress, will you not gratify me, my dear friend ^by informing me^ You may well be assured, only <u>dire</u> necessity, which I have never before, known, any thing about, would cause me to write so freely to you. The lace dress && is exquisitely fine, and was considered a bargain at the $3.500. I have also, the most magnificent white moire antique, that Mr Stewart[69] says he ever had imported, it was purchased last winter & never made $11, a yard, a yard wide. Some 16 yards in the dr[ess] I would sell at $125.[70] I am so anxious to have my boys, in a quiet hom[e] of our own, & without I make some exertion of the kind, disposing of articles, now unnecessary I fear I cannot succeed. If any of your friends would desire such articles, please advis[e] me, they are rich & beautiful. Taddie was very grateful for your magic toys

Your attached friend
Mary Lincoln.

In June 1876, Mary Lincoln regained legal control of her finances following the ordeal of her insanity trial and brief institutionalization in an asylum for the mentally ill in Batavia, Illinois. She had returned to Springfield, living with her sister Elizabeth since her release from Batavia, and she was enjoying the company of her sister's grandchildren. However, the deaths of her husband and three of her sons, combined with her continued estrangement from her eldest son, Robert, left her feeling alone in the world. For Mary, Springfield was simply too replete with haunting memories of her happy past. In addition, her notoriety as First Lady, a president's widow and now an insane old woman was taking its toll. She decided that exile in Europe would allow her to travel in anonymity and, hopefully, bring her some peace. She chose the resort town of Pau, France, in the Pyrenees, traveling there in October and making it her home for the next four years. From Pau, she wrote numerous letters to friends and family members, reporting on her travels, commenting on political matters and still sharing the emotional details of her continuing grief. She also penned nearly 100 letters to Jacob Bunn, the Springfield merchant and old friend of her husband whom she had chosen to manage her finances. This 1876 letter to him is typical of those business letters, and it demonstrates Mary's remarkably clear and capable mind. Also present in this letter, and in dozens of others, is the fact that even in her self-imposed European exile, American politics still fueled her spirit and stimulated her intellect.

———————

Mary Lincoln to Jacob Bunn[71]

Pau France,
Dec. 12th 1876.

Hon Jacob Bunn

My dear Sir:

The Pension paper, accompanied by your note, with instructions, have been received. I return the paper to you, signed by the proper authorities, M\ensuremath{^r} Musgrave Clay, is the Consul, connected with the American Consulate. Le Baron de Bennecker is one of the high authorities here & one of the Government officers. I observe, by my ^Daily^ Galignani of Paris, which receives constant news, from America, that gold on the 8th of Dec. was 107¼—quite a decline, making it however, so much better, if it continues, for the number of my francs. Living abroad, has greatly changed, <u>since</u> the war, between France & Germany & <u>this</u>, is a very expensive place. Doubtless the ag[it]ations caused by the difficulty of deciding, <u>who</u>, is to be our next President, overshadows everything, in our beloved Country. We can only pray, that no civil war, will occur, to blight our prosperous land.[72]

My sister, M\ensuremath{^{rs}} Edwards,[73] wrote me on the 20th of Nov, regarding the critical condition of M\ensuremath{^r} Dubois,[74] therefore I was <u>not</u> unprepared, to receive the sad & painful intelligence of his death. With many kind remembrances to your family, believe me,

Most respectfully &&
M\ensuremath{^{rs}} Abraham Lincoln

During her four years in France, Mary Lincoln satisfied a lifelong desire for sightseeing, of which all those years ago she had told her husband she was "so fond." From her home base in Pau, she made trips to Paris, Marseilles and Avignon in France; Naples and Rome in Italy; and other cities in between. By the end of her time in exile, however, her health was worsening, and her eyesight was failing. Perhaps surprising even to herself, she was growing homesick. Still estranged from her only surviving son, Mary had adopted as a surrogate son the young Lewis Baker, the grandson of her sister Elizabeth Edwards. Mary's correspondence with him over the years in France served as her most important emotional connection to her home, and this letter in the fall of October 1879 is illustrative of his importance to her heart in the fading years of her life. The letter also demonstrates that even as Mary's body failed her, her mind was still equipped for constructing and delivering sharp-edged political opinions.

Mary Lincoln to Lewis Baker[75]

Pau, France,
October 4th 1879.

My Dear Lewis:

I am sitting up, for the <u>first</u> half hour, within the past week. I have been really ill, with a very severe cold taken in the mountains, where I suppose I lingered too long. I am enveloped in flannels from head to foot, my throat

is almost closed at times, continual pain & soreness in the chest, & am coughing most of the time. I am well repaid for my love of mountain scenery, &
detestation of town in summer. Rather a poor prospect for me, for the coming winter. I enclose a card of my <u>exact</u> weight <u>nearly</u> a month ago, since
then, as a matter of course many pounds of flesh have departed. <u>Here</u>, in
France, they are compelled to be <u>rigidly</u> exact in their weights. I am now,
just the weight I was, when went to Wash in 1861. Therefore I may con-
clude, my great bloat has left me & I have returned to my natural size. It was
such a great pleasure dear Lewis to receive your interesting letter of the 8th
of September. I am so pleased also that you will visit the White Mountains
next summer, Lake George & pass a day or two at Niagara falls. I have visited
all these places & have always returned to Niagara with renewed interest.
I think 24-hours, <u>however</u> will suffice you, on the Tip Top house <u>One</u> 1st
of August, we ascended the Mountain from the Glen hou[se] where it was
<u>intensely</u> warm & found it snowing on top. There is so much pleasure, in
anticipation for those who have never visited these places

Without doubt, I must have been considered <u>quite</u> ill, as numerous cards
are daily handed me & notes of enquiry, flowers, &&. I lead a life of such
great quiet here that the <u>pleasant</u> thoug[ht] occurs to me <u>sometimes</u> that
I am not supposed to be in <u>this</u> latitude. How much I long to see you all, to
have a taste of your dear Grandma's good food—<u>waffles, batter cakes</u>, egg
corn bread—are <u>all</u> unknown here, as to biscuits, light rolls && they have
never been dreamed of, *not* to speak of <u>buckwheat</u> cakes. It needs no assurance of mine, to convince you, that a long period of absence from America,
is not agreeable, but to an oppressed, heart broken woman it is simply an
<u>exile</u>. You are spared a very long letter to day, my dear Lewis, for I cannot sit
up a moment longer. Since the commencement of this letter, the enclosed
card has been sent up to me. These <u>dignitaries</u> abound here & are so courteous. When you receive this letter, I hope you will <u>at once</u> write me. I see <u>no</u>
<u>American</u> papers. send me slips of news, all the time, when you write. I hope
our country, will never nominate for the Presidency, so <u>bad</u> a man as Roscoe
Conkling.[76] Adieu, for the present. With much love to all & a great deal for
your dear self

I remain your devoted Aunt,
Mary Lincoln

NOTES

1 Mary Lincoln to Mercy Ann Levering, 15 December 1840, Lincoln Collection, ALPL.
2 Ninian W. Edwards.

3 Matilda Edwards lived in Alton, Illinois, north of St. Louis on the Mississippi River, about
   ninety miles from Springfield. She was the daughter of Cyrus Edwards, who was a Whig in
   the Illinois State Senate (1836–38) and in the Illinois House of Representatives (1832–34,
   1840–42, 1861–62). Douglas L. Wilson, *Lincoln before Washington: New Perspectives on the Illinois
   Years* (Urbana: University of Illinois Press, 1997), 104; John Clayton, comp., *The Illinois Fact Book
   and Historical Almanac, 1673–1968* (Carbondale: Southern Illinois University Press, 1970), 203,
   205, 209, 223.

4 Aristocracy Hill.

5 Joshua F. Speed.

6 Edwin B. Webb.

7 Elizabeth Edwards.

8 Abraham Lincoln.

9 James C. Conkling.

10 Harriet Huntington married James Campbell. Mary and James Conkling attended the wedding.
   L&L, 21.

11 Martha Jane Lowry married Sidney Abell on September 22, 1840, and the couple lived in Chi-
   cago. *Illinois Statewide Marriage Index*, Sangamon County, Illinois State Archives Springfield, IL;
   Office of the U.S. Census, Seventh Census of the United States (1850), Ward 2, Chicago, Cook
   Co., IL, 169.

12 Mary R. Lamb married Joseph G. Bouman on December 21, 1840. *Illinois Statewide Marriage
   Index*, Sangamon County.

13 Whig General William H. Harrison defeated Democrat Martin Van Buren for the presidency in
   the fall of 1840.

14 The "Lionel" was the nickname Mary Todd and her friends gave to the Town Branch stream
   that ran through Springfield. *L&L*, 21.

15 Jacksonville, Illinois, was about forty miles west of Springfield and was the county seat of Morgan County.

16 John J. Hardin was Mary Todd's cousin.

17 Orville Hickman Browing, a lawyer and Whig Illinois State Senator. Usher F. Linder, *Reminiscences of the Early Bench and Bar of Illinois* (Chicago: The Chicago Legal News Company, 1879),
   83–84.

18 Matilda Edwards.

19 Lawrason Levering was a neighbor of Ninian and Elizabeth Edwards. Paul M. Angle, *"Here I
   Have Lived": A History of Lincoln's Springfield, 1821–1865* (Springfield, IL: Abraham Lincoln
   Association, 1935; reprint, Chicago: Abraham Lincoln Bookshop, 1971), 93.

20 Abraham Lincoln to Mary Lincoln, 16 April 1848, Lincoln Collection, ALPL.

21 This was the toddler's best effort to say that his father was at the capital.

22 Elizabeth Parker was Mary's maternal grandmother.

23 In November 1849, when the Lincoln family was visiting Lexington, Lincoln wrote a letter to
   the secretary of the navy, recommending John Parker for an appointment in the Hemp Agency
   in the state of Kentucky. Abraham Lincoln to William B. Preston, 5 November 1849, Lincoln
   Collection, Brown University, Providence, RI.

24 Robert S. Todd and Robert Wickliffe were political rivals, but Margaret and Mary Wickliff were
   Mary's childhood friends. William H. Townsend, *Lincoln and His Wife's Home Town* (Indianapolis,
   IN: The Bobbs-Merrill Co., 1929), 67, 124.

25 William Strong was a U.S. representative from Pennsylvania, who was serving in Congress with
   Lincoln. He was the brother Newton Deming Strong, who had married Matilda Edwards in
   1844. V. N. Bay, *Reminiscences of the Bench and Bar of Missouri* (St. Louis: F. H. Thomas & Co.,
   1878), 559–60; *Illinois Statewide Marriage Index*, Madison Co., IL, vol. 6, 62.

26 Mary Lincoln to Abraham Lincoln, May 1848, Lincoln Collection, ALPL.

27 Maria Bullock was the sister of Robert S. Todd. Daniel W. Stowell, Susan Krause, John A. Lupton, Stacy Pratt McDermott, Christopher A. Schnell, Dennis E. Suttles, and Kelley B. Clausing,

eds., *The Papers of Abraham Lincoln: Legal Documents and Cases*, 4 vols. (Charlottesville: University of Virginia Press, 2008), 4:113.

28 Frances Wallace was one of Mary's sisters in Springfield, Illinois.

29 Levi Todd was Mary's oldest brother.

30 Willie Wallace and Mary Wallace were the children of Frances and her husband, Dr. William Wallace. John Carroll Power, *History of the Early Settlers of Sangamon County, Illinois* (Springfield, IL: Edwin A. Wilson & Co., 1876), 478.

31 Samuel Todd was the brother of Robert S. Todd. Burial Record, Columbia Cemetery, Columbia, MO.

32 Betsey Todd was Mary Lincoln's stepmother.

33 Elizabeth Parker.

34 John A. McClernand was a U.S. representative from Springfield, Illinois, who was serving in Congress with Lincoln. His wife Sarah was a friend of Mary Lincoln.

35 Patty Webb, who was attending school in Lexington, was the daughter of Edwin B. Webb, Mary's former suitor. *L&L*, 38.

36 Eddy Lincoln.

37 Mary Lincoln to Emilie Helm, 23 November 1856, *L&L*, 45–48.

38 Abraham Lincoln.

39 John C. Fremont was the anti-slavery Republican candidate for the presidency in 1856. He lost to Democrat James Buchanan.

40 Millard Fillmore, the last Whig president, was the American Party candidate for president in 1856.

41 The Lincoln family employed some Irish domestic servants. Jean H. Baker, *Mary Todd Lincoln: A Biography* (New York: W. W. Norton & Co., 1987; reprint, New York: W. W. Norton & Co., 2008), 105–7.

42 In 1856, William H. Bissell won election as the first Republican governor of Illinois, defeating Democratic candidate William A. Richardson. Robert P. Howard, *Mostly Good and Competent Men: Illinois Governors, 1818–1988* (Springfield: Illinois Issues, Sangamon State University and Illinois State Historical Society, 1988), 109–15.

43 Lydia Matteson, the daughter of the outgoing governor of Illinois, Joel A. Matteson, married John McGinnis in 1856. *Illinois Statewide Marriage Index*, Sangamon County.

44 Margaret Kellogg was Mary Lincoln's stepsister.

45 Mary Lincoln's niece Julia was the daughter of Ninian and Elizabeth Edwards. She married Edward L. Baker in 1855. *Illinois Statewide Marriage Index*, Sangamon County, IL, vol. 3, 141.

46 Louisa Iles, a daughter of Elijah Iles, a founding father of Springfield, Illinois, married Timothy Carter in June 1856. *Illinois Statewide Marriage Index*, Sangamon County; Power, *Early Settlers of Sangamon County*, 400.

47 Julia Ridgley was the daughter of Nicholas H. Ridgely, a prominent Springfield banker and railroad developer. She did not marry Robert Scott. Joseph Wallace, *Past and Present of the City of Springfield and Sangamon County, Illinois*, 2 vols. (Chicago: S. J. Clarke Publishing Co., 1904), 1:723–24.

48 Charles Ridgely was Julia Ridgley's sister. Ibid.

49 Betsey Todd.

50 Orlando B. Ficklin was a Democratic congressman from Illinois. Linder, Reminiscences of the Early Bench and Bar, 110–12.

51 John H. Brown and his wife Clara lived in Springfield, Illinois, where he became the minister of Mary's church, the First Presbyterian Church, in October 1856. Office of the U.S. Census, Eighth Census of the United States (1860), Sangamon Co., IL, 141.

52 David Herbert Donald, *Lincoln* (New York: Simon & Schuster, 1995), 262, 265.

53 Mary Lincoln to David Davis, 17 January 1861, Lincoln Papers, ALPL; Edgar DeWitt Jones, *Lincoln and the Preachers* (New York: Harper & Brothers, 1948).

54 The *New York Herald* (NY) was a Democratic newspaper. James L. Crouthamel, *Bennett's New York Herald and the Rise of the Popular Press* (Syracuse, NY: Syracuse University Press, 1989).

55 Donald, *Lincoln*, 312–13.

56 *L&L*, 88; Philadelphia *Sunday Dispatch* (PA), reprinted in *The Crisis* (Columbus, OH), 30 May 1861.

57 Jefferson Davis was inaugurated as the president of the Confederacy on February 18, 1861.

58 Donald, *Lincoln*, 389.

59 Mary Lincoln to Abraham Lincoln, 2 November 1862, Abraham Lincoln Papers, LC.

60 Washington, D.C.

61 General Robert Anderson was the commander at Fort Sumter.

62 General Winfield Scott.

63 Nineteenth-century women rarely discussed such private female health issues with their husbands. Mary's candor here about a particularly difficult menstrual cycle indicates the level of comfort she had with her husband. Baker, *Mary Todd Lincoln*, 230.

64 Alexander T. Stewart was the merchant of an import store where Mary Lincoln had made purchases. She likely owed him money when he passed the letter to Lincoln to her. In his letter to Lincoln, Stewart recommended the promotion of Thaddeus P. Mott, who was a son of a New York surgeon. *L&L*, 140; Alexander T. Stewart to Abraham Lincoln, 31 October 1862, Abraham Lincoln Papers, LC.

65 Mary Lincoln to Queen Victoria of England, 21 May 1865, Papers of John Hay and Abraham Lincoln, Houghton Library, Harvard University, Cambridge, MA.

66 Queen Victoria of England to Mary Lincoln, 29 April 1865, Manuscript Division, LC.

67 1860 Census, Ward 10, Philadelphia, Philadelphia Co., PA, 227.

68 Mary Lincoln to Sally Orne, 31 August 1865, Lincoln Papers, ALPL.

69 Alexander T. Stewart.

70 Apparently, Sally Orne suggested no potential buyers. Two years later, Mary traveled to New York with Elizabeth Keckley to try to sell this dress along with other items. Elizabeth Keckley, *Behind the Scenes in the Lincoln White House: Memoirs of an African-American Seamstress* (Mineola, NY: Dover Publications, 2006), 113–41; *L&L*, 270.

71 Mary Lincoln to Jacob Bunn, 12 December 1876, Lincoln Collection, ALPL.

72 When Mary Lincoln wrote her letter to Jacob Bunn, the presidential election of 1876 was in dispute. Democrat Samuel J. Tilden won the popular vote and had edged Republican Rutherford B. Hayes in electoral votes as well. However, there were twenty unresolved electoral votes. In January 1877, the "Compromise of 1877" settled the election. The Democrats agreed to give Hayes the disputed twenty votes in exchange for the withdrawal of federal troops from the South, thus ending the period of Reconstruction. Michael F. Holt, *By One Vote: The Disputed Presidential Election of 1876* (Lawrence: University of Kansas Press, 2008).

73 Elizabeth Edwards.

74 Jesse K. Dubois, an old Springfield friend of the Lincoln family and former Illinois state auditor. *History of Sangamon County, Illinois* (Chicago: Inter-State Publishing Co., 1881), 522–23.

75 Mary Lincoln to Edward Lewis Baker Jr., 4 October 1879, Lincoln Papers, ALPL.

76 Roscoe Conkling had been a Republican congressman from New York during the Civil War. From 1867 to 1881, he served in the U.S. Senate. He played a prominent role in the Compromise of 1877, but he was never a candidate for the presidency. David M. Jordan, *Roscoe Conkling of New York: Voice in the Senate* (Ithaca, NY: Cornell University Press, 1971).

BIBLIOGRAPHY

Angle, Paul M., *"Here I Have Lived": A History of Lincoln's Springfield, 1821–1865* (Springfield, IL: Abraham Lincoln Association, 1935; reprint, Chicago: Abraham Lincoln Bookshop, 1971).

Baker, Jean H., *The Lincoln Marriage: Beyond the Battle of Quotations*, 38th Annual Robert Fortenbaugh Memorial Lecture (Gettysburg, PA: Gettysburg College, 1999).

———, *Mary Todd Lincoln: A Biography* (New York: W.W. Norton & Co., 1987; reprint, New York: W.W. Norton & Co., 2008).

Baringer, William E., ed., *Lincoln Day by Day: A Chronology, 1809–1865*, 3 vols. (Washington, DC: Lincoln Sesquicentennial Commission, 1960).

Berry, Stephen, *House of Abraham: Lincoln and the Todds, a Family Divided by War* (Boston: Houghton Mifflin Co., 2007).

Clinton, Catherine, *Mrs. Lincoln: A Life* (New York: Harper Collins, 2009).

Collins, Lewis, *History of Kentucky*, 2 vols. (Covington, KY: Collins & Co., 1882).

Darrin, Charles V., "Your Truly Attached Friend, Mary Lincoln," *Journal of the Illinois State Historical Society* 44 (Spring 1951): 7–25.

Donald, David Herbert, *Lincoln* (New York: Simon & Schuster, 1995).

Emerson, Jason, *The Madness of Mary Lincoln* (Carbondale: Southern Illinois University Press, 2007).

———, *Mary Lincoln's Insanity Case: A Documentary History* (Champaign: University of Illinois Press, 2012).

Epstein, Daniel Mark, *The Lincolns: Portrait of a Marriage* (New York: Ballantine Books, 2008).

Evans, William, *Mrs. Abraham Lincoln: A Study of Her Personality and Influence on Abraham Lincoln* (New York: Alfred A. Knopf, 1932; reprint, Carbondale: Southern Illinois University Press, 2010).

Fleischner, Jennifer, *Mrs. Lincoln and Mrs. Keckly: The Remarkable Story of the Friendship between a First Lady and a Former Slave* (New York: Broadway Books, 2003).

Gernon, Blain Brooks, *The Lincolns in Chicago* (Chicago: Ancarthe Publishers, 1934).

Green, Thomas Marshall, *Historic Families of Kentucky* (Cincinnati, OH: Robert Clarke & Co., 1889).

Grimsley, Elizabeth, "Six Months in the White House," *Journal of the Illinois State Historical Society* 19 (October 1926–January 1927): 43–73.

Helm, Katherine, *The True Story of Mary, Wife of Lincoln* (New York: Harper & Brothers, 1928).

Hickey, James T., "The Lincoln Account at the Corneau & Diller Drug Store, 1849–1861: A Springfield Tradition," *Journal of the Illinois Historical State Historical Society* 77 (Spring 1984): 60–66.

Humphrey, Mary E., "Springfield of the Lincolns," *Abraham Lincoln Association Papers* (Springfield, IL: Abraham Lincoln Association, 1930), 17–42.

Keckley, Elizabeth, *Behind the Scenes in the Lincoln White House: Memoirs of an African-American Seamstress* (Mineola, NY: Dover Publications, 2006).

———, *Behind the Scenes, or Thirty Years a Slave, and Four Years in the White House* (New York: G. W. Carlton, 1868).

Krueger, Lillian, "Mary Todd Lincoln Summers in Wisconsin," *Journal of the Illinois State Historical Society* 34 (June 1941): 249–52.

McCreary, Donna, *Fashionable First Lady: The Victorian Wardrobe of Mary Todd Lincoln* (Charleston, IN: Lincoln Presentations, 2007).

Neely Jr., Mark E., and R. Gerald McMurtry, *The Insanity File: The Case of Mary Todd Lincoln* (Carbondale: Southern Illinois University Press, 1986).

Ostendorf, Lloyd, *The Portraits of Mary Todd Lincoln* (Springfield: Illinois State Historical Society, 1969).

Pratt, Harry E., *Personal Finances of Abraham Lincoln* (Springfield, IL: Abraham Lincoln Association, 1943).

Pratt, Harry E., and Ernest E. East, "Mrs. Lincoln Refurbishes the White House," *Lincoln Herald* 47 (February 1945): 13–22.

Randall, Ruth Painter, *The Courtship of Mr. Lincoln* (Boston: Little, Brown & Co., 1957).

———, *Lincoln's Sons* (Boston: Little, Brown & Co., 1955).

———, *Mary Lincoln: Biography of a Marriage* (Boston: Little, Brown & Co., 1953).

Ross, Ishbel, *The President's Wife: Mary Todd Lincoln: A Biography* (New York: G.P. Putnam's Sons, 1973).

Sanburg, Carl, and Paul M. Angle, *Mary Lincoln: Wife and Widow* (New York: Harcourt, Brace, & Co., 1932).

Schwartz, Thomas F., "Mary Todd's 1835 Visit to Springfield, Illinois," *Journal of the Abraham Lincoln Association* 26 (Winter 2005): 42–45.

Schwartz, Thomas F., and Kim M. Bauer, "Unpublished Mary Todd Lincoln," *Journal of the Abraham Lincoln Association* 17 (Summer 1996): 1–21.

Schwartz, Thomas F., and Anne V. Shaugnessy, "Unpublished Mary Lincoln Letters," *Journal of the Abraham Lincoln Association* 11 (Spring 1990): 34–50.

Stoltz, Charles, *The Tragic Career of Mary Todd Lincoln* (South Bend, IN: The Round Table, 1931).

Temple, Wayne C., "Mary Todd Lincoln's Travels," *Journal of the Illinois State Historical Society* 52 (Spring 1959): 180–94.

Temple, Wayne C., ed., *Mrs. Frances Jane Wallace Describes Lincoln's Wedding* (Harrogate, TN: Lincoln Memorial University, 1960).

Townsend, William H., *Lincoln and His Wife's Home Town* (Indianapolis, IN: The Bobbs-Merrill Co., 1929).

Turner, Justin G., and Linda Levitt Turner, eds., *Mary Todd Lincoln: Her Life and Letters* (New York: Alfred A. Knopf, 1972).

Van der Heuvel, Gerry, *Crowns of Thorns and Glory: Mary Todd Lincoln and Varina Howell Davis: The Two First Ladies of the Civil War* (New York: E.P. Dutton, 1988).

Williams, Frank J., and Michael Burkhimer, eds., *The Mary Lincoln Enigma: Historians on America's Most Controversial First Lady* (Carbondale: Southern Illinois University Press, 2012).

Winkle, Kenneth J., *Abraham and Mary Lincoln* (Carbondale: Southern Illinois University, 2012).

INDEX